Shree Maa

The Life of a Saint

Swami Satyananda Saraswati

Devi Mandir Publications

"We are one family.
Respect is peace, respect is realization,
and respect is heaven."

Shree Maa

Shree Maa
The Life of a Saint, First Edition
Copyright © 1997 by
Devi Mandir Publications
5950 Highway 128
Napa, CA 94558 USA
Communications: Phone and Fax 1-707-966-2802
E-Mail shreemaa@napanet.net
Please visit us on the World Wide Web at
http://www.shreemaa.org/

ISBN 1-877795-71-2
Library of Congress Catalog Data
CIP 97-078038

Shree Maa
The Life of a Saint,
Swami Satyananda Saraswati
1. Hindu Religion. 2. Goddess Worship.
3. Spirituality. 4. Philosophy. 5. Biography.
I. Saraswati, Swami Satyananda

Table of Contents

Chapter Seven
Maa's Favorite Sadhu Teaching Stories

Shree Maa
The Life of a Saint

Introduction

She knew from her birth that she was divine. One of her most difficult realizations was the understanding that everyone was not so gifted as to have God Consciousness all the time, nor were they all endowed with the capacity to go into deep meditative states, called in Sanskrit *samadhi*, any time they choose. Can you imagine a life that never had any doubt of the fact that you came to this world as a divine messenger with a divine mission?

Her first recollection was the sound of the voice of the nineteenth century saint Shree Ramakrishna, who she considers to be her guru, saying, "Oh, you came again. Much more needs to be done in this Age of Darkness. You've got to show what divine life means, what is spiritual practice or *sadhana* and what is sacrifice." With that instruction her sojourn on planet earth began.

Shree Maa is one of the great women saints in contemporary history. She has been the subject of numerous books, and articles, interviews and stories in newspapers and magazines. She has inspired and contributed to the authoring of more than three dozen books in a dozen languages and has been the author of numerous songs which have been recorded on CDs and cassettes. Her picture stands on the altars of uncountable worshipers around the world. Yet she shuns publicity, prefers the solitude of her own spiritual discipline, loves the quiet regularity of her rhythm of worship, cooks and sews for her ever-expanding family of devotees, and sits for prayer, worship and meditation, ten, twelve, fourteen hours a day, every day of her life. Her advice is sought by politicians, leaders of industry, businessmen, educators and simple household people. Yet she remains the simple, objective friend of the universe, who wants nothing for herself but to share her life of prayer with all. She is Shree Maa, the Holy Mother of Kamakhya, and this is her story.

While we were writing this book, Shree Maa was chanting the complete *Chandi Path* three times a day, a commitment which takes from seven to nine hours a day. The *Chandi Path* is a Sanskrit scripture dating before the ninth century B.C., which describes the Divine Mother's victory over the forces of egotism and selfishness. It is comprised of seven hundred verses of praise to the Divine Mother, and it is still recited today as a spiritual discipline of self-control and purification by initiates into the mysteries of Divine Mother worship. This scripture has conveyed a significant inspiration in the spiritual growth of many saintly people from both ancient and modern times.

Such a commitment to spiritual life is an inspiration for future generations. Shree Maa lives her teachings with such sincerity. Please consider the love and devotion with which we have undertaken to share this most amazing life filled with the bounteous generosity of the grace of God. Shree Maa is a living manifestation of that grace. Our sharing of her story is only meant to convey the unlimited possibilities of a divine life.

Swami Satyananda Saraswati
Napa, California, 1997

Acknowledgements

This book was produced by a beautiful team of wonderful people working together as a labor of love. It is amazing how much effort was offered so selflessly. In addition to those who offfered stories, whose contributions have already been acknowledged, I want to thank all the behind the scenes efforts of typists, editors, graphics and layout people, who helped bring this project to fruition.

Agastya Seward
Arron Seward
Bob Jones
Devaraj Sylvian
Durga Nanda
Gautam Muni
Indrani Sylvian
Kalika Sales
Linda Johnsen
Linda Sehy
Mary Ann Jones
Savitri Goel
Seema Datta
Shantananda Saraswati
Steve Blake
Tapas Saraswati
Vittalananda Saraswati
Wes Wait

What a team! And the most thanks go to Shree Maa, without whom there wouldn't have been such an amazing example about whom we could write. Thanks to you all.

Chapter One

The Youngest Sadhu

Geographical Location

If you look at a map of India, and look to the very northeast corner, you will find a little tentacle of India that is one of the most fascinating areas of the world. Within a short distance to the north of the state of Assam is Tibet; to the northeast is China; to the east, Burma; to the southeast, the various tribes of Nagaland, Tripura and Meghalaya; to the south, Bangladesh; to the southwest, the Shillong district; to the west, lie Bengal and the rest of India; to the northwest, the various nationalities of Nepalese, Sikkimese, Bhutanese and Tibetans mingled into what is now called the hill states of Sikkim, Bhutan and Arunachala, and the entire range of the Himalayan populations.

Description of Upper Assam

In the Arunachala Range of the Himalaya Mountains are steep precipices with gorges which descend from the summits of Kanchanjunga and the areas to the east of Mount Everest. Waterfalls cascading from the majestic peaks shower the tall fir, pine and oak trees growing along the banks. The montage of greens from the dense vegetation forms a stark contrast to the foaming waters of the rivers below. The roar of sounds from the turbulent cascade is heard against the silences of nature, permeated with the harmonic whisper of the winds through the leaves in the trees. This is an area populated by white owls, rhinoceros, pythons, a variety of deer, bobcats and the famous Bengal tigers.

East Bengal

The Dhaka region of East Bengal is an area famous historically for having produced an abundance of saints and philosophers, artists and musicians. Famous in our time was Nagmahashaya, the great spiritual master who was a disciple of Shree Ramakrishna. Also from the region was Swami Prabhananda, who evolved in spiritual stature to establish the Bharat Seva Ashram Sangha, a public service religious organization famous throughout India. In addition there was the famous woman saint Anandamayi Maa who came from East Bengal, as well as other great spiritual adepts such as Khatya Baba, Lokanath Brahmachari, Bholanath Giri and Jagatbandhu, all highly respected for the intensity of their spiritual attainment.

Shree Maa's great uncle was Atulananda Saraswati, a *sannyasi* or renunciate who never married, but spent his entire life wandering from place to place. He never stayed in one place for more than three days. "I met him on a few occasions when he came to visit our house," said Shree Maa. "I remember when I was six years old my grandmother told me to cook for him. She instructed me on how to prepare the dishes. He was so happy to eat the food prepared by my hands. He fell in love with me and took me everywhere with him. He told my mother, 'One of your children will go to America.' Nobody ever thought it would be me."

One of her aunts was Renuka Sen, a famous poet and a friend and inspiration in the life of Rabindranath Tagore. Her family was descended from Ramprasad Sen, whose ecstatic songs in praise of the Divine Mother Kali are sung all over India, and are now becoming popular all over the world. It was from this heritage that Shree Maa took her birth.

Birth and Early Years

At the age of twelve, her grandmother, Abhamayi Gupta, was married to Sudhir Gupta, and bore a child every year until the age of twenty, seven boys and the youngest, a girl. When he got a job as stenographer in a British company, Sudhir Gupta moved the family from Dhaka to Calcutta. A few years later, he purchased a property in Digboi, and the family settled there in the region of Upper Assam. The little town of Digboi was the headquarters of the British Oil Company, and several of Shree Maa's relatives later became employees of this company. After moving to Digboi, her grandfather died, leaving her grandmother a young widow with eight children and responsible for supporting, raising, and educating the entire family by herself.

Although Abhamayi Gupta herself was not educated, she performed her task extremely well, and the seven sons became highly educated, and all of them found excellent employment. Five of them became officers in the British Oil Company, one of them became a professor of business management at the university, and one became the sole distributor in the entire northeastern regions for the Usha Sewing Machine Company. Ultimately, this meant that anyone who wore stitched clothing in the northeastern regions paid some kind of premium to the Gupta family.

Shree Maa's mother, Kalyani, was the youngest in the family of seven older brothers. She was the only girl, and like her mother, was married off young when she was only thirteen. Shree Maa's father, Sushil, was already in his twenties. He was the son of a wealthy family, and employed as a manager of a tea estate, where he lived with Kalyani after their marriage.

When Kalyani was fourteen, she and her husband went to visit the Kamakhya Temple to offer worship. In those days pilgrims had to climb to the top of the Kamakhya mountain by an arduous path of stones, which historically was said to have been built by Bana Ashura, an evil king. The story is told that Bana Ashura wanted to see the Divine Mother. She said, "I will show myself to you if you can build a stairway to my Temple before the crow of the cock in the morning." The king labored with all his men and all his might throughout the night, and just before dawn when he was about to set the last stone into place, the Divine Mother caused the rooster to crow. So the Goddess got a stairway to Her Temple without having to show Herself to the *ashura* king.

Kalyani and Sushil trudged up the path toward the top of the mountain. Suddenly, near the summit, there appeared Swami Bhuvananda Saraswati, a great saint and highly respected religious teacher who dwelt on the mountain at the Kalipur Ashram. "I've been waiting for you," he called. "You are going to give birth to a divine child, and I want to give you mantra initiation with the blessings of God."

Kalyani was filled with surprise. She wasn't pregnant. Maybe he was making a mistake. "No, no, it's you!" cried the ascetic.

The saint came close to the couple as they stood in awe on the path. He reached out his arms in blessings and recited several mantras. Then he placed his mouth to Kalyani's left ear, and recited the Gayatri mantra, one of the most sacred of all the Vedic mantras, honoring the light of wisdom. He anointed her with holy water and instructed the couple to return when Kalyani was two months pregnant.

In the next month Kalyani conceived, and both husband and wife knew that their child was destined to be a divinely inspired messenger. In the second month of the pregnancy both mother and father returned to the Kalipur Ashram near the top of the Kamakhya Mountain. The Guru was waiting for them and received them with the highest respect. After welcoming them to the ashram, Swami Bhuvananda Saraswati performed *puja* to the expectant mother, and offered a special offering with which to bless the progeny of Kalyani and Sushil. He then gave mantra initiation to the baby in the womb, and instructed the parents on ways to maintain a divine atmosphere conducive for the impending birth, and once again told them to return with the child when she was two months old.

The pregnancy was uneventful, but all of the neighbors could not help but wonder at how Kalyani was always shining. The birth occurred in the year when there was a great earthquake in Assam. Kalyani told the story that when the walls of the house began to shake, she grabbed her infant child and ran outside the house. One wall in fact collapsed.

Many records were destroyed in the earthquake. This perhaps explains why every official record in Shree Maa's life has a different birth date recorded on it, and the divergence is often extreme. It could be somewhere between 1938 and 1948, although it could easily be earlier or later, and there is no factual evidence to verify any date of birth.

From birth the child Shree Maa did not cry. In fact, no one could understand when she was hungry or needed to be changed.

When the child was two months old, both Kalyani and Sushil returned to the Guru's ashram at Kamakhya. Swami Bhuvananda Saraswati immediately took the infant into his arms, danced with her throughout the temple, and then whispered mantras into the baby's ears in the process of initiation. In later years Shree Maa remarked how she began her sojourn on earth with such clarity of mind. Never did she find herself in confusion but understood that this was the grace of the Guru's initiation.

Kalyani used to spend long hours in the family's shrine room with her infant child on her lap, reciting mantras throughout the day. Shree Maa grew up in a temple surrounded by a tea plantation and the jungles and forests of Upper Assam. She knew no fear and was a friend to every animal. As she learned to walk, she would wander outside, then sit and look at the scenery with great wonder.

At the age of three she would offer water, basil, incense and light to the sun, and began to learn the sun salutation, an exercise of bowing to the rising sun while reciting mantras in praise of God.

At the age of four she kept the one day Shiva Ratri fast with the other family members. After that she wouldn't take anything to eat without first offering it at the family's altar in the shrine room.

At the age of five she would perform worship every day, and would fast on every *Ekadashi*, the eleventh day of every fortnight sacred to Lord Vishnu. It was at this time when her parents were thinking about the education of their daughter, that they decided to send their young girl back to the joint-family estate in Digboi, where she could attend the good schools of their community, rather than the village-type education provided her at the tea estate.

When it came time for Shree Maa to begin school, she moved back to the family home at Digboi. Here she helped her grandmother with the chores in caring for the family, and attended school. It was in this environment that she learned so much from her first real guru, her grandmother. Throughout her life Shree Maa only spoke of two gurus: Ramakrishna and her grandmother. "Grandmother was my teacher," Shree Maa told us. "She taught me how to be efficient and she had a very strong discipline. She taught me with her every action, because she did *sadhana* or spiritual practice with every action. She did the morning prayer without fail. It didn't matter if she was late or had a busy schedule for the day; always the prayers were the first thing each day. This is the natural way to be. Our whole family was regular in our practice of our spiritual ideals known as *dharma*. This was our daily life: faithfully making offerings to the sun and taking care of the morning and evening prayers and *pujas*. Often we did this together.

"Every time she would open up a new bottle or package, grandmother would say God's name in a mantra. Every day she would offer some coins on the altar, even one cent, or twenty-five cents. At the end of every year she would invite people to share in God's bounty. She would say, 'If you save that money, you should use it to do good *karma*.' Every day when she would cook her one meal of rice and lentils, she would put a handful of rice aside for Annapurna, the Goddess of Food and Grains. Every year she would observe the festival of Annapurna, and offer God's food to feed the people of the neighborhood. A priest would come to perform the *puja*, and we would feed everyone.

"In front of our house was a Kali temple. On the occasion of Kali Puja, my grandmother would light hundreds of lights and decorate the temple with candles. I learned so much from my grandmother. She taught me that every morning when I first got up I should bow to the mirror. Only later when I grew up did I begin to wonder whether I should be bowing to the reflection I saw because I am divine or whether I should be bowing to the mirror, the reflector, the Consciousness which witnesses creation."

Viewing Shree Maa's childhood home and the surrounding area, today one can only imagine what may have been the quality of life during her youth. The sprawling joint-family estate is populated by five generations of her family tree. The residences are cut into tiers on the mountain slopes. Some of the houses are connected by breezeways, others by rails and stairways, separating kitchens and dining areas from the living parts of the houses. The estate contains a myriad of fruits, guavas, many kinds of bananas, mangoes, pineapples, jack-fruits, olives, pomegranates, and a variety of plantains, potatoes, grains, pulses and flowers galore. The rolling hills are high above the clouds, and they look out into the Himalayan mountains.

In her youth Shree Maa's school was located below the clouds at the foot of the hill, and she used to walk the three to four miles each day, along with the other children. The children never wore socks or mittens despite the fact that their home was almost always in the colder area above the clouds. Shree Maa walked regularly to school, and it was in this atmosphere that she became impervious to the cold.

Her grandmother being burdened with the responsibilities of raising a large family alone, was very strict in discipline. Quite naturally, Shree Maa learned a way of life which was to result in the optimum efficiency in her every action. Her grandmother insisted that every potato be cut to a uniform size and all the vegetables be cut equal in proportion, and thus aesthetic to the sight, as well as tasty to the palate. From the time of her arrival in Digboi, the young girl never had time to waste, and was constantly engaged in cooking, cleaning, helping with the laundry, and all the various household duties, while learning from every aspect of creation.

One of the great lessons Maa remembers from her childhood was learned after sweeping the house. "When I was a young child, even from the age of about five years old, I used to help my grandmother in the household chores. One day I was sweeping the floor, and when I had finished cleaning the rooms, I threw the broom into the corner where it was kept. Immediately I heard the voice of Shree Ramakrishna calling to me from within, 'Hey there! That broom is your very good friend. Why do you treat it with such disrespect? If it weren't for his loving service, how would you clean your house?'

"Quickly I went over to the corner, picked up the broom and said, '*Namaskar*, I bow to your divine essence.' Gently I placed it back in its proper place, and from that time on I tried to regard each and every thing as a manifestation of divine grace. Every atom of creation deserves respect. All are reflections of the Divine Purpose, so that all must be attended to with divine respect."

At the age of six Maa would take her bath in the river early every morning, and would not dress herself until she had offered water to Lord Shiva and to the sacred *tulasi* plant. During the Sanskrit month of Shravan, in July, when the monsoon rains were pouring down hard, the naked girl took water to pour on the *tulasi* plant and slipped in the muddy waters. When she fell, she broke her arm, but because she was naked, she did not utter a sound. Later in the morning when her uncles rose from sleep, they saw the plight of their young niece, lying naked in the rain before the *tulasi* plant with her arm broken. At once they lifted her into the house and sent for the doctor, who set her arm in a cast to heal the broken bone. From that time on Shree Maa observed the strictest rules of modesty.

In another story from her childhood, Shree Maa recalls: "When I was about six, I went to my uncle's house during summer vacation in another town called Tinsukia. They had a Kali statue at their house, which was three feet tall, in a separate temple shrine room which opened into a garden. That day I was alone at home, sitting before the shrine crying for Kali. 'Mother, Mother, please give me *darshan*, the vision of you.'

"Behind me there was a window with no glass, and the shutters were open in order to allow light to come in. I turned around and looked through the opening and there was a big cobra looking back at me. It must have been about fifteen feet long and totally black. It could have easily come inside, and I was so scared I ran into the other room, closed every door and stuffed cloth in every hole in the house. My body was shaking.

"After about half an hour, I came out and the snake was not there. I called for people to come, but they could not find the snake. After that, for a long time, I felt that the snake was slithering across my body. I was still so afraid that I developed a fever. I could not explain it to anyone.

"Later, I was sitting in meditation. I didn't wear any cloth when I meditated, just one sari wrapped around me for modesty. When I went beyond into deep meditation, I looked at my entire life as though it were on a TV screen. It was then that I saw what had happened: somehow I saw the whole miracle of my life. When I got to the part about the snake, Kali said to me, 'When I gave you *darshan*, you got scared.' Then I realized that it was the vision of the Divine Mother for which I had been praying, and that God will not necessarily give me realization of only one form of divinity. Who knows in which form God will come?"

At the age of seven, Shree Maa began to wander into the forests to meet with *sadhus*, people who have renounced attachments to worldliness in pursuit of spiritual life. She had heard that the company of holy people was the greatest blessing, and whenever she could find time from her household duties, she would roam into the forests to seek out the company of saints. Hurriedly she would complete her chores, and then without telling anyone, she would disappear to secretly visit all the spiritual people that she heard about. She met many kinds of *sadhus*. Some smoked *ganja*, an intoxicant like marijuana, from *chillum* pipes made of clay, some spoke of the Vedas and the highest philosophy of oneness. She met them all, listened most respectfully to each, and quickly came to know what would become important in her life.

At the age of eight she began to participate in the annual *Shravan Festival* for Lord Shiva. Wearing just one cloth with her feet bare, she would join the thousands of pilgrims of all ages who would draw water from the sacred river at Vashishta Ashram. Then, carrying two full bowls in baskets hung from either end of a stick balanced on their shoulders, they would walk sixty-five miles to pour the waters on Lord Shiva's head at the Umananda Temple located on an island in the middle of the Brahmaputra River just opposite from Kamakhya. For three full days she marched on singing "*Om namah Shivaya*, I offer my loving respect to Lord Shiva," every time her foot touched the ground.

At night she halted at a village temple, and the village ladies came with offerings of food for the pilgrims. All throughout the night she sat beside the roaring fire and joined in the singing and listened to the stories that the *sadhus* told. Shree Maa was particularly enthralled by the stories told by a kindly old *sadhu*. She asked him, "Sir, I have already met so many great *sadhus* like yourself. I cannot remember all of their names. What is your name?"

"What is the value of a name?" he replied. "It is only an external recognition. We must remember the inner qualities of the people we meet. Even seeing people who dedicate their lives to cultivating divinity is a benefit. You don't need to recall their names."

"What benefit can be gained by seeing someone?" asked the young girl.

The *sadhu* continued, "Just as when a person sits in the sun and its warmth penetrates all throughout the body, just so, in the presence of an illuminated soul, the inner light of spiritual knowledge travels all throughout the inner being. Without speaking many words, these people share profound truths. Keep the doors and windows of your mind open and listen to their words of wisdom with humility. Then you will feel the fullness of their understanding. When a great person sends us a letter, we will not concern ourselves with which pen he or she used to write it down. We will pay more attention to the message. Wise people are the instruments of God's communications. Concern yourself with the message. The messenger is of minor importance."

After that evening, Shree Maa never asked new people

their names. But every now and then, when she saw a new person, a name would spontaneously come from her mouth, and most often that is what that person chose to be called for the rest of his or her life.

By the age of nine she knew every tree in the forest, and had no fear of wandering off in any direction with only the clothes on her back. She would spend most of her free time sitting in meditation. Nature would always provide for her, and she became so convinced of this principle that she never had occasion to doubt or fear again.

By the age of eleven she knew almost every cave in the eastern regions of the Himalayas. She would disappear for hours at a time to commune in meditation. People who saw her sitting with her eyes closed marveled at her radiant aura, and whenever they got the opportunity to ask her what she was doing, they would only receive a radiant smile in reply.

Even by the age of twelve she had traveled in the mountains with *sadhus*, meeting yogis and learning the mystical traditions of Sanskrit. Wherever she heard of the presence of a holy person, she would rush to that place to receive spiritual teaching. She remembered the wisdom of the instruction she had received years earlier, and with humility she would ask questions and receive teaching from them all.

One *sadhu* told her, "The greatest power in the world is the mind. But the mind, like a restless unruly horse, does not remain still. When by the practice of yoga an individual disciplines the mind, the mind is then ruled by the all-pervasive soul. Such a person controls all the powers of the world."

Then Maa sought the secret of discrimination. A *sadhu* told her, "The good and bad of each one's actions must be evaluated every moment. In order to discriminate as to the value of an action there is one criterion: should I die this moment, how will my actions be regarded? Therefore, if one has committed error, it must be rectified immediately. Don't ever think it will wait for tomorrow. There comes a time for everyone when tomorrow won't come."

She loved learning about *dharma*, about the ideals of perfection. Wherever she went she asked the *sadhus*, and one *sadhu* replied, "The path of *dharma* requires the light of knowledge for its illumination. If the light is not visible, it becomes easy to stumble like the blind in darkness."

Then what is liberation? She climbed high into the mountains to meet a great saint who explained, "Where there is life, there is death. Where there is welfare, there is misfortune. If you try to grasp pleasure, pain will surely follow. Whoever can be detached from pleasure and pain, who can reside in the eternal wisdom of the soul, finds the true bliss. This is called liberation."

Why are the realizations of various individuals different? Maa wanted to know if there is one God, why do various people of wisdom propound various paths? She found a man who was sitting in a cave made of ice, who offered her a suitable answer: "Just as the rain falls equally on all vegetation, but one plant gives forth red flowers and yet another gives forth yellow leaves, just so, the same knowledge affects various people differently depending on their individual natures, tendencies and desires."

In the Kali Temple on the Kamakhya mountain a *sadhu* told her, "Words inscribed in stone are never erased, while what is written on water cannot remain for a moment. Do not allow anger or enmity to remain in your mind any longer than words written upon the water."

A wonderful woman renunciate told her, "There are many gifts more valuable than money: a kind word and a friendly smile often are regarded as the greatest wealth."

And another said, "Every being is a divine incarnation. But

caught in the illusion of our own importance, we forget who we really are. And then we search for liberation from our own bondage. This is the illusion of the Lord of Illusions."

Shree Maa incorporated all of these jewels of teachings into her life. It seemed she didn't need formal study of her school subjects. Common sense and the blessings of the saints made her an outstanding student at college where she won many honors for her scholastic aptitude. She frequently won prizes for her singing and dancing, and she charmed all the girls in her school with the way she styled her hair.

Her behavior at school made her extremely popular with both faculty and fellow students. She could always identify with everyone, avoided all conflict, and built bridges in all adversity. Even when her family affluence grew, Shree Maa would not engage in a lifestyle beyond the means of her community. After her uncle purchased a car, he would stop whenever he saw her walking in the road and ask to take her to the college on his way to work, but Shree Maa refused to ride in the car, saying that as all the other students had to walk, she would go on foot as well.

Community Service

Shree Maa quickly became the neighborhood *pujari* and was constantly involved in arranging festivals of worship for the entire community. Whenever any household in the neighborhood had any occasion for worship or celebration, like a wedding, birth of a child, or other occasion for rejoicing, they would always send notice to Shree Maa who would immediately come to assist with the organization and preparation of the ceremonies. It was as if she became the spirit of the whole community.

When she was in her teens, she became associated with the Netaji Forward Block, a social service organization, and organized all of her friends and the children of her community to prepare ground spices in their homes to sell to raise money for the poor. Later she used her organizing skills to dispatch mobile medical teams to villages, where free medical samples, which had been collected by Shree Maa and her friends, were distributed. In this way free medical treatment was provided to poor village people.

Mystical Experiences

It was in her early teens that Shree Maa began to experience extremely intense mystical states of consciousness. Daily she would sit for her worship and meditation, and every evening she would read the *Bhagavad Gita* and chant passages from the *Chandi Path*. It was as if an inner voice was calling to her to free herself from the bonds of material life.

One day while she was performing worship in the early morning, she felt an energy calling to her from behind. She turned around from her altar to see a large cobra standing with raised hood peering into the window. Her eyes met the eyes of the snake, and for some time the two stood transfixed staring at one another. Finally the snake lowered his head and slid away, whereupon Shree Maa lost consciousness. When she awoke, her entire family was standing around her bed imploring her to stop meditating and to give up all her spiritual practices. Many are the families that wish for their children to be successful in the world, and Shree Maa's family feared that her spiritual inclination would make her a burden to the family.

On another occasion, she was sitting in the shrine room of their family house when she felt an energy calling to her from outside. Immediately she rose from her worship and ran outside to the back of the house. Looking in all directions, she saw no one. But suddenly she looked down at the ground beneath her, where she found a small silver *trishula* or trident with the name "*Shankar*," a name of Shiva which means the Cause of Peace, written on it. To this day she wears it around her neck.

Jesus Won't Let Her Run Away

Throughout her high school and college life she became more introspective. No longer interested in family outings nor in other social functions, she enjoyed spending long hours in worship and meditation in her family's shrine room. Her family became very concerned and began to apply ever greater pressure upon her to desist from these metaphysical experiences. They began to put obstacles in the way of her worship. To distract her from her meditation exercises, they would constantly call her on the pretext of performing some errand or chore. The family couldn't understand why she was chanting so much, why she was spending so much time in the shrine room, in meditation, or running off to meet *sadhus*. And they couldn't understand why she wouldn't eat fish or chicken or eggs along with the other members of the family.

Shree Maa explained her convictions about food in this way: "My grandmother was a vegetarian her whole life, but the rest of our family ate chicken once a week. One day we were sitting at the table and everyone was trying to get me to eat chicken. Still, I would not eat it. They began yelling until finally I picked up a piece of chicken and put it close to my mouth. It felt like twisting... like everybody was twisting me. I felt the energy on my *crown chakra* began swirling, and I fainted. After that they would no longer make me eat meat. From that time I was slowly giving up my taste for all food.

"Another time I was sitting under my mosquito net at 2:30 in the morning, deep in meditation. One of my uncles got up to get a drink of water, when he saw me in meditation. 'What are you doing?' he called. When he began pushing me, it was like an electric current going through my body. At that time the braids in my hair opened up of their own accord, and I could no longer wear any ornaments. All jewelry fell off from me. In this way my family continually pulled me back from my spiritual yearning, but even so, from that time on I had lots of devotees, and they gave me support and inspiration."

After experiencing so many difficulties in the performance of her religious exercises, Shree Maa determined to run away.

In the darkness of night, Shree Maa quietly awoke, packed a few of her belongings, placed a note of farewell and started to leave. Over the door of their house was a portrait of Jesus, and as she reached for the door, she looked up into the eyes of the picture of Jesus. At once the artwork appeared so lifelike, so real, it was as though the Lord, Himself, was standing in front of the door blocking her way. Deep within her, Shree Maa heard a voice which said, "I am with you always. You don't need to run away to find me." She looked at the picture so deliberately that suddenly she went into *samadhi* and fell to the floor in a mystical trance. Jesus would not let her run away!

When she woke up in the morning, all of her family members were standing around her bed with great concern. "Please don't leave us," they said. "We won't put any more obstacles in your path. You can worship as much as you like and as long as you like, but don't leave our home and our family."

Shree Maa returned to her shrine room and sat for worship in the bliss of solitude. In the ecstasy of the deepest meditation, she looked at the picture of Shree Ramakrishna blessing her from her altar. Suddenly the voice of Shree Ramakrishna was clearly audible to her: "You must finish your college education. I have much work that must be done by you, and to accomplish that you must be educated."

The Last Years of Her Formal Education

Even after receiving this admonishment from her primary
Guru, Shree Ramakrishna, Shree Maa found her classes intol-
erably boring. Unable to find a way to apply all of the information she was required to memorize, she rarely attended
school, and remained mostly in the ecstasy of spiritual experience. Her classmates would find her sitting on a rock gazing at
the Himalayan vistas or down by the river staring into the
meandering waters. For hours she would sit with her eyes
closed.

All too soon the time of her examinations came, and Shree
Maa felt herself totally unprepared and at a loss. That morning
she sat in her meditation and moved into the delight of mystical experience. She called to Thakur Ramakrishna, "What will
happen? I am not prepared."

Shree Ramakrishna replied, "Be without fear. I am with
you."

Shree Maa grew angry and turned the photograph on the
altar around until it faced the wall. "Because you have been
with me, I have not been with my studies. You are the cause of
my not being prepared! Everyone else has been studying!"

Shree Maa stormed out of the shrine room and went to the
college. To her amazement she found all the students milling
about the entrance. The college was closed due to a strike, and
the examination had been rescheduled for two months into the
future. She raced home and immediately went to the shrine
room and bowed down. She caressed the photograph of Shree
Ramakrishna and danced around the room. Now, realizing the
seriousness of her predicament, she began to study in earnest,
and a few months later, passed her exam and was awarded her
bachelor of arts degree.

Chapter Two

Wandering Years

Kamakhya Temple and Wandering Years

After Shree Maa's graduation from college, her grandmother became very ill. Shree Maa attended to her grandmother's needs night and day, but her divine aspiration was calling, and she felt the need to move into deeper *sadhana*. In her deepest meditation, the vision of Shree Ramakrishna told her, "You have to go to your own place." He gave her a date to leave the house, and she made a reservation for the train to Gauhati.

When the day of departure approached, Shree Maa went to take leave from each of her uncles. First, she asked for the blessings from the oldest uncle, who was adamant in his displeasure because he had his heart set on seeing Maa continue her education. "If she studies," he thought, "maybe she will become someone important."

Shree Maa went to each of the other uncles in turn. They expressed their disapproval as well. Then Maa went to her grandmother, who was advanced in age, in failing health, and truly dependent on Maa's help for performing the duties of running the household. Maa's grandmother gave her blessings without hesitation, saying, "It is your time now. Go! You should not be present at my end. Your preparation is complete, and I will be watching you from above."

Then Maa realized that the one who needed her most could let her go without selfishness, but the others who had no need, bound her with attachment to their own desires.

It was a calling of divine inspiration, a magnetic force which drew her towards a destiny she could not conceive. She felt powerless to resist its attraction, and had no recourse but to follow. She did not consciously plan her movements, but was led on by a divine power, unconscious of any motivation to achieve "something," to go "somewhere" or to become "somebody." She was one with her own inner self, and experienced no necessity to become something "other."

With just the clothes on her back and a copy of the *Chandi Path*, Shree Maa boarded the train to Gauhati. She went first to the Kamakhya Temple where she offered worship. And she began to dwell on the holy mountain. Sometimes she was found in an unconscious state sitting on the rocks beside the Brahmaputra River. Sometimes she would stay in the caves in the mountain or at the Bhairavi Temple on the top of its summit. At the Bholanath Giri cremation grounds she was often seated next to the funeral fires. At Pan Bazaar she was often found sitting in the Durga Temple. She became very famous as the Goddess of the Mountain.

She wandered into the jungles of the interior of Assam, oblivious to any impending danger. She had truly become the "Friend of the Universe," and never imagined that her safety might be in jeopardy. "What risk, what fear?" she later joked with disciples. "When I am one with the soul of existence, how will any one or any thing cause me harm?"

Tribal villagers knew her well. They found her sitting on rocks, beside the river waters, at the foot of a tree, or in the caves in the Himalayan foothills. Her renunciation was legendary. She carried only the simple cloth she was wearing, and went for days at a time without any food, just sitting at any conducive place with her eyes closed, looking inside to some greater reality few can comprehend. She would experience such deep *samadhi* for such prolonged periods that an aura of illumination would radiate whenever she sat to meditate.

The little beings of the forest would congregate around her wherever she sat in an isolated place: chipmunks and sparrows, snakes and squirrels (the myriad of forest dwellers would forget the presence of each other because of their attraction to her being.) She sat in the mountains and concentrated on the peaks of the Himalayas. She sat beside the rivers and followed the flowing water to its union with the sea. She would walk in any direction with such grace, exuding love and power and confidence, as though her naked feet had never felt the prick of a thorn. And she never looked back at her former life. Once she walked forward, she never looked back.

Once, while walking in the mountains of Shillong, moved by inspiration, she sat down to meditate. She looked deeply into herself and for some hours became absorbed in *samadhi*, unaware of any movement in the outer world around her. When she opened her eyes and returned to the awakened state of reality, she found several hundred village people sitting before her in silent respect. These people had heard of the meditating yogini in the forest, and left their jobs and homes to come for her *darshan*.

All were overjoyed to see the now famous saint opening her eyes. They greeted her silent gaze with dancing lights in their faces. Suddenly Shree Maa began to sing. With a voice choked with emotion, she sang her own songs of longing for the divine spirit in every form. Her voice of unselfish abandon in supreme love, conveyed her spontaneous offering to God. She communicated such a vibration that inspired the entire village. Overwhelmed, they invited her to return with them to their village, the whole village united in preparing a feast and in celebrating the presence of the saint. In the dark of night while the village people were gaily singing devotional songs, Shree Maa quietly and unceremoniously vanished into the silence of the forest.

Just as the famous Babaji became a tradition in the Himalayas, so also Shree Maa became a legend throughout Northeastern India. Thousands of people will swear that it was she who came to their rescue in their time of need. Each one of their stories is more wonderful than the next: how she helped with Annubha's marriage or Sangeeta's baby or

Sushil's employment or Prasad's school.

One time in the foothills of Darjeeling, she sat in deep contemplation before a temple to Goddess Kali just adjacent to a tea plantation. Hearing of the presence of the saint, the wife of the plantation's manager came immediately to the temple, sat down in the doorway and began to cry. Rising from her meditation, Shree Maa went over and began to comfort the troubled lady. What was the problem? The lady began to tell her story. "Our community has too much conflict between disputing interests. How are we to live in such a situation?"

"As a Divine Mother who loves all of Her children equally!" came Shree Maa's reply. "Inspire them all to surrender their selfishness. Each of the members of your family loves their own favorite dishes, and because you love them, you cook for each according to their individual desires. You are that Divine Mother who loves all your children and gives to each according to his or her need. The fish at the bottom of the pond is always in the mud, but never dirty. Serve all of your children with love, but don't let your service be a bondage," was her advice.

Hundreds of tourists have visited the famous caves near Tejpur, Assam. Near to where one alights from the bus, after passing through the row of tea stalls and the cacophony of sounds inviting visitors for cold drinks and snacks, stand the huge entrances of the caves carved into the rocks. The large chambers which were used for community worship are adorned with sculptures of the various deities.

What most tourists do not know is that one mile to the north of the caves is a small footpath leading into the mountainous terrain. Winding into the back country along the small path, after three miles one reaches a stream. Again by following the stream for a little more than a mile, one will come to a series of pools — clear, fresh, deliciously inviting pools, near the city of caves. What a civilization it was!

The ancients constructed rock hewn troughs carrying running water to each structure, with special drains to carry away waste. They had elaborate stairways to reach the higher elevated dwellings. This whole complex of caves is now abandoned, populated only by wildlife and an occasional wandering monk. It is perfect for performing the most sublime *sadhana* or spiritual discipline.

Shree Maa trekked up the mountain side alone, carrying a bundle of provisions. Finding the entire area vacant, she selected a cave, set down her things, and then bathed in the clear waters of the nearby pool. Returning to her seat, she began to recite the mantras of the worship ceremony for occupying a new dwelling. After her worship and meditation, she began to clean and organize the cave. The last occupant had thoughtfully left everything ready for the next, which is a tradition among *sadhus* wherever they travel. Spirituality means giving more than we take. A *sadhu* will want to leave an environment in a condition at least as good as it was found.

Shree Maa made a wood fire and cooked a small quantity of rice with a potato boiled in its center, and then made offering of the food before her altar to Lord Shiva and her guru, Shree Ramakrishna. She ate in silence, relishing each morsel as she looked out at the expanse of natural beauty around her. By the time she had finished eating her meal and cleaning up, darkness had fallen, and she sat on her small bed of leaves and went into meditation until sleep overtook her.

It was three o'clock in the morning when she awoke and sat up on the blanket spread upon the hard ground which was her bed. She recited mantras for Ganesh, Shiva, the Divine Mother and Ramakrishna, and performed *japa*, recitation of the rosary, until the first light of dawn. When it was easy to see the terrain, she rose and attended to the calls of nature, and having bathed and washed her clothes, returned to her fire for a cup of tea.

Now she established her *asana* and began to sing the *Chandi Path*. Her chanting was so melodic! How skillfully did she weave the Sanskrit mantras in and out throughout the recitation, and her *pranayam* or rhythmic breathing was so regular that each breath was exactly equal in length. She sat for hours like a statue, without the slightest movement. Except for the turning of the pages of the text and the sweet tones of chanted Sanskrit there was nothing to indicate that the form sitting there was alive. Only the radiance of her light and those marvelous tones of chanting could indicate the presence of a life force. And the chanting went on.

It was late afternoon before she stopped, her face beaming with light. She was radiant in every detail and there was no one to share it with but the universe. She was love made manifest — radiating the power of that love into her communion with the Soul of Life.

Rising from her seat, she took a bath and washed her cloth, and sat down on her bed at the mouth of the cave to look out into the eternity of nature. She was Mother Nature, she was the mantra, she was the divinity she was worshiping. And she knew she was *Chandi*, the Divine Mother Goddess. Her meditation grew deeper and deeper until she merged into *samadhi*.

The winter passed by in but a moment. One hundred and eight days merged into one continuous offering of spiritual practice and contemplation. Shree Maa was all light. She was all peace. Every day as she read the *Chandi*, when she reached the last chapter the Supreme Goddess would ask her, "What do you want?" And each day Shree Maa requested, "A life of pure devotion and blessings for all your creation!" And the Goddess said, "*Tata-stu*. I grant you that!"

Here she was, Shree Maa transformed into radiant Light!

Having completed her vow of one hundred and eight days of worship, she restocked her campsite for the next spiritual practitioner, and in a state of divine intoxication, wandered off towards Bengal. She was full of God. She had become the Divine Mother!

In Bengali the term for this state is *mast*. In English it must translate as "blissful, full of joy, total freedom and lack of limitation." All of those adjectives try to describe that state of divine intoxication which became Shree Maa's natural orientation to life. It was inconceivable for a woman to travel around India alone. It was even more inconceivable for a woman to travel alone without money, possessions or care. Shree Maa never knew any fear. She always said, "*Lajja, grihna, bhaya - tin takite nai:* Shame, hatred, fear — these three will not remain."

That is why so many looked at her with such awe. She traveled in ways that men dared not. And she experienced no difficulty in doing so. One look at the radiant aura wrapped around her tender frame, and not even the bravest among fools dared to approach her with impure motives. Her purity was her shield, and all who saw her readily understood who she was and what she had come to offer.

It was no surprise to find her sitting in the forest of Arunachala at the break of Spring singing the *Chandi Path* beside a flowing mountain stream. On some days she would alternate between the *Chandi* and the *Bhagavad Gita*. "*Gita*," she said, "is the definition of the goal. It says again and again, 'Whatever you do, do for God. Surrender your attachment. Give up your selfishness.' The *Chandi* shows us how to do that. The *Chandi* says, 'Sit down in one *asana*, in one posture, and recite. Don't move your knees until it is complete. Watch the Divine Mother cut down your attachments. Away with your anger, away goes desire. One by one She takes them away.' The *Chandi* is the path to the realization of *Gita*."

Shree Maa was high in the mountains of the Himalayas. She would sing the *Chandi* in the morning, the *Gita* in the afternoon, and sit in silent meditation throughout the night. After a few days her rations were finished and yet she remained. The *bhava* or feeling was too beautiful to leave. The density of the tall fir trees which covered the mountain sides for as far as one could see, the lush shades of green of the foliage, the snow caps of the Himalayas above, the crystal clarity of the stream, and the sweet music of the flowing waters dancing between the banks, tripping over rocks, singing as it ran, all created an ambiance — an environment conducive to *sadhana*. So she stayed and fasted and smiled at nature and reveled in her inner Self.

After four days with no food, she began to grow concerned. "I don't know how far I will need to go before I find provisions," she thought. "Tomorrow I had better leave."

Just as she was contemplating her situation, she suddenly heard a sound like a bell. "There it is again. How strange!" she thought. She climbed to the top of the hill overlooking the path that followed the stream up the mountain coming from civilization. Then she heard the sound again. Up the path, coming over an incline, she saw a goat with a bell on its neck! Shree Maa was overjoyed!

Then followed the sound of a second bell! And a third! And then a chorus! Staring at the rise in the path, Shree Maa saw a whole herd of goats and sheep, followed by a horse packed with provisions and a family of shepherds guiding their flock, Mama and Papa and three little children, two walking with sticks and one in the arms of his mother, and their dog. That family walked up to where Shree Maa was camped and stopped.

Right on cue, without a word being spoken, they unpacked

their horse. They rolled out a bright carpet in which was wrapped the possessions of the entire family: big brass pots, cooking utensils, bedding and clothes. Within a few minutes the dog had gathered the flock, the children were milking the goats, and the mother was making tea over a roaring fire that father had started. Then the "Papa" sat and smoked his water pipe while the kids went off to bathe in the stream.

A few minutes later the wife came over and stood before Shree Maa, bowed humbly, and presented her a pitcher full of tea made from fresh goat's milk. With great joy Shree Maa accepted the offering, and after a short negotiation as to which language they would speak, the two ladies sat down to cultivate their friendship.

This family lived outside under the trees twelve months a year. They made an annual pilgrimage to the plains in the winter and up to the high mountains during the monsoon. This was their life. They knew every tree in the forest. They knew all the edible herbs, when to stock up on which commodity, and how to live in harmony with nature. Shree Maa decided to join the family in this year's pilgrimage.

How joyous were her days traveling in such simplicity. Daily she performed her *sadhana*, and was ready by the time the family broke camp. In the evenings she would bathe in the rivers and streams, then sit for meditation into the dead of night. And she continued to radiate her glory!

One can only imagine the state of consciousness of this *sadhika*, a female renunciate, as she roamed the North of India! She stayed at Vashishta Ashram, the hermitage of the famous sage in Central Assam, where she studied with other *sadhus*. She was often found in Parashuram Kunda, a sacred lake in Upper Assam, and practiced spiritual disciplines in the many sacred forests and groves throughout the area. For more than eight years her daily meal consisted of a little piece of turmeric and basil leaves, washed down with some sandal paste mixed with water. In 1980, she weighed only sixty pounds, and her very name had become a tradition throughout Northern India. The stories about her are unending.

There are just too many stories to tell of her wandering through the countryside of Assam, Sikkim, Bengal, Bihar, and even the Himalayas of Bhutan, Nepal and Uttar Pradesh. If you say the name of Shree Maa in almost any village, you will hear many stories describing her peaceful demeanor, her loving service and her teachings of wisdom.

The stories of the villagers made Shree Maa a legend. Now new devotees brought her greater fame and her capacities continued to grow. A school principal brought her into contact with the State Board of Education; an attorney brought her into association with the State Department of Justice; a businessman introduced her to a relationship with the Ministry of Economic Development. Soon she was introduced to the Inspector General of Police and then the Chief Minister of the State of Bengal, and then there was a continual stream of politicians, government servants and businessmen, farmers, villagers and housewives flocking to see Shree Maa wherever she went.

One day she traveled to the banks of the Brahmaputra River in Gauhati with a number of disciples. Seeing her approaching, the boatmen along the river ran up and bowed before her on the sand of the river bank. They asked in most respectful terms, "Maa, Maa, where are you going?"

Shree Maa replied "I want to take my disciples to the Umananda Temple, on the island in the Brahmaputra River opposite from the Kamakhya Temple."

"Maa, Maa," the boatmen called. "Please ride in our boat."

With great reverence the boatmen escorted the group to their boats. The boatmen told the few passengers who were waiting, "Get up from my boat! Shree Maa will sit here!" They emptied the boats completely, and Shree Maa and her group were seated within.

As the boatmen rowed out to the island in the center of the river, one middle-aged man told his story in coarse and rustic Assamese language. He said that when he was a young man, one day there was a great storm in the area of Gauhati. "I was working on the boats with my family that day, and Shree Maa was a passenger. The boat began to toss about on the rough waters of the river, and everyone began to cry with fear. Only Shree Maa sat silently at the front of the boat uttering prayers. All of the other passengers were struck with terror, fearing that the boats would be sunk or capsized in the howling winds and turbulent waters. But seeing Shree Maa's composure, everyone took courage, and suddenly, as quickly as the storm had arisen, the winds subsided.

"By the time we reached the shore, everyone knew that it was Shree Maa's blessings by which we were all saved. Since that time, all of the boatmen regard her as the Goddess of Kamakhya. I was a young man at that time, and Shree Maa looks just the same today as she did then. Nobody knows how old she is, but we know her as the Eternal Goddess of the River."

Durga Temple at Parashuram Kunda

Near Parashuram Kunda, there was a large tea estate. The manager of the estate was a Punjabi man by the name of Prem Singh. Mr. Singh was a practical business man, and as a Sikh, had no devotion towards the Hindu religion. But every year the Hindu coolies who harvested tea leaves at the tea plantation celebrated their festivals with great devotion. One year Shree Maa attended the festival and experienced such a state of ecstasy that Mr. Singh was taken aback. Mr. Singh's wife had been disturbed by various physical ailments for many years. Mr. Singh brought Shree Maa to his home, where she performed worship and instructed him to support the devotional celebrations of the Hindu coolies. He accepted her advice and by the climax of the period of worship, his wife's complaints had subsided. He was so ecstatic that he built a temple for the Goddess Durga, and for many years Shree Maa shared in the annual worship.

At Shree Maa's recommendation, Mr. Singh employed a Hindu man from Bengal as the *pujari* or priest of that temple. Many people were astounded at the unorthodox manner of his worship. He threw the flowers in every direction and sang songs to the Goddess that he spontaneously composed.

In Gauhati, Shree Maa met a young girl who was suffering from leprosy. The young girl implored, "Maa, what can I do to become free from this disease?"

Shree Maa told her to go to the Durga Temple at Parashuram Kunda, and ask the priest to offer worship on her behalf. When the young girl approached the priest to help her become free of her disease, he said to her, "You stay here and shine the utensils that I use for my worship every day. The more the utensils shine, the faster your cure will come."

The young leper girl was amazed at such a possibility. It is rare in India that lepers are even allowed entrance to a temple, much less to actively participate in the worship of God, touching the utensils with which the Goddess is served. Appreciating this opportunity, the young girl moved into the temple and began to shine the utensils. She was so filled with the bliss of her new-found existence that she hardly noticed the passage of time. No longer was she aware that she had a disease, nor did she notice when the disease vanished. She grew into a radiant gentle young woman, and took the greatest delight in serving her guru and performing the ceremonies of worship to the Divine Mother.

One day an American doctor who had been traveling in the area as part of a team working with the World Health Organization came into the temple after having heard of the reputation of the *pujari* and of his unorthodox ways of worship. After meeting the priest and offering *puja*, he saw the young lady silently performing her duties at the temple with such love and purity of devotion. He looked at the radiance of her beautiful smile as she prepared for the worship, and he said to her, "You are my Durga. Come with me and share with me your light and inspiration." Some years ago they were married and they now live in New York City where he has his medical practice and she is an active participant in the Hindu Temple community.

Maligaon and Bholagiri Cremation Grounds

High above the hills in Maligaon, a *sadhu* lived in an ashram surrounded by a small terraced farm. When Shree Maa came wandering past one day, the *sadhu* came running out of his hut and called to her, "Mother, Mother, please come and let me have the privilege to serve you." Calling his family of disciples, he explained to them, "Quickly prepare the best you can. Do you know who this is? *Maa Janani*. She is Shree Maa of Kamakhya." He seated her upon his own *asana*, washed her feet and began to feed her with his own hands. "Maa," he said with great concern. "Please take care of yourself. In your future lies the future of many. Your influence will expand around the world."

At Bholagiri Cremation Grounds one young widow accompanied the funeral party to perform the last rites for her deceased husband. She was a well-educated young lady with a seemingly brilliant future, but an unfortunate accident had claimed her husband at a young age. In her grief she refused to leave the cremation ground where she just sat writing and writing. Shree Maa went regularly to visit her and over the years requested all of her disciples to make sure that the lady had enough supplies. "Give her clothing, give her blankets and give her enough paper and ink," instructed Shree Maa. "Make sure she is provided for." Often Shree Maa would wander down to the cremation grounds to visit the unfortunate widow.

In Maligoan there was a railway colony which housed the workers employed by the eastern railway department. Many disciples and devotees came from the railway colony and when Shree Maa expressed a desire to travel, they provided her with a first class railway pass to cover all the expenses en route to her destinations.

It was during these journeys that she visited Calcutta, and went on from there to have experiences all over India. In Calcutta she began her sojourn in a railway colony, but she soon made many friends in and around the Ramakrishna Mission. Thus, it wasn't strange that she was invited along with delegates from around the world to an ecumenical convocation, a World Conference of Interreligious Harmony, held in the Netaji Subash Chandra Bose Stadium in Calcutta. Prior to the convocation, Shree Maa sat in her room for some days writing a lengthy philosophical treatise, which she delivered to the president of the Ramakrishna Mission, who had it read and quoted from it frequently during the convocation.

One day the archbishop of the Bandal Church sent devotees to invite Shree Maa to attend the Sunday service. She went along with a group of her own devotees, and was delighted at the presence of Jesus in the church and the mutual respect and harmony between the two spiritual leaders. She spoke with the archbishop at length, and they discovered a fine relationship in working together toward inspiring mankind to pursue the noble path of *dharma*.

Resemblance to Shree Sarada Devi

In Jayrambati Shree Maa became the guest of the Ramakrishna Mission and was provided the old house of Shree Sarada Devi for her lodging. A number of people congregated outside the house, especially the older residents of the village who had known Shree Sarada Maa, Shree Ramakrishna's wife. They were amazed at the striking physical resemblance between Shree Maa and Sarada Devi. But when Shree Maa began to speak, many were astounded at hearing her words. "The voice is the same!" they proclaimed. "And the sincerity and integrity with which she speaks is the same. She is not speaking words from books, but just like Sarada Maa, she is communicating from her heart and personal experience."

Daily devotees would congregate outside the room where Shree Maa was staying. Maa would come out every evening and sit on a bed on the veranda and conduct *satsangha*, sharing spiritual inspiration, stories and songs with the visitors. Sometimes she would sing, but mostly she would sit in silence with her eyes closed. Everyone was moved to meditation in Shree Maa's presence.

The abbot of the Ramakrishna Math in Jayrambati came to visit her. After sending away the crowds he confronted Shree Maa in private. "Have you come to destroy our Ramakrishna Mission? Don't divide devotees from the administrators of the rules and regulations of our community. You know, if Shree Ramakrishna were to come here according to our rules, we would not be able to give him a place to stay! We are now bound by the rules. Don't make yourself so accessible to the public!" And with that he stormed out in a huff.

Mr. Ganapati Mukerji, the oldest living descendent of Shree Sarada Devi came to visit Shree Maa. In his possession were the relics of the Holy Mother. He sat Shree Maa down upon the *asana* of Sarada Maa, washed her feet and fed her from the same utensils which Sarada Maa had used. To him it was the highest respect he could offer. Even many years later Shree Maa said, "Ganapati is one of my children."

Rath Festival at Jaganath

Shree Maa arrived alone at Jaganath Puri during the *rath* (car) festival of Jaganath. It was evening, and of course there were no vacant accommodations anywhere in the town. Shree Maa sat down in a *rickshaw* outside of the railway station. "Where shall I take you, Mother?" the *rickshaw* driver inquired.

Shree Maa replied "I will need some place to stay."

The *rickshaw* driver was puzzled and said, "There is no place to stay in all of Puri. I will take you to Bharat Seva Ashram. Perhaps they can guide you to a safe place for a woman traveling alone."

He took her to the Bharat Seva Ashram and left her in the waiting hall, which was filled with pilgrims looking for accommodations.

Somewhat aloof from the distraught and distressed pilgrims, Shree Maa stood in total comfort at the end of the line. Suddenly, from one of the doors came a priest of the temple, who walked right up to Shree Maa and asked, "Where are you staying?"

Shree Maa replied, "I don't know yet."

He grabbed her small bag and said. "Maa, please stay with me!"

"All right," said Shree Maa and followed him to his very fine house at the side of the temple. She was given a private room where she sat for long hours of meditation.

After a long time, when Shree Maa did not come out of her room for food, the pundit became disturbed. "That poor woman is sitting in her room all by herself, afraid to go out-side, having no food," he thought. He decided to bring her a platter of food. Entering the room he saw Shree Maa sitting in the ecstasy of *samadhi*. After hearing of his experience, other priests and *sadhus* from around the temple began to pay visits to Shree Maa.

She rarely spoke and when she did, she said very little. But around her was an aura of light. Groups of devotees would congregate in her room and sing *kirtan*, songs about God, while she sat in the ecstasy of spiritual communion. During those days in Puri her face had the shine of mystical light, and people from all over India began to come to take blessings from the saint known as Shree Maa of Kamakhya.

One day Swami Vishnu Deva Vairagi, a highly respected religious authority, came to visit Shree Maa. He asked, "What *sadhana* have you been doing to come to this state? What kind of *tantra* have you been practicing, you who come from Kamakhya, the seat of *tantra*?"

Shree Maa looked at him with tender compassion. "She answered, "I know no *tantra*, I know nothing of *sadhana*. I have only been listening to the orders of Shree Ramakrishna all my life, and I do what I do because of his orders," was her answer. The swami bowed down in respect before he took his leave.

Shree Maa returned to Calcutta as a great celebrity, and wherever she would stay, crowds of devotees, rich and poor alike, would congregate. Every night there was *kirtan* and var-ious forms of devotional singing. Sometimes Shree Maa would begin to sing. Pin-drop silence would permeate the atmosphere. Her songs came from the depths of spiritual feel-ing, and her music would inspire the wandering minds to silence. At other times she would just sit with closed eyes, immovable as a stone statue, radiating the blessings of divine presence to all who would come to her.

Chapter Three
With Devotees in India

Pilgrimage

One time a number of wealthy devotees decided to take Shree Maa on a pilgrimage. They took her first to the guest house at the Temple of Rameshwaram, where Ram had offered *puja* to Lord Shiva for a successful victory over the demon King Ravana of Lanka. The next morning, the chief priest of the temple came to visit Shree Maa, Mr. Prasad, Mr. Parbat and other devotees in their entourage. "We would like to perform a great *yagya* fire sacrifice for you," proclaimed the priest. "We would like twenty-one priests of our temple to recite the texts of the Yajur Veda before the *homa* fire within the temple."

Mr. Prasad inquired innocently, "What *dakshina* (priestly fee) would you like for such a wonderful sacrifice?"

Shree Maa smiled to herself.

The priest replied in all seriousness, "We would like 10,000 rupees."

Mr. Parbat, who was the secretary of education in the government of West Bengal, fainted on the spot. The priest was stunned by this reaction and shouted in dismay, "Call the doctor! Get some water!"

Shree Maa sprinkled water on Mr. Parbat's head and when he slowly regained consciousness, he looked into Shree Maa's eyes and said, "*Amar darshan hogaya* (I just had the vision of God). No need to go back to the temple!"

The chief priest apologized and said that whatever worship Shree Maa wished to perform would be done at no charge. He summoned the other priests, and together they escorted Shree Maa to the main gate of the temple.

At the main gate of the temple was a large elephant, who reared and trumpeted through his trunk when he saw Shree Maa. The elephant took a wreath of flowers from his *mahut* (caretaker) and put the garland around Shree Maa's neck, bowing in salute. Then the chief priest took a large silver scepter and placed it in Shree Maa's hands, and with a band playing temple music, led the procession around the entire temple complex. They took Shree Maa to the innermost sanctum of the temple and allowed her to personally worship the deity. Mother took a leaf of the *bel* tree prepared in gold and offered it to the Rameshwaram deity, just as Shree Sarada Devi had offered some fifty years before.

Returning to their room in the guest house, Mother astounded the entire group by saying, "I must return to Calcutta now. We will have to cancel the rest of the pilgrimage. One of my devotees is calling me, and I must go."

"But, but...," they all protested. "Maa, we have come so far, and have organized this pilgrimage at great expense, taking leave from our jobs. Can't we stay a little longer?"

"No, let us return to Calcutta immediately!" came her emphatic answer.

Everyone packed their belongings and went to the railway station, taking the first train to Calcutta.

Reaching Calcutta unannounced late at night, Shree Maa made a mad dash to the taxi stand and called to the driver, "Lelua Railway Colony!"

After twenty minutes of riding in the cab, she pointed out a house to the driver. He stopped his cab and let her out. Though it was late at night, she climbed the stairs of the tenement house and knocked on the door. When an astonished husband opened the door, Shree Maa slapped him on his cheek. She then walked right past him to see his wife who had been sitting at her altar for two days calling Shree Maa's name.

The wife rose up and bowed with great delight. "I knew you would come!" she cried. "I knew you would come!"

That lady was a real devotee, but her husband was fighting with her about Shree Maa. The wife said, "If it is true that

Shree Maa is the Holy Mother, I'm not getting up from this
seat until she comes and gives her blessings." The lady had sat
for two days and did not give up. When Mother came to her
house, she got up from her seat and said, "My Mother is true!"

Vashishta and the Lotus Flower

Vashishta's long white beard was tied in a knot at the base
of his chin. The locks of his white hair were wrapped into a
bun on the top of his head. His frail body gave evidence of
many years of deprivations and the wrinkles around his eyes
shared the delight of his exploration. Maa called him Vashishta
because, just as Shree Maa looked in appearance to be the
image of Sarada Devi, just so, Vashishta appeared to be the
ancient sage who had bequeathed great wisdom to all of pos-
terity. His real name was Prabod Chatterji, a Brahmin from
one of the villages of West Bengal. Born a Brahmin, Vashishta
was educated in the school system established with British discipline.

After finishing his education, Vashishta's parents instructed him to marry. Instead, the young man fled to his guru's
ashram. "Guruji, I have no desire to marry. Please save me!
Talk some reason, put some sense into the heads of my parents, who are demanding that I enter into a life of bondage,
even when I have no desire for the enjoyments of worldly
pleasures. Please let me take refuge in your ashram. Let me
stay and live with you. I will be a *sannyasi*."

The compassionate guru looked at the distressed young
man and said, "My dear Prabod, no one can run away to
become a *sannyasi*. *Sannyas* is an attainment. It is a fact of
life, not a discipline of life. If you will be my disciple, I want
you to become like a potato."

"What do you mean to become like a potato?" asked the
incredulous disciple. "Potatoes are known as inert dullards

which produce nothing."

"No," replied the guru. "My dear son, potatoes grow everywhere, and are loved by everyone. They nourish all people in all lands. In fact, do you know of a country where potatoes are not grown? You, my son, will be like a potato."

Vashishta married Savitri and became an engineer for the Indian Railways. He established an image of Goddess Kali in his house, and he became her ardent devotee, a most devoted *pujari*. Daily he left for the train station at 3 a.m. for the departure of the 5 a.m. train, but this odd timing did not stop him. Every day he would rise at midnight, bathe in the pond behind his house, gather all the materials necessary for the worship of the Divine Mother, and fervently engage in *puja*. This continued for many years until he heard of a saintly woman named Shree Maa.

Shree Maa was staying in a home in the Lelua Railway Colony, approximately seven miles from Vashishta's home in Belgachia. Every day he would walk the seven miles to Lelua carrying fresh milk from his cow to be offered for Shree Maa's tea. Suddenly he had found a new *puja*, the worship of a living Goddess! When he returned from his day's work journeying on the railway lines, he would milk his cow, put the milk into a closed container, and walk to deliver the milk at the residence where Shree Maa was staying. With such joy he wandered through the back streets, narrow alleyways and lanes separating the two communities, singing all the way. Many times he did not get the privilege of seeing Shree Maa, but contented himself with presenting the milk to other members of the household or other devotees who were present.

In this way several months passed. Vashishta had been working hard to decorate the temple in his home, and it was on the occasion of Kali Puja in the month of November (corresponding to the Indian month of *Kartik*) that Vashishta moved the altar of the Goddess from the eastern wall, where it had been situated, to the northern wall facing south. This was in keeping with his newly discovered understanding that priests whose primary worship is in the morning face toward to rising sun, while those whose primary worship is in the night should face toward the north pole to be in harmony with the magnetic forces of energy. For this occasion, with sincerity and pure humility, he requested that Shree Maa be a guest in his home and bless him by attending the installation ceremonies.

Shree Maa compassionately agreed.

In what must have been an inordinate expense for a man accustomed to walking to and from his work and errands, Vashishta hired a car and driver, and drove with Shree Maa from her Lelua residence to his home. He welcomed her with the waving of ceremonial lamps, gave her a garland of flowers, and brought her into the sanctuary of his temple. He offered her an *asana* or seat upon which to sit, and placed a large platter under her feet.

Reciting the Vedic texts of mantras, he ceremoniously washed her feet. And with the greatest of devotion, with his own cloth that he was wearing, he started to dry her feet. He looked into her eyes to find that Shree Maa was gone. She sat in the *samadhi* of perfect stillness. She was radiating the bliss of communion as he tried to lift her feet from the plate of water and milk. But much to his amazement, the dish stuck to the bottom of her feet. Try as he might, with all of his power, he could not separate her feet from the dish. Struggling in this way for some time, he ultimately broke down in tears and sobbed and bowed down to the Divine Mother. Just as all the warriors of Ravana's court could not move Angad's foot and just as all of the allures that a gallant presents cannot stir the heart of a truly devoted woman, just so, Vashishta could not lift Shree Maa's feet from the plate.

Overcome with emotion, Vashishta began to pray and sing the Sanskrit texts proclaiming one's devotion to the Divine Mother. At last Shree Maa regained consciousness and permitted Vashishta to complete his ceremonial worship. It was very late in the night when the *pujas* were completed and dinner finally was served.

After dinner Shree Maa said to Vashishta, "Vashishta, I will make *arati* in the morning with a lotus flower."

Vashishta replied, "Mother, it is very late. I don't have a lotus flower and the bazaar is closed. How will I find a lotus flower, Mother?" asked Vashishta.

Mother said, "My son, I always make the early morning *arati* for Kali Puja with a lotus flower. I am sure you will make some arrangements so that my tradition will not be broken when I am a guest in your house." Thus speaking, Shree Maa retired to her room to take rest.

Vashishta was beset with worry. "How will I find a lotus flower in the middle of the night, without which, I will certainly be embarrassed for my inadequacy in fulfilling the Divine Mother's wish? Where will I find a lotus flower?"

It was late in the night when he woke up his two sons. "Boys, do you know where there are any lotuses growing? Quickly, we must find a lotus flower."

"Father, you must be joking. It is the middle of the night. Where will we go to find a lotus flower in the middle of the night?" asked the older boy.

The father said, "Sons, you must know of some ponds where there are lotuses growing."

"Father," answered the younger, "I know of one pond where there are lotuses growing, but it is so far away that I cannot be back before sunrise. How could I even go so far in the dark? How will we swim out into the middle of the pond in the darkness of the night in order to pick a lotus for you? I am sure the Mother will forgive us. Can't it wait until morning?"

"Go to sleep, my children," said Vashishta. He went to his room and lay down on his bed, and although it was past midnight, unfortunately he could not sleep. He tossed and turned and experienced various states of unrest throughout the night, but could not find an answer to his problem. By four o'clock in the morning, he was apprehensively ready to begin the ceremonies of the day. He rose and washed his teeth, and then went to take his morning bath in the small pond at the back side of his house. He jumped into the pond, dunked his head under the water three times as is customary for a Brahmin's oblations, and then dove and swam to the bottom of the pond.

Amazed, he asked himself, "What is this I am touching?" he thought. "It feels like some type of vegetation at the bottom of the pond!" Filled with wonder, he grabbed it and quickly rose to the surface gasping for breath. "Aah! It's a lotus! I found one!" he called with joy. Hearing the commotion, the occupants turned on all the lights in the house. All the members of the household came running down to the pond to find the jubilant Vashishta.

Making his way to the bank of the pond holding the prized lotus in his hand, with tears in his eyes he approached Shree Maa, and bowed down presenting her the lotus flower. When she took it into her hands, he cried, "How long will you play with me, Mother? Please, take your lotus and perform the *arati* to your delight!"

What an *arati* it was! Shree Maa rang the bell and showed the flower of Vashishta's devotion to the Divine Mother, and this is only one story among the many blessings received by Vashishta.

Vashishta's Umbrella Story

After the worship in Vashishta's temple was completed, Vashishta began to travel with Shree Maa. He took trips to Assam, Mathura, Vrindaban, Benares, and many other holy places of pilgrimage. Back in Calcutta, one day he went for the *darshan* of Shree Bharat Maharaj, who was the president of the Ramakrishna Mission at Belur Math.

"Oh, Prabod, how have you been?" inquired the swami, seeing his old friend and devotee.

Vashishta told him about his divine love affair with the saintly Shree Maa, and how he was joining her in travels to various places of pilgrimage around India.

"Where will you be traveling next?" asked the swami.

Vashishta replied, "We will be going to temples in the Himalayas."

"Well then," replied Bharat Maharaj, "you will need an umbrella to take with you to the Himalayas. Please take my umbrella."

Vashishta was overjoyed to be the recipient of a present offered by such a great man. "I will certainly worship this umbrella and regard it as the highest blessing," he replied.

Shree Maa, Vashishta, Rathan and other devotees began to wind their way into the Himalayan foothills. Traveling by bus and on foot from Haldwani through the various pilgrimage sites of the foothills, the party visited Bimtal, Sattal, Nainital, Bhowali, Kanchi and Almora, before arriving in Jageshwar. They performed *yagya* for some days in the ancient temples of Jageshwar, bathed in the mountain rivers, and prayed to Lord Shiva in the ancient temples which were built stone upon stone with no mortar. They wandered in the forests of fir trees and worshiped the numerous Shiva lingams established throughout the forests.

Ultimately, the party climbed through the mountains to

Julai Jageshwar, the beautiful Temple of Lord Shiva from which the entire Himalayan vista is visible. To the right is Mount Kailash, straight ahead Badrinath, to its immediate left Kedarnath and further left, Gangotri, Yamunotri, and the entire expanse of snow-capped peaks. They admired the broad valleys of green rising up to the white peaks of snow, shimmering in the radiance of the morning sun. These are the vistas of the Himalayas, and in Upper Jageshwar the party settled into a rhythm of worship. Every day the *Chandi* worship was performed and the *Chandi Path* was recited before the divine fire.

One day in the midst of this discipline, Shree Maa proclaimed, "Our rations are running low. I will take Rathan with me and go to the market. We will buy enough provisions for another week, and be back by evening."

"It may rain, so you had better take an umbrella with you," warned Vashishta.

"I will be all right. Don't worry about me," replied Maa.

Vashishta turned to Rathan. "Rathan," he said. "Take my umbrella with you. In case there is a storm, make sure that Shree Maa does not get wet."

Rathan took the umbrella and his pack, and set out on foot with Shree Maa to walk the distance through the mountain paths to the nearest bazaar, which was several miles away.

When they reached the market, Shree Maa purchased supplies and filled Rathan's pack. All through the day back at the temple, Vashishta and other devotees were constantly engaged in worship and recitation of scriptures, and at evening time Shree Maa and Rathan returned.

"Did you have a successful journey?" inquired Vashishta.

"Yes," responded Shree Maa. "We bought everything that we need."

"Did you encounter any rainstorm on the way?" asked Vashishta.

"No," replied Shree Maa. "The weather was clear all the way."

Vashishta then asked Rathan, "Where is my umbrella?"

Rathan looked dismayed and asked Shree Maa, "Maa, where is Vashishta's umbrella?"

Maa asked, "Did you take Vashishta's umbrella?"

"Yes," replied Rathan.

"And you had it with you all through the day?" asked Shree Maa. "Do you know where the umbrella is?"

"No," replied Rathan.

Vashishta was getting agitated listening to this dialogue. "Where is my umbrella?" he inquired again. "That was a very special umbrella. It was given to me by Bharat Maharaj of the Ramakrishna Mission. Where is my umbrella?"

Shree Maa looked Vashishta in the eye and said, "I gave it away!"

Vashishta couldn't believe it. "Do you mean you gave away my umbrella that was given to me by Bharat Maharaj, the president of the Ramakrishna Mission?"

Shree Maa said to him, "You have come to the Himalayas to perform *sadhana*. You want to do *tapasya*. You have come high into the mountains in order to meditate on the eternal reality, and still you have attachment for an umbrella. I gave it away! No more needs to be said! I gave it away! It is gone!"

Vashishta could hardly control his agitation. Silently he lay in his bed pondering the meaning of Shree Maa's words. The next morning Vashishta arose and prepared himself for worship. Just as he was about to sit in the *asana*, Shree Maa came before him. "Maa," he inquired. "Did you really give my umbrella away?"

"Yes, Vashishta. I really gave your umbrella away. You who want to contemplate the eternal reality, you who want to attain the heights of self-realization, why is it that you are asking me again and again about a silly old umbrella? I gave away your umbrella!"

Vashishta's worship was performed with a fragmented mind. Thoughts kept weaving in and out of his meditation and it became impossible for him to sit still. Finally he asked Shree Maa one more time, "Mother, did you really give away my umbrella?"

"Yes, Vashishta. I gave away your umbrella," came the reply.

The next morning, Shree Maa went early in the morning to visit the temple of Jageshwar, where Lord Shiva is manifest as the Supreme Lord. She offered her worship with great sincerity, at the end of which she said, "Shiva, if I am true, give me back that umbrella. I want to share my truth with my devotee."

Three days later, when the vow of spiritual discipline was complete, Shree Maa packed up all of her belongings and along with the entire party boarded a bus. The day was very dark and grey and heavy rain was falling. All of the windows of the bus were closed and the breath from the passengers made clouds of fog that stuck to the glass, so that no one could see in or out of the windows.

As the bus pulled away from the temple, jerking down the muddy road, Vashishta looked behind at the temple one more time, and then turned to Shree Maa and asked, "Maa, did you really give away my umbrella?"

Shree Maa ignored him completely.

After about an hour of bouncing over the rutted roads, the little bus came into a bazaar area and pulled up beside a tea stall to let some passengers out. As the bus was grinding to a halt, Shree Maa noticed a young boy running beside the bus crying, "Mataji, Mataji."

When the bus finally stopped and the passengers began to alight, the young boy fought his way through the doorway like a fish swimming upstream against the current. Running down the aisle between the seats, the boy cried out, "Mataji, Mataji, here is your umbrella!" He presented her the umbrella, which had inadvertently been left behind in a shop.

Shree Maa smiled at the young boy and took the umbrella in her hands. Turning to Vashishta she said, "Here, take your umbrella! If you still have such attachment to this world, you will need all kinds of worldly things!"

Shree Maa gave her blessings to the young boy, and the bus pulled out of the little village and proceeded down the road.

Purnima

Purnima Talukdar was the chief nurse in charge of the operating theater at the Lelua Hospital, just across the river from downtown Calcutta. A stylish and socially inclined lady, she had numerous friends throughout the colony of railway employees where she lived, as well as in and around the community of greater Calcutta. Many of the neighbors from her area began to speak to her of Shree Maa, the saintly woman *sadhika* from Kamakhya. One day Purnima decided to pay her a visit. When Purnima reached the home where Shree Maa was staying, she was surprised to find a messenger greeting her at the front door, saying Shree Maa was not available to meet people today.

A few weeks later Purnima decided to try again to meet Shree Maa. However, when she reached the house where Shree Maa was staying, she was disappointed to find the door was locked and no one was at home. Sometime later, Purnima attempted to meet Shree Maa again, only to find that she had left town. In this way more than a year passed with Purnima again and again unsuccessfully trying to meet the Holy Mother.

One day several months later, while Purnima was at work, Shree Maa visited her home. Shree Maa knocked on the door and a servant woman let her in. Shree Maa, along with devotees, cleaned the entire house, established a beautiful temple shrine in the drawing room, cooked a delicious meal and offered beautiful worship with flowers, shining utensils and dancing lights.

That evening when Purnima returned home from her work, she looked in amazement at the transformation of her home. She saw the cleanliness and orderliness that Shree Maa had brought to her home. She saw that God had been offered a seat of importance in the drawing room. She saw the beauty of the *pujas* and turned to the servant and asked the question in a tone which betrayed that she already knew the answer, "Who did this?"

"Wahi," came the reply. "She, the same lady, the Holy Mother Shree Maa, whose *darshan* you have been denied on so many occasions."

Purnima looked around her and sat down upon the *asana* before the altar which Shree Maa had established and began to cry.

She took her bath, put on a sari, and walked out of the house. As she walked through the neighborhood, searching for the house where Shree Maa was living, all the neighbors were amazed to see Purnima wearing a sari and no makeup. They had never seen her in anything but fashionable western dresses. She found the house where Shree Maa was staying, entered the house without obstruction, and walked directly into the room where Shree Maa was seated upon a bed. A number of devotees who had congregated were seated on the floor below. Purnima immediately walked between the members of the seated congregation right up to Shree Maa, bowed down to her feet, and took a seat on the floor in front of the guru and began to cry.

When Purnima began to perform the daily worship of the Divine Mother Goddess, the effects reverberated throughout the community. The changes were far-reaching. Her home became a center of *satsangha*, and Shree Maa, herself, began to stay there. Purnima organized her life and her household, the operating theater in the hospital, and later the office of the Director of the hospital, and then went on to organize the entire nursing staff of the hospital. Everyone felt the changes. She joined Shree Maa in organizing buses with doctors, nurses and devotees who went out into the villages offering medical counseling, administering medicines, and relieving a number of ills of the poor villagers.

She helped to collect medical samples and resources from the railway hospitals and to help Shree Maa's devotees in sharing the wealth of the city life with the poor of the villages. Shree Maa would often be found in some remote village performing worship, singing, meditating, and conducting *satsangha* with her devotees. Around her there would be a team of doctors, nurses, lawyers and teachers striving to help all who came because of their love and devotion to the Holy Mother. Purnima was a part of that sharing and she became a beloved daughter. Often she would travel with Shree Maa and join in the *satsangha* in various places. Later, she even came to visit Shree Maa in America.

Hanumandasgunda

In 1971 the Nakshal *gundas* were killing and stealing whatever they wanted from wealthy families, and there was a river of blood flowing all over West Bengal, especially in West Calcutta. The Nakshals were political activists, but a *gunda* is a thug or a thief, a character whose life is filled with deceit and violence. The union between the two groups was an invitation to disaster. The Nakshals wanted to support a Communist government, but the *gunda* element only wanted an excuse to steal. They would kill anyone with only the slightest cause, even women, babies and young children. They did not care for anything or anyone, having so much frustration in their lives with no vision for the future. After 1971, the police forces became mobilized and supplied with more modern equipment, and much greater capacity to protect the citizens. Many of the Nakshal *gundas* ran away into hiding and disguised themselves as *sadhus*.

One day a well-organized police patrol was in hot pursuit of Hanumandasgunda, one of the most notorious thieves in all the districts of Calcutta. He had been a cause of terror to many citizens, and now he was fleeing for his life. On the same day a number of devotees had assembled at a home in Bamangachi Railway Colony to enjoy *satsangha* with Shree Maa. Seeing the congregation at someone's home, the fleeing thief in order to hide came running into the room where Shree Maa was sitting. The meditating devotees were terrified when he entered the room, but Shree Maa sat silently upon a cot with her eyes closed in meditation. Hanumandas took a seat on the floor in the back of the room, and all of the devotees immediately closed their eyes and made a pretense of being in meditation.

Some time passed before Shree Maa returned to waking consciousness. When she did, she began to moisten her lips by moving her tongue around the interior of her mouth. Slowly she took elongated breaths, and thereafter opened her eyes. Seeing her open her eyes, a devotee immediately brought a glass of water and set it on the cot beside the divine yogini.

Just then, a fly alighted upon the surface of the water and began to drink. Suddenly it began to flutter its wings, unable to lift itself from the surface. Shree Maa glanced down and observed the predicament of the struggling fly, and then looked to the back of the room directly into the eyes of

Hanumandas. Hanumandas was astounded by the clarity of focus of the eyes of the Holy Mother, and even more surprised when she quietly summoned him, "Would you please come here?"

Hanumandas pointed to himself as if to ask, "Who, me?"

There was no escaping from Shree Maa! Once again she beckoned to him, "Please come here."

Slowly he rose from his *asana* and climbed through the crowd seated on the floor. He bowed his head at Shree Maa's feet. Shree Maa looked him straight in the eye, then at the fly struggling in the glass, and again back to Hanumandas. Then she asked, "Will you save him?"

Hanumandas looked at the struggling fly in the glass near Maa's feet, and without a word immediately picked up the glass, scooped out the fly to safety, and let it fly to freedom from the palm of his hand. Maa looked at Hanumandas and asked, "If you would do it for a fly, then why don't you do it for the rest of us?"

Hanumandas looked at Maa with great apprehension and asked, "What do you mean?"

And Mother said, "Will you save us?"

Hanumandas began to cry. He fell on his knees before the Holy Mother, held his head in his hands and began to cry.

Hanumandasgunda and the Bamangachi Yagya

One can only imagine the changes that occurred in the locality of Howrah after Hanumandasgunda became Shree Maa's devotee. He wanted to stay with her, to become a *sadhu*, and to follow her wherever she went. But Mother denied him that privilege, saying that he couldn't hide from his past by pretending to be spiritual. Instead she prevailed upon some devotees to arrange a job for him as a supervisor in an iron foundry.

Maa had arranged to perform a *yagya* in the railway colony of Bamangachi, one of the most notorious areas in all of Calcutta. A large circus tent was pitched in a field near the railway tracks, and inside the tent an image of the deity Durga was installed. A large *hawan kunda* was prepared in which worship would be offered to the sacrificial fire. For nine days, from sunrise until late into the night, Shree Maa worshiped continuously either at the altar or at the fire, and a crowd of people grew until the worshipers filled up the entire field.

The Bamangachi Railway Bridge was the dividing line between two different gangs of thieves. The gang on one side of the bridge used to rob the people coming to its side of the bridge, while the gang on the other side would rob victims on their own side, and then the two gangs would fight across the railway line, the line of control demarcating the boundary between opposing armies. Throughout the night the sound of gunfire frequently reverberated through the air, and a sense of hostility and fear of violence was often in the atmosphere. Every day bombs exploded, and the police felt powerless to do anything about the situation. It was in such a locality that Shree Maa chose to perform this worship.

Shree Maa sent Hanumandasgunda as her ambassador, and summoned the chief leaders of the two opposing gangs to come to her tent one night. Shree Maa appealed to the gangs of both sides of the bridge, "I want to do worship here, and I want you to help me."

The gang leaders were totally at a loss. "Maa, how can we help you?" they inquired.

Shree Maa replied, "I want you to protect my *puja*. I want you to guard my entire *puja*, to ensure that nothing wrong happens here."

The leaders of both the gangs immediately acquiesced, "Certainly Mother, we will protect your *puja*."

Then Shree Maa said, "We are performing a *yagya* here, and we will be worshiping day and night. Could you keep it quiet until we are done? Don't allow any noise that would disturb our worship. Whatever you must do, do it quietly."

Again the gang leaders looked at one another and both said, "Yes, Shree Maa."

From then on the members of both gangs were standing side by side to protect Mother's *puja*. The worship grew in intensity from the first day to the ninth. Every day men, women and children of all persuasions, of all religious affiliations, joined together in the worship of the Supreme Divinity, and Shree Maa went from worship into *samadhi* and back to worship without rest.

On the ninth day of that festival of worship, Shree Maa had a vision that the women should dance at the *arati*. Several of the female devotees who were keeping the vow of worship came to Shree Maa and asked permission to dance at the *arati*. Shree Maa replied, "I have just received that instruction from the Divine Mother. Today the women will perform the worship of *arati*, the dancing with lights." She told all the female devotees to wear red-bordered saris, and had a rope tied around the entire perimeter of the tent.

That evening the ladies wore saris of white silk with red borders. Shree Maa herself raised the light, the drums began to roll, and the ceremony of *arati* commenced. When the ladies saw Shree Maa waving the *arati* lamps in front of the deity of the Divine Mother, they picked up pots of burning coals, sprinkled frankincense upon the coals, and streams of smoke poured forth. Some ladies had lights, some had pots of burning incense, and some were dancing while playing musical instruments. All of the ladies moved into the inner circle and began to dance. The drums were rolling and everyone was chanting "*Jaya Maa!* Victory to the Divine Mother!" The excitement, the effervescent spirit of pure devotion rose up in the hearts of all and was expressed in the singing and dancing in praise to God. After a few moments, the boys could stand it no longer. They jumped over the ropes and joined the ladies in dancing. The desire to dance overcame the crowds in the field, and everyone began dancing together and shouting, "*Jaya Maa!* Victory to the Divine Mother!"

Shree Maa began to hug everyone in the crowd and bless them all. And everyone began to hug everyone else! When devotees who had formerly been members of opposing gangs began to hug each other, everyone shouted with triumphant joy! And the entire town was filled with peace and JOY! Words cannot explain!

Hanumandasgunda and the Lost Briefcase

There is one more story about Hanumandasgunda which ought to be shared, about Dr. Chakravarti, a devotee of Shree Maa, who had inadvertently left his briefcase in a Calcutta taxi cab. Dr. Chakravarti arrived at his office and found that the briefcase containing many valuable papers and his wallet and keys was no longer in his possession. He had left it in a taxi which was now in some unknown place in greater Calcutta.

Dr. Chakravarti was further dismayed when he realized that a check to himself for a considerable amount of money was also in the briefcase. Everyone said, "What will you do?"

Dr. Chakravarti immediately went to visit Shree Maa, where it just so happened that Hanumandasgunda was sitting enjoying the *darshan* of the Holy Mother. A distraught Dr. Chakravarti started to explain his problem to Shree Maa, but before he completed his story, Hanumandasgunda interrupted and said, "I think I can find your briefcase. I will try to help as much as I can."

Dr. Chakravarti asked, "How can you help find my briefcase? I don't think all of the police of Calcutta can find the missing bag."

Hanumandasgunda replied, "How would the police know where to look? I know every *gunda* in Calcutta, and whoever took your briefcase will also be pleased to bring it back."

The next day when Dr. Chakravarti came to his office, his secretary greeted him at the stairway with miraculous news, "Your briefcase has been returned."

Hastening his steps, Dr. Chakravarti ran into his office to see the briefcase sitting upon his desk. He opened it and found everything just as he had left it. How far Hanumandasgunda had come since his days as a thief!

Hanumandasgunda now runs a charitable dispensary and a school for the poor children of his locality.

The Maidservant

There was one servant woman from the lower caste who would bow down to Shree Maa every day before she went to her work of cleaning houses. She was thinking inside herself, "Mother is always around rich people. She will never come to my house. I am so poor. I cannot invite Shree Maa to my house."

One day Shree Maa told some devotees, "I would like to go to that servant woman's house."

"Mother, she is not home. How can we find her home? We know the direction of her home, but not the exact location."

Mother said, "Then let's go. We'll find it."

So Shree Maa, along with a couple of devotees, went in search of the home, and after numerous inquiries, found the one-bedroom servant's quarters on the fourth floor of a tenement house. When she got into the room, she found a young child about two or three years old all alone. Shree Maa went into the kitchen, and after cleaning the whole place, prepared food. She cooked a number of dishes, made sure the child ate, offered everything with flowers upon the counter, and then returned to where she was staying and sat down as though nothing had happened.

The next day the maidservant came to where Mother was staying and told everyone that somebody cleaned my house and prepared food for me. "Who would do such a thing? Do I have to take my baby to work with me and lock the door of my room? Who would cook for me, a lowly servant?"

One of mother's devotees began laughing and she could not stop. Finally she told her, "It was Mother that came to your house and prepared your food."

Then the maidservant began to cry. While the maidservant was crying, Mother came and hugged her.

The Man Who Cleaned the Toilets

Several hundred people were gathering around Shree Maa. Most of the people came near and tried to bow to her. But there was a man at a distance, who cleaned toilets, and he did not come close because he was an untouchable with an unclean profession. It was not appropriate for him to go close to a saint.

Mother left the crowd and walked straight up to him. He was chewing a betel leaf. Mother told him, "Open your mouth."

The man was surprised and opened his mouth. Mother took the betel leaf from his mouth and put it into her own and started to chew, while the man who cleaned the toilets began to cry.

Mother is truly a Mother! On the earth the man was considered an untouchable, but Shree Maa saw that he was a pure soul.

The Greedy Man

During this time of her life Mother was very often in deep meditation. She spent long hours in *samadhi* and whenever she would wake up there would be very little talking. Devotees would come and ask her questions, but she would talk very little with them. She felt that little could be communicated with words.

One time Mother was in *samadhi* from morning to evening. Suddenly she felt a painful burning sensation. It was like a knife stabbing her. Her whole body started burning. Mother was furious when she woke up. She looked with angry eyes at everybody and then looked at her lap, where a couple hundred rupee notes had been deposited. Shree Maa took the notes, tore them up, and threw them at the man who had placed them there. "You came to see Mother with a bribe!" she scolded. "What is the relationship between Mother and child — tell me? Give me an answer! You take bribes and you give bribes! You cannot buy the grace of God!"

The man started crying, saying it was his mistake. Mother told him never to keep a relationship between money and Mother, and to try to be pure. "Give up your greed," she told him.

The Dying Husband

One day a lady came whose husband had just had a stroke. The doctor told her that her husband would only live three days at most. The distraught woman came to Shree Maa at night with the request, "Please take care of my husband."

Mother went to the woman's house along with a devotee and blessed the man. His wife had so much devotion and faith in Shree Maa. "Mother will take care of my husband," she thought. "I don't believe the doctor."

The recovery was miraculous. His wife's pure devotion

made her husband live for many more years. The woman told Shree Maa, "Mother, you have made my husband alive."

Mother replied, "God gave everybody equal power. You just have to wake up your pure devotion and you can do this also." Mother said to all the devotees, "This woman with pure devotion made everything happen. I am nothing."

Other Devotees

It is difficult to tell all the stories of all the changes that took place in the lives of the devotees. Vasanti was a lawyer and the granddaughter of the Maharaja of Kashmir. She owned an English medium school in central Calcutta. One day she came to visit Shree Maa and was so touched by their meeting. Once anyone visited Shree Maa, they invariably returned with all their friends. With Vasanti came Joy Dip, who is the owner of another English medium school. Later came the principals, the school teachers, and then the secretaries and ministers in the Department of Education, and then the clerks and other officials of other governmental departments. Shree Maa's purity and selflessness, her availability and approachability, her Motherly nature, honesty and sincerity, spread across the North of India as if riding on the crest of a wave. And the numbers of devotees grew.

Shree Maa never asked people their names or occupations, but would call them by whatever name came to her mouth. And that became the name by which that individual was known by the entire community. Maa never declined to become actively involved in solving the problems of those who came to her. She would always listen to the difficulties of those who wished to confide in her, and invariably would end the interview with the words, "I will pray for you." No sooner had the visitors left, than she would turn to a devotee and say,

"Call so and so. Tell him or her that Mother is remembering them."

The list of devotees reads like a Who's Who of both Eastern and Western culture.

Chapter Four

Traveling With Swamiji

Meeting with Swami Satyananda

I first met Shree Maa under extremely curious circumstances. I had been in India for more than fifteen years, studying Sanskrit, philosophy and the systems of worship with many gurus, and moving from temple to temple on foot. I used to spend my summers in the Himalayas and the winters in the Bay of Bengal. When I found a suitable temple, I would befriend the *pujari*, and make arrangements to stay for a prolonged period of intense worship. In this way I completed vows of nine days, of thirty days, of one hundred and eight days, and on at least three occasions, a vow consisting of one thousand days of worship at a time without going outside of the temple, a little more than nine years in all.

In this way I moved into the Ramakrishna Tapomath in Bakreshwar, a small temple in a small village about six hours by bus outside of Calcutta. I locked myself in the temple enclave, all alone for one hundred and eight days with a statue of the Goddess Kali holding a picture of my face in Her hand. Pachu was a young man of the village who used to help me prepare for my daily worship. Every morning he would pick flowers and fruits for worship, and then take the brass and copper utensils out to the hot spring just outside the gate, where he would shine them. After returning and completing all the preparations, once he was assured that I was comfortably seated in the temple, he would close the gate and lock it with a padlock on the outside. He would then throw the key in through the window in order to ensure that no one could disturb me.

After about sixty days had passed in the performance of this *Shata Chandi Vrat*, I began to think about what I might do upon its completion. I thought that I might go to the Kamakhya Temple to make my next vow of worship. I had always wanted to go there, as it is written about in the *Devi*

Gita, saying, "That of all the places of the Goddess, there is no place as holy and pure as Kamakhya." Now I felt the Goddess was calling me to come there.

About this time, without my knowledge, Shree Maa was meditating in the Kamakhya temple along with a group of her devotees. One day, she got up from her meditation and turned to some devotees and said, "Who is Satya?"

The devotees said, "We do not know any Satya."

She closed her eyes for a few moments, and then again opened them and said, "Where is Bakreshwar?"

One of the devotees replied, "Maa, I have lived most of my life in Calcutta, and there is a small village named Bakreshwar about six hours outside of Calcutta.

She said, "Let's go to Calcutta."

It was a few weeks later when one morning Pachu came into the temple from the hot springs carrying all of the utensils which he had just washed, and he said to me, "One Mataji is here looking for you. She wants to take *darshan* in this temple."

I said, "Pachu, I haven't seen anyone in more than three months. We have only got another few weeks to go. Please don't bring anybody into the temple now."

He said, "She is a really radiant and pure soul and has a whole group of devotees with her. They just want to look at the temple and see the place where you are worshiping, and then they will go."

"All right," I replied. "But make it quick. I am going into my room. Make sure that they leave quickly, because I don't want to be late for my worship. If I start late, I won't finish until late, and you know very well that if I finish late in the night, I have to light the hurricane lantern to see the last mantras of the text. My nose gets black from breathing the kerosene fumes. It is always a hardship. But I will accept the inconvenience of their visit, if you make sure that they leave quickly."

"No problem," said Pachu.

I went into my room and saw through the crack in the door that several people were walking into our little temple. And they all sat down and began meditating. They were like sardines in a can, but there they were sitting in meditation.

I called Pachu and said, "Pachu, you said that one Mataji was going to come in and pay her respects and then go away. Now all of these people are sitting in the temple meditating. Get them out! Give them some *prasad*, a *tilak*, bless them, and send them to the next temple. I have got to begin my worship!"

Pachu said, "I can't send them out. They are meditating in a temple. I can't tell them that they can't meditate in a temple! That is why we make temples!"

He wasn't much help. I got up and went outside the door to the temple and started pacing back and forth. They didn't move. I started to cough and clear my throat. I tried to make myself as much of a disturbance as I possibly could. Nobody moved. They all sat there. It had been about forty-five minutes already, and I was getting angry. "You get out of my temple," I thought. "I have got to worship! I don't know who you people are. All I know is that you came from the city. We are village people. Get out! Go! Go visit somebody else's temple. This is my temple! There are so many other famous temples in this area. What are you doing in my temple?" So my thoughts raged.

Finally one man came out. He looked at me and his eyes lit up. He was ecstatic. "Oh, you are a foreigner! Have you seen the Taj Mahal?" He started to question me about all of the sights of India.

I blew my cool. In the nicest village slang I knew, I said, "You are the foreigner. This is my temple. You people are disturbing my meditation. Pick yourselves up and go sit in some-body else's temple. I've got work to do! Don't come talking to me about the Taj Mahal and making me late for my worship!"

Hearing the commotion, all of the people came out from the temple. I couldn't imagine there were so many people in our little temple. We thought it was big enough for only four or five people comfortably, but more than twenty people came out from the temple. They were all city people, wearing pants and shirts, respectable city-type clothes, not like the dress of the people of our village. We were villagers, wearing torn dho-tis, and they wore coats, terry-cloth shirts, and the women wore silk saris.

I tried to recall the best city Bengali that I could fake, and in the best diction I could pronounce said, "Please excuse me, but I don't have any *prasad* that I can offer you, because I have not yet performed the worship. So if you will please go away, I will perform the worship, and maybe you will come back some other time and share in the fruits of my offering. *Namaste*. I bow to you. There is a beautiful temple over there," I said pointing to the other side of the hot springs and pond.

As if on cue, the people parted and formed two lines on either side of the doorway. Shree Maa came out from the Temple and walked up the aisle between the devotees. Her face was more radiant than anything I could have imagined. She had been crying, and tears were rolling down her cheeks. She was luminous, so majestic. She walked right between the group of people straight toward me. She looked me in the eye, and I knew her immediately. She was the deity that I had been worshiping.

My jaw fell open in astonishment, and so gracefully, with-out the least hesitation, she reached up and put a sweet into my mouth, and just looked at me. We stared into each others' eyes for what must have been an eternity. Then she put a flower on my head, turned around and walked again between the two rows of people. Without looking back, she walked right out through the gate. Then all of the people turned and followed her out. No one spoke a word. Then Pachu followed behind them all. He closed the gate and locked it. And I was alone with a flower on my head and a sweet in my mouth!

Alone, I stood there staring at the locked gate in disbelief. She was the Goddess I had been worshiping, and I had made such a fuss about being late for worship. It was She whom I had been calling, but I didn't recognize Her when She came. Who was She?

I went into the temple and looked into Kali's face. It was just the image of Shree Maa. I sat down and started the morning worship. There were eighteen days left to the performance of my vow. I performed the *puja* and completed the *homa*. But all I could see was Shree Maa's face.

"Who was she?" I wondered. "Where was she from? Where was her ashram? Who were all those devotees?" All these questions continually came to my mind as I recited the texts for worship.

Pachu was of no help. He couldn't find out anything from the other people of our village. All he knew was that a group of tourists came from Calcutta, spent a few hours in the temples of our area, and left. There was no information from anyone.

The time of my vow passed and I completed my worship in that temple. I performed a large *yagya*, made rice pudding for the whole village, fed all of the *brahmins* and gave cloth to the needy. Now what? What was next in my life? I decided to go to the Kamakhya Temple to repeat this wonderful experience there. There is nothing in life so wonderful as living according to a regular rhythm of worship.

I packed up my few belongings, gave my respect to the

people of Bakreshwar, took a bus to the train, and made my way to Calcutta. Whenever I went to Calcutta, I always visit-ed Dakshineshwar, the temple where Shree Ramakrishna attained his realization. In Shree Ramakrishna's room, above the bed upon which he used to sit, there is a picture of the great saint sitting in meditation. When sitting there it feels like I am sitting in his holy presence.

At one time in my life, I sat there every day for almost two months. I slept on the veranda of the temple just outside his door, along with the other *sadhus*, ate the food from the tem-ple offering, which is served regularly to all, and spent three to four hours each day just sitting at the foot of that bed in front of his picture. That room has so much *bhava*, such intense feeling!

This day I had come to his picture full of excitement and said, "Thakur, I have just completed a *mahayagya*, a great spiritual vow. Every day for one hundred and eight days I sang the entire *Chandi Path*, performed the complete worship, and sat before the *homa* fire. I fed the *brahmins* and made rice pud-ding for the entire village. I gave cloth to the poor and did as much as I possibly could, just as is described in the scriptures. Now I have come to say 'Thank You' for this success. Thank you very, very much!"

For more than four hours I sat in very deep meditation. It was extremely blissful. When I awoke, I was filled with so much love, joy and a sense of successful accomplishment. I was all prepared to go to Kamakhya to do it over again. Suddenly I heard a voice inside my head. It was a strange sound which I didn't recognize. The word was *belgachia*. I didn't know what it meant. It was a word I didn't recognize. I couldn't even tell to what language it belonged.

I rose from my *asana* and went outside. The first person I met was standing by the doorway and looked like someone from the Hindi-speaking areas of northern India. In Hindi language I asked him, "Brother, can you tell me the meaning of *belgachia*?"

Somewhat surprised at a foreigner speaking to him in his own language, he replied, "*Bel* is a fruit and *gach* is a tree. *Belgachia* is a fruit tree."

That didn't really mean much to me. At least it didn't solve the mystery. I went to the Ganga and jumped in, swimming for a while to refresh myself from the heat of the day. When I had cooled off, I came back to the stairs to dry off and change my clothes. Near me there was a Bengali gentleman standing on the stairs changing his dhoti. I asked him in Bengali, "Sir, can you tell me the meaning of *belgachia*?"

"*Belgachia*?" he said considering. "*Bel* means a fruit and *gach* means a tree. *Belgachia* means a fruit tree."

"Do you know of any other meaning of *belgachia* than fruit tree?" I asked him.

"Yes," came his reply. "There is a bus stop by that name."

Thanking him, I went to the bus stop. I saw a ticket collector standing in the road and said in Hindi, "Where is the bus to Belgachia?"

"There are two stops named Belgachia. One is in Calcutta. The other is in Howrah. To which one do you want to go?"

"Where is the bus to the Calcutta Belgachia?" I asked.

"The bus stand is over there, but the bus left a few minutes ago. The next one will be here in an hour," he replied.

"Where is the bus to the Belgachia in Howrah?" I asked.

"It is over there," he replied pointing. "They are just boarding."

So I went to the Howrah bus and purchased a ticket to Belgachia. I told the collector to please tell me when we got there, because I wouldn't recognize the stop, and he said that he would.

We went across the bridge, and drove down toward Howrah. After about forty minutes, the ticket collector came to me and said, "This is Belgachia."

I got down from the bus to find there were three roads connected to a circle. In the center of the circle there was a little island, and there in the middle of the roundabout was a fruit tree. Of course there were a number of rickshaws around the fruit tree. Some of the drivers came over to me and started asking, "Where do you want to go?"

Not really knowing the answer, I suddenly remembered the Divine Mother, who I had been worshiping the last fifteen years and said, "Where is Maa?"

One of the rickshaw drivers replied, "Maa is everywhere!"

I didn't know what I was looking for, or where I was going. "I want to see Maa," I said.

He called the youngest of the rickshaw drivers and said in the Bhojpuri language, "You've got a great fare here. Take him on a tour of the city, and show him a temple of Kali."

I didn't even ask him the fare. I sat in the rickshaw, and he took me up one alley and down another. I felt every bump in the road of the whole Belgachia suburb. That *rickshawala* took me out to the farthest edge of the community to a little tiny Kali Temple, far away from the main bazaar and there he stopped.

I said to him, "Please wait here."

Inside the temple there was a small statue of Kali. The *pujari* appeared astounded to see me. He immediately gave me a *tilak* or spot of red powder over the third eye and a blessing, and was waiting for an offering. He gave me some holy water and asked, "Do you speak Bengali?"

"Yes," I replied.

He said, "May I ask you a question? This is the most amazing thing. All of the foreigners that come to Calcutta go to

Belur Math, they go to Dakshineshwar and Kali Ghat. How did you happen to come to this temple? You are the first foreigner to come here."

"I am looking for Maa," I replied.

"Do you mean Shree Maa?" he asked incredulously.

"Of course I mean Shree Maa," came my reply. "What Maa isn't the respected holy mother, Shree Maa. How can there be a Maa that isn't Shree Maa? Of course, I am looking for Shree Maa."

"She is in that house across the street," he said pointing.

I still didn't understand what he was telling me, because I didn't know Shree Maa's name was Shree Maa, nor could I imagine who it was that I was going to meet.

I told the rickshaw driver to wait, walked across the street, and knocked on the door.

Suddenly the door opened and a little old man with long white hair and a flowing white beard tied at the base of his chin grabbed me. He was the same man I had seen at the temple in Bakreshwar. He hugged me and dragged me inside saying, "She said that you would come! She said that you would come!"

I went into the house which was filled with people singing *kirtan*, songs about God. When they saw me enter, they all lit up and sat up straight.

"Maa has been meditating in her room on the roof since yesterday," came Vashishta's explanation. "All of these people have been waiting for her *darshan*, and she hasn't come down from her room yet. She's been sitting in the same posture for more than twenty-four hours, and hasn't eaten anything at all. She hasn't even gone to the bathroom. She has just been sitting in the same place without the slightest movement. But now that you are here, she will surely come down!" he said emphatically.

He escorted me to the temple in his house. Not even ten minutes later, Shree Maa came down the stairs and entered the temple. She was the same Divine Mother I had seen that day in Bakreshwar. We just sat there looking at each other, and it was a very profound and deep meditation.

After a lengthy time our meditation broke, and we returned to waking consciousness. I had forgotten about everything. I didn't even notice that Vashishta had paid the rickshaw driver and sent him away. It was a very hot day, so after some time I excused myself and asked where I could take a bath. They directed me to the pond behind the house, where I disrobed and placed my cloth in a dressing room, which had been erected adjacent to the pond. Reciting the mantras customary to the bathing ceremony, I plunged beneath the water.

After a few moments of swimming beneath the cool water of the pond, I arose and wrapped myself in a *gamcha*, a thin towel made of Indian village cloth. Rinsing out my old clothes, I returned to the dressing room where I would put on a new set. Much to my dismay, I found that all of my clothing had vanished. In its place, neatly folded upon a bamboo hanging rod, were brand new expensive clothes, which had recently been procured from the bazaar.

I called out loudly to anyone who could hear, "What happened to my clothes?"

It was Shree Maa's voice which gave the reply. "They were dirty, so we took them to wash. Put on the new clothes."

Having no option, I dressed in the fancy clothes that were provided, clothes that my friends from the villages could never aspire to wear. I turned to the shelf and found a brand new toothbrush with toothpaste already spread across the bristles, alongside which was a new comb and a mirror. I felt very much that I was welcome!

Having cleaned and dressed myself, I returned to the temple in Vashishta's home. From the doorway I peered in to a scene of highly polished, gleaming brass and copper platters bearing fruits, sweets, flowers and all of the articles required for worship. For so many years, I had been offering as substitutes dry leaves or flowers in lieu of the expensive items. Large bells and copper spoons and bowls were gleaming, as they are described in Bengali, *chack, chack,* gleaming, radiantly gleaming. I looked at Shree Maa and then to Vashishta, whereupon both of them motioned to me to be seated upon the *asana,* upon the seat directly before the altar, and immediate terror filled my heart.

For so many years I had been worshiping behind the closed doors of a village hut, at the foot of a large tree, or beside the singing waters of a brook. This day I was required to offer worship in front of people. How my heart trembled on that first occasion of performing *puja* in public! With no recourse but to take the seat, I hesitantly sat down. Silently I began to pray: "Mother, if you scare me so much, I'll forget the mantras. Please let me forget the people and remember only You!"

Suddenly my mind was filled with the vision of the grace of the Divine Mother. She took me to the memory of a scene from the days of my growth and development under the tutelage of my guru, Swami Amritananda Saraswati. For three years we had been traversing the length and breadth of the Himalayas, having taken the spiritual vow that we would never sit underneath a roof or behind a closed door. What that experience yielded only my heart can sing.

My life was much different then. We slept under the moonlit starry skies and listened to the crickets chirping until the sound faded into the silence of the night. We rose with the first chirping of the morning birds, sat in harmony with the cadence of the flowing streams, and bathed in the cold glacial waters which streamed forth from the white snow of the mountains. We chanted the Sanskrit mantras of the scriptures and prepared our daily meal upon the fire where we would offer worship. In this way we studied the scriptures, lived in harmony with wisdom and nature, and basked in the love and respect for the highest wisdom of God. What a way of life it was!

One day Guruji spoke to me as we sat beside the fire drinking our morning tea. He said, "This part of your training is complete. Today we will go down."

"Down?" I inquired. "Down where?"

"First to the plains of India, then to the cities of men, where we will embark on another phase of your education."

"Guruji," I inquired. "What phase of education is it of which you speak? What are you talking about? These years we have been together studying Vedas and Vedanta, history and philosophy, the systems of worship to the Divine Mother and all of the Gods. Now what practice am I to perform?"

"How to share what you have learned with mankind. You must give it away in order to make it grow!" came his response.

How astounded I was by the time we reached Howrah Station in Calcutta, the largest and most active railway terminus in all of Asia. What an amazing experience it was! Hawkers walked up and down the aisles of the trains shouting out their wares. Bauls, traveling ministrels and whole families of troubadours got on the train and sang and clapped and danced and rang the bells on their feet as they played accompaniments on their homemade instruments! As the train progressed toward Calcutta, beggars and *sadhus* came aboard as well as whole families carrying so many possessions that the coolies were struggling to find a place to put them all. When the train reached Howrah Station, coolies jumped aboard and struggled with one another over who would carry whose lug-

gage, and the crowds pushed and shoved their way out from
the railway car.

Landing on the platform, my Guru said to me, "It is morning and time for us to perform our worship."

"Where will we sit?" came my incredulous voice. "Here
on the railway platform?"

His reply was stern. "It is easy for you to meditate in the
Himalayas. Now control your mind even in the midst of the
rush of society!"

The two of us sat down on our seats on the railway platform and began to recite the *Chandi Path*. His voice was as
melodic as always, just like the voice I had always heard by
the banks of the rivers in the high mountains of the Himalayas.
While I struggled to even pronounce the words, a gang of
coolies carrying large loads upon their heads, came cursing us
in Bhojpuri language. They called out to us to get up from our
seats in the middle of the platform and get out of their way. We
were blocking their way and disturbing the flow of traffic. My
guru didn't miss a syllable, as I cowered and flinched under
the immediate threat approaching us. When finally the coolies
had passed us, more passengers came kicking and spitting and
dropping things upon us. The surge of people upon us was like
the flow of a river, the torrents of water cascading from the
Himalayan vistas!

Finally, when our recitation was completed, Guruji looked
at me with a smile of satisfaction upon his face and said, "Now
you come here every morning and recite the *Chandi Path*. And
when you will not miss a syllable, even while sitting in such
an environment, I will ordain you to teach."

There I was sitting in front of the statue of Kali in the home
of Vashishta remembering those experiences of my past, and
the vision of the Howrah Railway Terminus came to my mind.
Suddenly my heart filled with love. Placing my palms togeth-

er in a traditional gesture of respect, I began to pronounce the first mantra, "Shreeman Mahaganadipataye Namah." I can't recall how many hours passed. There was such a stillness and silence in the room, and even though the whole house was full of people, only the vibrations of the mantras echoed within.

It must have been 2 a.m. when I began to wave the lights of offering in the dance of devotion called *arati*, the closing ceremony of the worship. Suddenly the energy in the house became alive. Shree Maa herself took a large bell and mallet and began to beat the cadence to the songs of *arati*. I could not stop dancing, and after some time I held two bells, one in each hand, and I was ringing them vociferously. While the house swelled with people, the whole neighborhood became awake. Even little children in their pajamas were standing in the street screaming, "*Jaya Maa!* Victory to the Divine Mother!"

It was well after sunrise when I finally put the bells down. Shree Maa also put down her mallet and bell, and everyone sat down for meditation. At mid-morning we all rose, took our baths, and wearing fresh clothes, returned to the temple. Once again we offered worship, after which a feast was served. The Bengalis of Calcutta surely know how to eat!

Over the next few days, the electricity continued to grow. The house was full by the early afternoon and by late evening the streets and lanes in the immediate vicinity were completely blocked by people coming to share in the loving devotion of the worship. I really didn't know what was going on in the outside world. There was only one person, Manju, who could understand the dialect of Bengali which I had learned in my village. She, too, used to spend most of her time with Shree Maa, and very occasionally came to ask me if I needed anything. All of the other visitors mostly gathered around Shree Maa with a very scant interest in me, and they spoke rapidly in their dialect of sophisticated urban Bengali.

So I was quite at a loss, when one day Manju came to me and, speaking in our village dialect, said to me, "Go downstairs and sit in the car."

I certainly wasn't prepared for that. While living as a *sannyasi* in the jungle, I didn't do such things as riding in cars. I was not accustomed to receiving an order from anyone and I was quite amazed to receive Manju's instructions to go downstairs and sit in a car. I immediately went downstairs and very politely asked Shree Maa, "Maa, where are we going?"

Her reply caught me off-guard and struck me with amazement. In her very soft Bengali she said, *"Jani na. Vasho.* I don't know. Sit down."

I tried to probe her for deeper understanding, but immediately realized it was of no use. So with nothing but the clothes on my back, I sat down in the car.

It is difficult to express what that meant to me, to sit in somebody's car, with no money, going to some place I didn't know, possessing only the clothes I was wearing, in a foreign land where very few people, if anyone at all, could even understand the languages I spoke. I sat down in the back of the car, and then my stomach rose to my throat. Shree Maa sat down in another car. I thought, "Oh my God, here I am in an unknown car, with an unknown driver, going to an unknown destination, with no possessions! I am totally alone, and even Shree Maa, whom I trust implicitly, is sitting in another car. She, too, does not know where we are going? This has got to be the meaning of surrender."

In a few moments the engine started up, and the cars slowly wound down the narrow alley. The caravan of cars pulled out onto the main thoroughfares of Calcutta. As we inhaled the pollution and smoke from vehicles darting in and out between horse-carts, rickshaws and barefoot coolies carrying tremendous loads upon their heads we slowly worked our way out of the traffic of the congested city. After more than an hour, the car stopped in front of a house and the driver bade me, "Get down."

Shree Maa's car was already parked ahead, and Shree Maa was entering the house. I scurried to keep up with her group. I walked into the house behind Shree Maa to see the owner of the house washing her feet. He had placed a platter upon the ground just before his doorstep, and requested that Shree Maa step into the tray. Using the warm scented water which his wife was holding in a brass urn, he washed Shree Maa's feet before she stepped into his house. I tried my best to keep up with her as she entered the premises.

Much to my surprise, the host stopped me at the doorway and suddenly a clean shining tray appeared at my feet. The host bade me to step upon it for him to wash my feet as well. I chanted the mantra of offering, knowing fully well that they were washing the feet of the wrong person. I folded my hands and requested: "Please God, make me worthy of this honor." Suddenly my hands raised in blessing, just like every *sadhu* of ancient India, proving the proverb that whenever one bows down, one gets a blessing. Then I followed Shree Maa to the inner sanctums of the temple of that home.

Shree Maa motioned for me to be seated in front of the deity, and I knew what to do. I sang the mantras and made the offerings of the orthodox system of worship. Forgetting all the new circumstances, I focused on the deity before me. At the completion of the closing prayers, I raised my hands in blessings, partook of the offerings of the worship, and then followed the others as once again we sat down in the cars.

Who can tell how those days passed? The names of the cities, towns and villages that we visited escape me. We performed worship in every home and in every temple where Shree Maa was invited, and the devotion grew as we visited the *tirthastans*, the places of pilgrimage famous for the saints and deities of the Hindu traditions.

At Kamarpukur and Jayrambati

Among the pilgrimage places which were the most favorite of Shree Maa was the little village of Jayrambati, the birthplace of Shree Sarada Devi. Many of us believe that Shree Maa is an incarnation of Shree Sarada Maa. She would never say so herself. She constantly responds, "All of us are incarnations of God." But she speaks of things which do not come from any book, and tells them with such conviction that no one can doubt that the observations come from firsthand experience.

Shree Maa talks about the life of Shree Ramakrishna in a way that is not recorded in any book. She not only tells about the kinds of food he ate, but also cooks those same foods in the very same style. She not only tells us of the inimitable village language that he used, but she also speaks such language herself. And she speaks of him and demonstrates his teachings with such a clarity of conviction that can only have come from firsthand knowledge. Also her physical appearance is so strikingly similar to Sarada Maa that if one were to imagine Sarada Maa in action, there is no finer example than the life of Shree Maa.

When Shree Maa began her travels around India, she went to Kamarpukur and Jayrambati, the birth places of Shree Ramakrishna and Shree Sarada Devi. As she walked through the lanes of the villages, which are only fifteen minutes apart by bus, she started telling stories of the life in those times. "People got attracted, and I was telling stories even I do not know how they were coming from my mouth," she told us. "I wanted to stay there, so I sat down at the temple. An old lady came and asked me where I would like to stay, and then she suggested that we go ask the president of the Ramakrishna Mission for permission to stay in the Mission Guest House. Going to the office, she said, 'A lady from Kamakhya has come to see you. Thakur Ramakrishna gave her the order to come here.' He yelled at us, 'Without a letter of introduction nobody can stay here!' Then he looked at me, and said, 'Don't worry, I will give you a place to stay.'

"After that I was sitting in the temple and the president came to me and said, 'You have to eat. Where are you taking your meals?' Then they brought me some food. They gave me pudding, which I placed by my side as I drifted into meditation. Meanwhile, a cat came and ate all my pudding.

"That old lady was always behind me. 'Sarada Maa always offered her food to a cat,' she said with laughter.

"Throughout the whole night that lady was walking with me, while I was telling stories about how it was. Everything had changed since Ramakrishna's time. She was crying. 'You have to come to my house.' 'OK,' I said. We stopped at a little tea stall to drink tea. She was from the Lahata family. When Ramakrishna got married to Sarada Devi, they borrowed ornaments from the Lahata family because we were so poor (notice we) that we had none of our own.

"I used to wake at three in the morning and chant until sunrise. When I would step out to walk around the village, many people would follow me. Such a reception they gave me! One old man was crying when he saw me and said, 'I knew you would come! I knew! My aunt told me you would come!' He was extremely pleased to see me. I was very happy to stay there."

One day Shree Maa asked me to accompany her with a number of devotees to the village of Jayrambati, the birthplace of Shree Sarada Devi. Jayrambati is a small village in the interior of Bankura District, very remote from the communications of modern India and quite inaccessible. We traveled by bus and then by rickshaw, and ultimately reached the Ramakrishna Mission, which had purchased the ancestral property of the Mukapadhaya family. There they had constructed a large temple and a guest house for the men, and had turned the original cottage of Sarada Devi and her family into a nunnery for the female devotees. As a matter of course, all the males of our party were lodged in the men's guest house, and all the females resided with Shree Maa in Sarada Devi's cottage.

Very early the next morning I felt some force pulling me from my sleep. It was still dark while I bathed outside, and wandered into the lanes of the village as if a magnet were pulling me. I came directly to the window of Sarada Devi's cottage, where I heard the sweet music of Shree Maa's recitation of the *Chandi Path*. Grabbing the ledge of the wall, I pulled myself up, peering through the window to look at the scene within. There was Shree Maa in the early morning hours, sitting by the light of a candle, plucking the strings of a tambura and reciting the melodious harmonies of the *Chandi Path*.

Her voice was so soothing and her tone so captivating, that I found myself enraptured by the music which poured forth. I sat upon the wall and listened intently, totally oblivious as the night faded into dawn and the sun rose upon the eastern horizon.

Suddenly, some of the women within the room began to laugh. I opened my eyes from an ecstatic trance. They were standing at the window gazing at me, a *sadhu* sitting upon the wall of the ladies' quarters peering at them through the window. Laughing, they invited me into the ladies' chambers. Quickly I slid down the wall and climbed in through the window. Then the ladies accompanying Shree Maa offered me tea and biscuits, while Shree Maa completed her devotional worship.

How joyous were those days in Jayrambati! After we broke the ice that day, and made the understanding between us that the female quarters were not off limits to all the males, then every morning I arose in the dark before sunrise, and my feet knew the way into Shree Maa's chamber. The ladies would have the door open for me, and I would sit in meditation and listen as Shree Maa sang.

One morning Shree Maa said to the entire group, "I have a desire to eat Govinda Bhog rice. I am tired of eating the fat short-grained rice that the ashram is providing. Would somebody get some first quality rice for me?"

I immediately stood up and walked out from her chamber. As I went out from the female quarters, I found Rathan, one of the male disciples who was accompanying our party. He asked me, "Swamiji, where are you going?"

"I am in search of Govinda Bhog rice," I replied. "Shree Maa has requested some good rice to eat."

He said, "Please let me accompany you." And he did.

When we returned to the convent and presented the rice, Rathan gave this report: "Wherever Swamiji went in this village, everyone knew him. They invited him into every single house and when he told them the nature of his search, what he was looking for, they immediately directed him to the farmer who gave us what we wanted."

Just then Ganapati Mukapadhaya, Shree Sarada Devi's oldest living relative, came to the convent door. "Maa," he said bowing with great reverence. "How is it that you are traveling with this Swamiji?"

Maa replied, "We have been doing *pujas* together for a few months, and he said that he had never yet seen the village of Jayrambati. Therefore, I brought him here for *darshan*."

"What do you mean, 'he has not seen the village of Jayrambati?'" replied the astonished Ganapati. "He lived with me in my house for three months and did *tapasya* under that tree!"

Shree Maa looked at me delightedly and exclaimed. "Oh, so you've never been in Jayrambati? Well then, with great privilege I will eat this rice presented by a great thief. You want to steal the *darshan* of God? You will force Her to give to you, whether She is ready or not!"

That afternoon a number of people assembled before the room in which Shree Maa was staying. Seeing so many people trying to look inside the room, Shree Maa said, "Let us go to the Vipatarini Mandir, the village temple, where we can all sit together." Shree Maa led the entire congregation to the mandir, where everyone joined in song and meditation, and the entire village experienced the conviction that their Sarada Devi had once again returned.

Pujas and Yagyas

The festival season approached and devotees from many places began to request Shree Maa to join in the celebration of the various Hindu rites. In Maligaon, near Gauhati, the deity of Durga was prepared and installed in a circus tent at one end of a large open field. The *yagya* fire blazed and from morning until night worship was conducted with great devotion. The whole community joined in the celebration of Durga Puja as Shree Maa led the chanting of the mantras offered before the sacred fire. Thousands of voices joined in recitation. The rhythmic beats of the *dhaki* drums set the pace of the *aratis* during which devotees danced with ecstatic fervor. The *homa* fire was fed with wooden railway ties and the roaring blaze attracted even greater numbers of people.

When the expressions of supreme devotion reached their

climax, Shree Maa sat before the deity and merged into *samadhi*. The shimmering glow radiating from her body and the softness of her peaceful smile disseminated her attitude of serenity. The vision of her peaceful countenance was the greatest blessing the people could have received.

Hearing about the delightful *pujas* and festivals of worship in Assam, the devotees in Calcutta sought to recreate the exper-ience in their own communities. In a school playground just outside of Belur Math, a large tent was erected in which the Goddess Durga, along with the image of Shree Ramakrishna, was enshrined upon the altar. Shree Maa led the worship, singing, chanting, and offering oblations to the sacred fire for each mantra of the *Chandi Path*. Throughout the nine days of worship the intensity of devotion increased. Even the *sannyasis* dwelling in Belur Math, upon hearing of Shree Maa's worship, left their monastic confinement to join in the celebrations.

Shree Maa's reputation for the sincerity and clarity of her worship spread across northern India and she was regularly invited for festive occasions to guide various communities in prayer. Many such festivals were observed under her guidance in private homes, in temples, and even in the jungles of Bangladesh. One *puja* stands out in particular as an example of Shree Maa's universal love.

Late one night, a few dozen people gathered around the *homa* fire to chant the Sanskrit mantras. They were enjoying the offerings and spiritual communion, when suddenly out of the darkness appeared a group of more than five hundred Muslim men, each carrying a large staff in a very threatening manner.

The Muslims surrounded the sacrificial area and fear of an impending confrontation swept through the worshipers. Shree Maa, with her delicate frame, gracefully stood up and walked directly to the Muslim leaders and very politely invited, "Please, will you join us in our worship?"

The leaders were stunned. Never before had their presence been accepted in Hindu homes or functions of worship. Mother lost no time. She said, "Please sit down and join us in the offering." She grabbed one of the men's hands and led him to a vacant seat at the fire. Some of the Hindu devotees moved aside to make room for their Muslim brethren, while others wondered in amazement why a Hindu saint was inviting Muslims to participate in an orthodox Hindu ceremony of worship. They could do little save watch what happened next.

The Muslims looked on in astonishment as well. An orthodox priestess was welcoming the Muslims instead of rejecting them. As the cadence of the mantras became more intense and the rhythms grew stronger, the Muslim leaders were shown the ritual of *homa*. Gradually an attitude of relief descended upon all of the participants, which later became a joyous peace.

Later that evening, all the devotees, Hindu and Muslim alike, sat together at the *satsangha* with Shree Maa. She looked at a young Muslim man at the back of the room and requested in Urdu, "Will you bring me a glass of *pani* (water)?" He was startled since Muslims are not allowed to touch any possession belonging to a Hindu devotee, let alone that of a respected Guru. A Hindu boy sitting nearby immediately rose to bring water.

"Not you," called Shree Maa. "I want that man to bring me water," pointing to the Muslim man.

Embarrassed, the Muslim man nevertheless fetched the drink and handed it to Shree Maa. Drinking the entire glass of water, she said in Bengali to the Hindu boy, "Now, you can bring me a glass of *jal* (water)." He promptly rose and soon returned with the water, which Shree Maa again drank completely.

Then she turned to a Western devotee and in English requested the same of him. "Bring me a glass of water." As she finished drinking this last glass of water, she turned to the assembly and said, "Don't you see? What is the difference between *pani*, *jal* and water? It's all the same. Whether you say it in Urdu, Bengali, Hindi or English, we all drink the same thing! Why are you fighting with each other? What's the purpose? We are all the same. Just the names are different. Why do we not respect each other? Don't you want to make heaven here? We are breathing the same air, drinking the same water, feeling the warmth of the same sun. Why are you making differences? Follow Mother, the Divine Mother. Mother has no discrimination. She treats all Her creation the same."

Some of the men began to weep, while others smiled in great delight. Perfect silence permeated the room and a feeling of unity, harmony and peace filled the atmosphere. Shree Maa closed her eyes and went into deep meditation. After that no one ever disturbed our worship. Some Muslims started to come back to hear Swamiji speak and to learn from him. One of the Muslim men said about Swamiji, "He is from a Western country and he is following Hindu philosophy. He has a picture of Mecca on his altar. He is a good example for us." They were moved by such a universal philosophy and invited us, "Please come to my house to wake up knowledge."

After this incident, in all future festivals all the religions were given equal respect and importance. Everyone worshiped together according to the dictates of their religion, and the festivals grew larger and more delightful. People were provided with holy books of their choice and everyone sat before the altars reading the scripture of their *dharma*. People of all faiths came to celebrate their devotion to their path, and to receive the blessings and *prasad* from Shree Maa. In this way all throughout India Shree Maa inspired community worship and religious harmony.

The Doctor in Bangladesh

One family with which we stayed in Bangladesh had a young girl who was to have a gall bladder operation to be performed by a famous surgeon in Dhaka. This doctor was a Muslim who had completed his education and training in London and had quite a reputation in his country. We went to visit him in his chamber, and quite naturally the chamber was full of patients, some who were in terrible condition. At exactly 11:30 he got up and left the chamber, and walked right out without a word to anybody.

Shree Maa walked up to the secretary and asked, "Where is he going and when will he be back?"

The answer came, "The doctor went to pray."

After half an hour the doctor returned and called Shree Maa into his private office for the interview. Shree Maa said, "I am really pleased with you. You keep your prayer."

The Doctor replied, "I am in His hands. I am nobody. Why should I give up my Allah? When Allah has made this time of prayer, then Allah will take care of my patients while I am giving my remembrance to Him."

Shree Maa's eyes filled with tears and she thanked him for being a pure guru to every patient.

Yagya in Rishikesh

The Devaloka Ashram was situated on the banks of the Ganga in the Mayakunda section of Rishikesh. A large brick wall surrounded the property and two wrought iron gates swung out to the sandy shores of the river. Within the one acre garden stood a small Shiva Temple, adjacent to which was a single room house. The garden was filled with trees bearing mangoes, guavas, bananas and papayas. One hundred and eight red hibiscus flower trees encircled the perimeter, and neat rows of marigolds lent a golden hue in contrast to the var-

ious shades of green and red. Within the garden were egg-
plants, taro root, okra, zucchini and various other forms of
squashes; carrots, radishes and potatoes were in sufficient
quantity so that occupants only required some oil, spices, flour
and a little salt from the market.

Within the garden was a large *hawan kunda*, a pit for the
sacrificial fire, and it was here that Shree Maa sat with
Swamiji and other devotees for one hundred eight days performing the *Chandi Yagya*. What a *yagya* it was! The chanting
was so vibrant and the meditation so deep. The sound of *kirtans* and *mantras* resounded throughout the neighborhood,
while Shree Maa sat deeply in meditation.

It was on the evening of a great festive occasion toward the
end of the worship when Shree Maa determined to cook a
large meal for all of the participants. She had set the pots upon
the stove, laid down her spoon, and sat down listening to the
tones of the sacred mantras as they were offered before the
divine fire. In this condition she became totally absorbed in
her meditation and totally oblivious to the pots of food sitting
upon the stove. Even after the mantras of the text of worship
and the *arati* had been completed, Shree Maa sat in the bliss
of her communion in *samadhi*. Swamiji and the other participants sat looking at the radiant glow of her aura as she was
obviously lost in communion with another reality. Ultimately,
everyone became tired and went to sleep without partaking of
any of the food.

It was very late in the night when Shree Maa awoke from
her meditative trance to find all of the devotees deep in sleep.
Looking at the stove, she found her dinner burnt beyond
recognition, and the stove itself had long since run out of
kerosene, extinguishing its own flames. Suddenly, Shree Maa
felt a pang of guilt for having neglected her duty of feeding all
the participants. It had been her vow to provide the food offer-

ing for the worship, and she had neglected her duty. Feeling very badly, she started banging on the pot lids and calling in a loud voice to awaken all who were sleeping. "What," she exclaimed. "You have all gone to sleep without taking your food! Why didn't you awaken me from my meditation?"

The groggy participants sat up in their beds rubbing their eyes. "Shree Maa, you looked so beautiful in meditation that we felt that you should remain there."

"No. No. That will never do," exclaimed Shree Maa. "You cannot put me in debt to you. I must fulfill my responsibility too. Now our dinner has become ruined. I will have to cook another dinner for you."

"But Mother," called the devotees. "It's almost morning already. We have to get up in another hour or two. There's no need for dinner. Just let us sleep."

"No," said Mother. "All of you get up! It will only take a few minutes. Here, help me wash these dishes and we'll start all over again."

Then one by one the devotees climbed out of their bedrolls on the floor and started scrubbing the pots, washing and cleaning new vegetables, filling the stoves with kerosene, and helping Shree Maa to fulfill her obligation.

It was early morning by the time everyone had eaten and finished cleaning up. They all went down to the bank of the river and took their bath, ready to begin the new day's worship.

At Guhyeshwari Mandir

The devotees followed Shree Maa on many pilgrimages, as Shree Maa was determined to visit as many of the *Shakti pithas*, places of worship of the Divine Mother, as possible. Along with Swamiji, she performed *yagyas* and *pujas* at forty-two of the fifty-one places sacred to the Divine Mother. Near

Kathmandu in Nepal, Shree Maa performed a special sacred worship at the Guhyeshwari Mandir. Sitting in an alcove just beside the temple, she and Swamiji recited the *Chandi Path*. After a short time of recitation, a number of local residents came and congregated in front of the two chanting *sadhus*. As they heard the recitation in rhythmic *pranayam*, they started to talk to one another in hushed tones, "Look at the purity of the Mother's devotion."

Along came a local pundit and the village people asked him, "Punditji, why do you not chant in such rhythmic *pranayam*?"

The pundit drew closer to listen, but after a few minutes he shook his head and turned away in disgust. "No, no. What can these people know, a foreigner and a lady from India. They can't possibly know how to chant in proper Sanskrit. It's improper for you to even sit here and listen to them," he declared. "Everyone go about your business!" he ordered.

When he walked away, all of the local devotees began to disperse. They followed the pundit down the street and around the corner. No sooner had the pundit turned the corner, then all of the devotees returned. They sat where Shree Maa and Swamiji were chanting and by the end of the recitation a great number of people congregated at Mother's feet.

They witnessed the spiritual integrity and sincerity with which Shree Maa was chanting and listened to her musical tones. They felt in the depths of their spirit a purity which permeated the worship. At the end of Shree Maa's worship, the devotees bowed to her in reverence and laughed at their own pundit, who, thinking he knew, actually knew not.

Tapas Chakravarty

Tapas Chakravarty was a doctor who worked at the Northern Indian Railway Hospital. After a serious spinal inflammation, he was confined to a wheelchair, and he went to the Ayurvedic Hospital in Kotakhal, Kerala for treatment. He asked Shree Maa and Swamiji to accompany him and the entire family took a suite of rooms in the hospital. Many of the other patients in the hospital were wealthy Muslim patrons, who came from the Gulf states of Kuwait, Dubai, the Emirates and Saudi Arabia. Much to the chagrin of these visitors, Shree Maa and Swamiji made an altar in their room and began each day with *Mangal Arati* and the beating of drums and blowing of conch shells at the break of dawn each morning.

Throughout the day, Shree Maa was performing the functions of worship, reciting the *Chandi Path*, ringing bells and singing songs. An atmosphere of joy filled those rooms of the hospital. Often the orthodox Muslims would congregate outside the room, snickering to one another, and they nicknamed the room the Ding Dong Room because of the amount of celebration and bell ringing which was taking place. Together they went to complain to the management that this was not the proper ambiance for a medical facility. The hospital was managed and maintained by orthodox Hindu Brahmins who could not find anything distasteful in the worship that Shree Maa was performing, but tried as best as they could to appease all of the guests.

One young Muslim man from Kuwait named Samir began coming to Shree Maa's room. Every time he heard the bell ring, he would come and ask, "What is the cause of your joyous celebration?"

After a few days of his coming, the other Muslim patients became concerned. They saw this young man came earlier and stayed later each day, and every time he left the room, he had a bright smile upon his face. Soon his joy became so obvious that the orthodox Muslims thought it was their duty to save one of their brothers who was falling into temptation. They began to protest with greater strength to the management, and persuaded them to make Shree Maa at least stop the ringing of bells and blowing of conch shells.

What happened next was an even greater curiosity. The family of the management was devoted to the worship of Lord Krishna, and had erected a large temple at the far end of the hospital complex. They invited Shree Maa to move her worship from the hospital room to the temple. When Shree Maa began to worship in the temple, people from the village came bearing offerings. Soon the entire community was involved in a festive celebration of divinity. Many homes prepared sweets and platters of fruit and other offerings. Then that Muslim boy started to come to the temple every day. He sat with Shree Maa and listened to explanations about the meaning of *dharma*, and with a contented heart, he developed a greater respect for different traditions around the world.

Ultimately the doctor's treatment was completed. Shree Maa blessed Samir, and returned with her entourage to Bengal.

Under The Tree In Karnaprayag

We were staying under a large Pipal tree in front of the Shiva Temple at Karnaprayag. The Shiva Temple is located on the far side of the bridge, across from the bazaar. Whoever follows the path down the steep precipice, will arrive at the confluence of the Alakananda and Pindari Rivers. On the shores of that confluence stands the Shiva Temple. Outside the temple is the great Pipal tree, around which a large stone *bedi* or platform has been erected. Sitting upon the platform, one can look at the vistas of nature, listen to the roar of the rivers as they converge, and see the different colored waters mingling together as they flow into one stream.

It was in this wonderful scene that Shree Maa sat with a group of devotees and practiced meditation. I remember so very clearly the dialogue that took place one afternoon as we sat under that tree. I had asked Shree Maa, "Mataji, there are so many various schools of philosophy. To which school do you belong, and to which branch of philosophy should your devotees owe allegiance?"

Shree Maa looked at me with great joy in her eyes and said, "What schools of philosophy are you referring to?"

I immediately answered her, confident of all the studies I had performed, "Mother, in Sanskrit literature there are seven classical schools of philosophy. Each of them advocates a different position. *Charvaka* says that everything we think of comes from our senses. 'No,' says *Nyaya*, the next school of philosophy. There are many things in our minds which have not come directly from the senses. There are inferences of deduction and induction, testimony and intuitive perception.

"The third school of philosophy is called *Vaisheshika* and this asks us, 'What is it that you know through all of these means of knowledge?' When you analyze the substance of all thought or speech, all we can know of the world is material. The *Sankhya* school of philosophy says that matter alone will not explain the evolution of existence. There must be some other phenomena in addition to matter. In addition to *prakriti*, we require *purusha*. In addition to a body, life requires a soul.

"*Yoga* is the next system of philosophy. The purpose of life is to unite the two. The *purusha* must unite with the *prakriti*. *Citta vritti nirodh iti yogah*. The cessation of change or modification within the objects of consciousness is union. The highest wisdom is the perfection of union, and the path of *Yoga* enumerates the eight steps by which union can be attained.

1. Take control of your life. Define your goals. Organize your life.

2. Create a discipline. Budget your time, budget your resources, budget your energy, budget your mind.

3. Put your body into harmony. Every movement of the body is a reflection of the movement of mind. Make your body sit still.

4. Put your breath into harmony.

5. Bring your senses inside.

6. Contemplate.

7. Meditate.

8. Realize the ultimate peace.

"The next school of philosophy is called *Purva Mimamsa*, otherwise known as *Tantra*. The synthesis of all worship with devotion will lead seekers to their goal. *Tantra* means to synthesize, to weave together the various disciplines of spiritual practice into one holistic spiritual offering which we call Life. The seventh school of philosophy is *Vedanta*, where there is one and only one. All is in the perfection of union.

"Shree Maa, to which school of philosophy do you belong, and which philosophy is appropriate for your followers?"

Shree Maa, who was listening very intently, withdrew inside and sat very still for a long time. After some time a beautiful smile of recognition came across her face. Slowly she moved her tongue around her mouth, moistening her lips, and opened her eyes, which were radiant with compassion. Then she gave her answer. "The philosophies which you have described are not really different schools of philosophy. Actually, the Sanskrit term is *shakha* — branches. They are all branches of one philosophy, and taken together they are the one path to self-realization.

"Every child in its infant state knows only what the senses tell it. A child seeks the warmth of its mother, and cries for food instinctively, not because of a logical deduction. As we evolve, we begin to judge, and we learn how to discriminate using our mental faculties as a test of propriety. Sometimes we seek to discriminate between our changing nature and our changeless reality. Again we seek to unite the two. Through devotion to our worship we arrive at the realization of *Vedanta*, the unity of oneness. Mankind is constantly moving between the various forms of worship, the various schools of philosophy. Regardless of whether you call yourself a devotee or an intellectual, regardless of whether you perform with understanding or without, each of us in our every action is acting in accordance with one philosophy or another. Therefore, we all belong to all the schools of philosophy, as they are the elements of one path to unity.

"When a bird rises into the atmosphere it can see for a great distance. When one rises to the top of a high place and looks down upon the scenery, even the tallest of mountains appear to be small from the perspective of height. When the soul looks down from the heights of self-realization and sees all of life, it frees itself from attachment. The actions that one encounters in life appear to be very small, just as the mountains upon the earth. As high as the soul will rise, so great a distance can be perceived both before and after, the actions which will happen in the life of that soul, as well as its past experience. Just as from the heights above, one can see that even beyond the most difficult of mountains lies a beautiful valley, in the same way one can see the probable results of actions. This is what is called a perceiver of past, present and future.

"The ignorant is like a person who is sitting beside a mountain of gold, yet still remains a beggar. When a person has met their guru, and with an open heart allows the guru to show how to see, that person discovers the wealth that is with them, that person is known as wise.

"Experience Truth for yourself and don't rely only upon the experiences of others. Truth has only one reference for verification -- personal experience. If a teacher says 'I have seen, but you cannot see,' please do not accept such a one as a guru. Whoever will say, 'I have seen, and now I shall show you how you may see,' you should make such a one your guru. You can trust in him or her."

"Please tell me by what means is a true guru known, and by what means is a pretender known," I asked.

"A true guru is always thinking for the welfare of others, whereas a false teacher is always thinking for his or her own personal gain or even of destroying others. The true teacher does good even to those who do him or her harm. Just like the sandlewood tree: if anyone cuts into the tree, even still, the tree gives forth its beautiful fragrance. The saintly being is always engaged in striving for the upliftment and welfare of everyone. An unsaintly being is known by the capacity to do harm to others and do harm even to himself in the process."

I was truly astounded to hear her words which were so simple yet so wise, and emanated from such strength of character. All through my sojourn with various teachers, with various disciplines, I had always heard the sectarian views that "our philosophy is correct, and in some way better than all the others." Shree Maa was someone who had harmonized all of philosophy into a way of life. It was not theoretical knowledge confined to books. It was a living, vibrant way of life.

I looked at Shree Maa sitting under the tree. I peered out across the Himalayan vistas, looked down at the raging waters below, and merged into meditation.

Himalayan Yatra

The view from Kausani is one of the most spectacular of all the Himalayan vistas. The Gandhi Ashram is situated upon a high peak which looks out upon the summit of Nanda Devi in the Himalayan range. At sunrise all of the residents of the ashram, wrapped in blankets, sit upon a stone wall watching the marvels of sunrise in the Himalayas.

At the crack of dawn, the dark of night transcends into a gradient of illumination and a wash of colors, as the sun's faint glow becomes apparent on the horizon. The blues and purples turn to pinks and reds, and then oranges and yellows as the sun's rays rise above the mountain peaks. The white glacial formation of Nanda Devi reflects the entire spectrum of color, and the radiant reds and golds shine like a treasure chest of the wealthiest kings. This sunrise's golden reflection finds verbal expression only in the poetry of the Vedic *rishis*.

Traveling with Shree Maa through the Himalayan vistas was such an incredibly unique experience. She knew the mountains like the back of her hand and was known throughout the regions from the Kumoan Hills, Pithoragarh and Gharwal, throughout Himachal, and even as far as Lahulshpiti. Everywhere we traveled, we found acceptance and wonder. At Patal Bhuvaneshwar, we descended into the cave in which spiritual aspirants have meditated for many thousands of years. Patal Bhuvaneshwar looks over the lush valleys of the foothills, and when the clouds rise, the entire Himalayan pantheon from Kailash to Yamunotri can be seen.

The cave is unspeakable in grandeur. The first flight of steps descends fifty-five feet vertically, like a steep ladder hewn into the rock. In many places visitors must lie on their bellies, pressing their bodies against the wet and muddy rocks to squeeze through the tight places. But once inside, it is a wonder of amazement. Perhaps the largest hall can seat more than fifty meditating *sadhus* at one time. Where those meditators sat, the stones have been rubbed perfectly smooth.

The cave obviously dates back several millennia before Christ: tunnels and grottos, an entire underground community, something like a Kishkinda for *sadhus* of prehistoric times. The rock configurations are perfect *murtis* of the entire Hindu pantheon, and water drips from various sources, making channels with moss and ferns growing throughout. All the Gods are present and one can feel the *rishis* are still sitting in meditation.

A *hawan kunda*, a pit for the sacrificial fire, sits just before the entrance to the mouth of the cave. The priest of the temple made all of our arrangements and we chanted the *Chandi homa*. Completing the *homa*, we invited the entire community to share, and as we were chanting the worship, suddenly the clouds parted and the most clear vision of the Himalayas was exposed. A shudder of chills ran up my spine, as we could see from Mount Kailash to Badrinath, a little to the left was Kedarnath, and then Gangotri and Yamunotri. Taking in the majestic view, I began to shake with astonishment. We continued to sing as the setting sun turned the glistening western slopes progressively golden and then orange. Then it began to grow dark and the view faded back into the clouds.

Every day was a unique experience. Sometimes we ascended high mountains, and sometimes we descended into valleys. Always we kept the name of God upon our lips, and we would stop regularly to share the most inspiring conversations.

This day we climbed into the high mountains to cross a pass above 8,000 feet. The valley grew steeper as we began the ascent and the sides became lined with jagged rock formations. I looked up to see a cover of clouds hugging close to the ridge of the mountain, obscuring a portion from view. But between the breaks in the clouds I could see the white snow-capped peaks and patches of blue sky. The air grew thinner, cold, fresh and invigorating, and I became absorbed in the energy. It was so soft, yet so strong. So many times along the trek we stopped just to gaze out upon the scenery, the falling waters melting off the glaciers, the river below, occasional trees, and the cold, fresh breeze — all of it so unique and so spectacular. I felt drawn into it, as though I was an integral part of nature, a tree standing beside the mountain holding it in place. There was so much energy.

Pausing for a moment's contemplation, I observed that I had been walking out my thoughts, trampling them beneath the dust of my feet, and now I had entered into the rhythm of just walking. I gazed out at the clouds. They hugged the mountains with such serenity, like a blanket keeping the peaks safe and warm with softness and gentleness. It was as though I was a mountain, being caressed by the love of a cloud. Inside was silence and I became one with that scene of nature.

We moved with a certain vigor, absorbed in vision. We would silently recite our mantras as we walked, attaching one syllable to each footstep. Sometimes we would even forget that we were walking. We became so absorbed that only the prayer of God was walking on the mountain footpaths. The trees towered above us as we proceeded along the banks of a river. The shallow waters of the tumbling creeks moved quickly, splashing over the rocks, bending and twisting, foaming white, before returning to pour into a shallow pool. The scenery remained incomparable: the high peaks of the mountains covered with trees, the changing colors of the days. Life is all around. And I feel so very much alive!

The morning sun was warming and its light glistened through the dew-moistened leaves of the trees. The sky was clear, a soft breeze gently flowing, causing the limbs of the trees to make dancing shadows upon the earth beneath. A bird sang its morning song; a butterfly moved beside us, flitting back and forth between Shree Maa and me, as if a representative of the welcoming committee. Somehow this day everything appeared more green, more lush, more alive. For this was the day when we joined a family of shepherds, and Shree

Maa was to lead our ascent of the Chota Booboo, a mountain pass two meters wide at an elevation of over 12,000 feet.

For some time we had been wandering in the foothills of Himachal Pradesh, when we joined with this group of nomadic shepherds, who were moving their flocks to the north to graze during the monsoon rains.

How simply these people lived! All the possessions of a family could fit onto one pack horse, which was loaded and unloaded daily. Their life was so quiet and so rhythmic; they never slept in other than a natural shelter and they knew more of the forest than could be imagined. They knew what things to carry with them from one place to another, sometimes taking wood, sometimes grass for the animals, occasionally stocking up on some herbs that would not be available in the next campsite. Silently they exhibited a respect for life and the members of the family were bound with such complete loyalty and devotion.

We marched about fifteen miles in a day, breaking camp at sunrise and moving continuously until midday. Then, at the issuance of a silent command, the camp quietly unfolded from the two large sacks upon the back of the horse. Father went off to gather wood, Mother unpacked the vessels, spread out the carpets and went in search of herbs and ferns. The children cut grass for the horse and another brought water. When they had finished their appointed tasks and met at the camp, Father sat by the fire, smoking his big water pipe, while Mother cut the vegetables, and the children bathed at the nearby spring. Twelve months a year they lived in this manner — walking along the scenic mountain trails, singing in the evenings beside a hot, blazing fire, drinking the fresh milk of their goats, loving, laughing and living with such utter simplicity.

That morning we rose well before dawn and completed our bathing and devotions before the first light. It was a cold morning to be camped there in the valley, surrounded by tall fir trees, above which steep mountain peaks rose into jagged, glacial formations, rugged and white. We sat huddled by the fire, caressing our hot cups of steaming tea, as so many others were doing. This day, over five thousand sheep would move through the two-meter wide pass between the two jagged peaks of the glacier.

We got off to an early start and, with our light packs and blankets, the freshly cut staffs in the form of shepherd crooks presented to us the night before, and abounding energy rising to the occasion, we waded our way through the stream of babbling sheep, winding over the path which twisted back and forth up the side of the mountain. Straight up it couldn't have been one and a half or two miles, but as the path crossed back and forth, it became five or six miles, and even though well-graded, it was steep and the altitude caused shortness of breath.

Shree Maa leaped ahead with a bounteous stride, her frail figure floating with grace. The trees loomed overhead, the river below. We had to ford the river a number of times as we worked our way back and forth across the face of the mountain. The path became steeper and suddenly we were above the tops of the trees.

Shree Maa continued to climb, I behind her, and below me, five thousand bleating sheep moving along as the men, women and children poked at them, called to them, and encouraged them up toward the summit. As we looked up, the sun was shining between the two peaks which outlined the pass, gently sending streams of refracted light down the face of the mountain into the valley below.

The sun's light glistened from the fir needles of the trees, danced upon the gushing waters of the river, and highlighted the magnitude of the mountain with shades of green and yellow. The air was fresh and cold, and as I looked down upon the scene, I could imagine the tempo being picked up with full orchestration, the steering sounds of men and animals on the move. Now we approached the top and then, as I lifted my eyes from the jagged stones we traversed, I saw Shree Maa standing above in the center of the pass.

It was a vision I shall long remember. Her hair was fluttering in the breeze as she stood regally, streams of sunlight pouring down from around her body. Her smile was luminous and her eyes brilliant. She stood there with the shepherd's crook in her hand like Moses surveying his flocks of Hebrew children. An aura of contentment, majesty and triumph glistened about her.

Trumpets were blaring in my ears. The sheep and their calls, the men and horses, women and children, the two giant pinnacles of ice between which stood this glowing ember transformed into light, the figure of Shree Maa, radiating warmth and love against a background of ice.

When I reached her, she gently caressed my shoulder, turned me around, and together we surveyed her domain. We looked over the broad expanse of landscape, across the Himalayas as far as the eye could see: animals and men winding their way over the course we had traversed, nature reflecting such power as I had never known before, and men stepping out to ascend her peaks.

What a privilege to travel the Himalayas with such an illuminated soul! Badrinath, Kedarnath, Gangotri, Yamunotri — she knew the paths to them all. What a power, what *bhava* we felt sitting in meditation in the cave of Shankaracharya at Joshimath. More than a thousand years of pure vibrations permeated our being. The richness of philosophy manifested in pulsating sensations as we sat in the stillness and felt ourselves a part of this heritage.

Wherever Shree Maa sat, under the trees or beside the bank of the river, her communion was so total and so rich that the radiance of her aura as she fell into ever deeper states of *samadhi* created an ambiance of awe for all who were privileged to see her.

She sat with such stillness and radiated such clarity that there was no mistaking the intensity of her absorption in communion. She is Divinity in manifest form, and Her light, Her love, and Her silence are a testimony to that Divine realization.

It was very curious that day, as we sat upon the rocks beside the Mandakini River near Agastya Muni on the old footpath to Kedarnath. I remember asking Maa, "Mother, there are eight forms of behavior described as appropriate for spiritual seekers. Which form of behavior do you recommend?"

Maa asked, "Which eight forms are you speaking of? Define them for me."

"Mother, first is *Vaishnava Achara*. According to the text, this means devotion, the behavior of devotion. Cultivate an inspiration. The second form of behavior is called *Vedic Achara*, the behavior of learning. Learn about that which inspires you. Number three is called *Shaiva Achara*. Practice that which you have learned. The fourth is called *Vama Achara*. Some people called it the left-handed path, but Vama Deva is not the left-handed deity. He is the Beloved Deity, and *Vama Achara* means Beloved Behavior. Make every action you perform as an expression of your love, perfect in efficiency.

"Number five is *Dakshina Achara* which means the Preferred Path. This indicates the behavior which reduces our necessity to act in the world. When desires are less, the actions required to fulfill them become less. Number six is *Siddhanta Achara*, the behaviors described in scriptures as capable of leading us to Divinity: namely, *puja* (worship), *path* (recitation), *homa* (sacred fire ceremonies), *sangeeta* (singing), *nreeta* (dancing), *pravachan* (explanation), and *arpana* (offering). These seven functions of *Siddhanta Achara* are called *Karma* Yoga, the actions which leads to union.

"The seventh type of behavior is *Yoga Achara*, the Behavior of Union, and the eighth is called *Kula Achara*, the Behavior of Excellence. Whether sitting in meditation, or acting in this world, we maintain the same attitude of absorption in the love of God. Mother, which of these behaviors is appropriate for us to practice? Are we *Vaishnavas* or *Shaivites*? Should we follow the path of wisdom or the path of devotion? Please enlighten my confusion."

Shree Maa reflected upon the question put before her, and for a long time remained silent, looking within. After some time, she opened her eyes and a faint smile of delight radiated from her face.

"All the behaviors which you have described," she said, "are the stepping stones on the path to Supreme Union. These forms of behavior are not exclusive, but rather, comprise the path of Divine Union. Take your inspiration and learn. Take your knowledge and practice. Refine your practice to perfection, and then reduce the necessity to act. Step by step, each of these attitudes defined by scriptures will bring you into the perfection of communion.

"Wisdom is like a light. Devotion is like a jewel. Both of them give forth light. When you understand either of them, darkness flees. In all four directions there is illumination. In order to make a light you need a container, some oil and a wick. But a gem or a jewel shines by it's own effulgence. From the winds of desire, anger, greed and ignorance the flame of the light can be extinguished. But greed, anger, desire or ignorance can never extinguish the light of the jewel of devotion. That jewel shines by the power of its own self-effulgence. In this way, in whoever's heart true devotion resides, no desire, no greed or other limitation can ever have an effect upon that heart.

"The enemy of wisdom is ego. One can fall because of ego. The devotee is always humble; therefore, how can he fall? Wisdom is a man. *Maya* is a woman. Even a wise man can be afflicted by the passions for *maya*. Therefore he may fall. The man falls for the woman. But devotion is a woman. And devotion, a woman, can never fall for *maya*, a woman. A woman rarely falls in love with another woman. Therefore, *maya* has little or no power over devotion."

"Then what is the relationship between a devotee and someone who follows the path of wisdom?" I asked.

Shree Maa replied, "The attitude of a devotee is like the relationship between a mother and her small child. If the child were to grab hold of a snake, or in any situation of danger, the mother will always protect it. But when the child is bigger, a young man like the wise person, she would think that the child could protect himself. The responsibility does not remain with the mother. Therefore, God will always protect a devotee who is like a small child. And like a grown young man, God will leave the wise people to their own devices."

"There is only one path and we are all on it. Do not try to dissect spirituality into a number of fragments. Spirituality means giving more than we take. That is the behavior I would like my disciples to practice."

How her teachings speak to my heart!

We made our camp one night on the banks of the Ganges, high above Uttarkashi, on the way to Gangotri. After our evening meal, we sat by the sacred fire, silently communing with the stars and the moon and the sparks which were singing and dancing. Suddenly, Shree Maa broke the silence.

"What do you call the native land of your birth?" she

asked.

"Maa, we call it the Fatherland," came the reply.

"Very interesting," observed Shree Maa. "Here in India devotees call the land of our birth Motherland, and now I understand the meaning of the vision I saw last night."

"What vision was that?"

"I saw deeply in my meditation that Ramakrishna came to me and said, 'The Motherland and the Fatherland must be made one. You, my children, shall perform worship in the West as you do in the East. There is no need to build community temples, but a temple should be established in every home and in every heart. For that purpose you shall go to new places to teach people how to worship.'"

"Swami," she said. "We will have to obey Thakur's order."

"Shree Maa," I replied. "I will not leave India. India is the place for spiritual life and the West is the land for material concerns. People have no desire to learn to worship in the West. In order to learn to worship, one must desire to sacrifice selfishness. And that sacrifice demands that the student come to the guru. The guru does not go to the student. Therefore, I think your interpretation is wrong."

"Still," said Shree Maa, "tomorrow we will begin our descent to the plains. I have received Thakur's order."

Back to Calcutta

After the morning devotions were completed and the camp packed, Shree Maa and I began the walk back to the motor road. Finding the pavement of a Himalayan highway, we followed the road until we came to a tea stall. After some time, we found a bus to Uttarkashi and by evening we were in Rishikesh.

We took the train toward Calcutta and by the second morning had reached Asansol, where we were recognized by a ticket collector on morning duty. We couldn't have imagined that he would wire ahead about Shree Maa's coming to Howrah Station, and upon receiving the announcement, at least a few hundred beloved devotees gathered at the station terminus to welcome the Himalayan pilgrims. When other travelers in the station saw the commotion, they all rushed to get a view, and soon there were thousands of people congregated on the station platform in anticipation of Shree Maa's blessings.

Viewing the commotion, the station master sent the Central Railway Police to escort Shree Maa to his office. Tea was served and *kirtan* began, and suddenly, the entire station was reverberating with the sounds of joyous worship. The devotees became ecstatic singing *kirtan*. Shree Maa danced around the station master's office and then outside into the lobby, where she was greeted with exuberant devotion. The devotees escorted her to waiting cars, and in this way Shree Maa returned to Calcutta.

Leaving India

It was the Spring Festival of 1984. We were in Calcutta, performing the *Navaratri* with a large group of devotees. I had just gotten up from my *asana* in front of the sacred fire, where I was chanting the *Chandi Path* every day, and I was sitting upon a bed made of rope in a small room nearby our site of worship.

Damaroo came into the room and said, "There is a policeman from the Foreigner's Registration Office outside who wants to see you."

"What does he want?" I asked.

"He says he must talk with you personally."

"Show him in," I said.

In a few moments the policeman entered and handed me a piece of handwritten paper. "It's for you," he said. "I need your signature."

"What is it?" I asked.

"You have been ordered by the Government of India to leave the country within seven days. The Government cannot give you any more extensions of your visas."

"What?" I replied in consternation. "I'm in the middle of a big *yagya*. You can't put me out right now!"

"Swamiji," replied the officer. "You have been here almost twenty years now. When were you not in the middle of a *yagya*? Everyone knows what you have been doing here. That is why we ignored the matter so long. But now an order has come from the Central Government in Delhi, and we have no choice but to serve as their messengers. You have seven days to leave the country."

"What is the problem?" asked Shree Maa as she was escorted into the room by a number of devotees.

"The Government of India has determined that it is time for Swamiji to return to his own country," replied the officer. "The people over there are desperately in need of good teachers. Look at the chaos they are creating around the world. They are supporting unjust governments and economic exploitation everywhere. He must leave India. It's the Government's order! He should go to his native land and teach the people there how to live in peace." He showed the paper to Shree Maa.

"I have been telling him the same thing," said Shree Maa. "Swami, you cannot disobey Ramakrishna's order."

"Tell him to sign the paper and date the paper," requested the officer.

Maa looked at him with gentle warmth. "Could you let us finish this *yagya* first?" she requested.

"How much time do you need?" he asked.

"If you could give us one extra week, then it won't disappoint the devotees."

"All right," replied the officer. "I can do that much. Date it with next week's date."

"Go ahead and sign it," said Shree Maa, passing the paper to me.

Tears filled my eyes as I read the contents. I took the pen and signed it and dated it a week in advance.

That *yagya* went by so quickly. After every *yagya* in Calcutta, we retreated to Vashishta's attic. He had converted it into a little room for us, which no one even knew existed. He would put a padlock on the outside, and we would remain silent for three days after every *yagya*. No one in Calcutta could imagine to where we had disappeared.

I was determined not to leave. "We will go to Kathmandu and get a new passport," I suggested.

Shree Maa was poised with equanimity. "I think we had better go," she said. "It is Thakur's order."

"No, Maa, don't send me to the West. Let me try to stay."

"All right, go ahead and try. But I think we had better go. Ramakrishna has work for us in the West."

"No, Maa, it can't be!" I replied.

A few days later we were in Kathmandu. After getting a new passport, I went to the Indian Consulate. "We have orders not to give you any more visas," came the reply. "You have been in India quite a long time already. The Government of India has determined that you should go back to your country."

"But we haven't made any arrangements to go. All of our necessary papers are in India."

"I can give you seven days."

Back in Calcutta with three days left, no one could help us extend our stay. Shree Maa said, "Swami, I think it is time for us to go."

"No, Maa, let me try in Dhaka."

In Dhaka too came a refusal. There we were penniless, with the clothes on our backs, a few Sanskrit books and a pair of tongs for the fire, when we took refuge with a family in the Madhupur jungles of Taingal District in Bangladesh. I wired my family for assistance, and in a few weeks our packet of papers arrived at the American Embassy in Dhaka, where Shree Maa received a business visa for the United States as an international representative of a manufacturing firm.

While the papers were being processed, we wandered around the Chakma Mountains above Chittagong and performed worship in the various shrines which had survived the Muslim domination.

It was just after Durga Puja in 1984, when we received our approval to enter America. We got a plane to Hong Kong, another to Tokyo, and a few days later, with a bundle of clothes tied up in a blanket by a piece of string and a few books, we landed in Los Angeles.

The international travelers were as curious to see us as I was to see them. How life had changed since I had left America! Everything was astounding to me: jetwalks in the airports, computers everywhere, fashions, everything had changed so much. Shree Maa wasn't the least bit excited or surprised. I remember going into a supermarket to buy some food. The checker pulled the items over a scanner, and the prices lit up in an electrical display. In one store the checker put a few potatoes on the weighing machine, and an automated voice called out, "Three pounds of potatoes... $1.47." I was looking all around for the voice of whoever said that. Shree Maa stood with perfect equanimity.

We visited an office where they had a computer on a desk. When I had left America, a computer took up the top floor of the university. We all had packets of IBM keypunch cards, and the computer would be rolled around on wheels. Now computers were springing up everywhere. Shree Maa asked, "What can you do with a computer?"

"You can write, do bookkeeping, run a whole business," came the reply.

"Swami," she said. "It looks like a very efficient tool. I think you had better learn how to use one of these."

Little could I have imagined that the little computer was going to become one our most important tools for sharing the ancient wisdom of the Himalayan traditions. Today I smile when I think how right she was in seeking a union between the spirituality of the east and the technology of the west. With Mother's blessings we were able to share a lot.

Shree Maa with devotees at the Kamarpukur Temple,
marking the birthplace of Shree Ramakrishna.

Getting Started in America

Within a few hours of our landing in America, we were rescued from the airport by relatives of devotees from India and immediately set up camp in a suburban home in Southern California. No sooner had Shree Maa arrived than she began to redecorate the home and transform the living room into a temple of God.

Within a few days, the house was full of people and we brought a bale full of straw, dug the soil from the garden, and began the process of constructing the clay image of the Goddess Kali. How I remember that first *yagya* which we made in America! We went to the East West Aurobindo Ashram in downtown Los Angeles and asked permission to use their facility for a great fire sacrifice in worship of the Goddess Kali.

The manager of the ashram was named Fred and he asked us, "How are you going to advertise your worship?"

Shree Maa looked at him incredulously and said, "Why would we want to advertise?"

"Well, who is going to come to your worship?" asked Fred.

"Mother Kali," came Maa's reply. "Who else should come to our worship?"

He was so astounded that he could not help but agree.

People gathered inquisitively to watch as we put the finishing touches on the clay statue of Kali and transformed the parking lot into an area of sacred worship. We drew the *yantras* and invited the Divine Fire.

Within half an hour of the commencement of our chanting, the sound of sirens reverberated through the air and the sounds grew louder and louder until we could discern that they had stopped just a few feet away. Looking over my shoulder, I could see the hook-and-ladder fire truck with an entire crew of firemen climbing down with hoses. The captain of the fire brigade approached with curiosity.

"What is going on here?" he requested.

"This is the sacred worship of the Goddess Kali," we replied.

"Do you have a permit?" He appeared stern and unrelenting.

"No, I'm sorry. I never knew we needed a permit for worship."

"Shall we cite them for an illegal burn?" asked the lieutenant.

Shree Maa looked puzzled and asked, "Are they going to put you in jail for worshiping?"

"No," said the captain. He turned to the lieutenant, "Leave them alone. Just make sure the fire doesn't get out of hand."

Fred showed the captain that we had an extinguisher nearby.

How strange it was to worship in America!

Only a handful of people came to visit our worship, but one of the sincere devotees invited us to visit his house in Palm Springs. A few weeks later we started out to explore and eventually ended up in this devotee's house. This devotee explained to us that there were many ashrams already established in America and Shree Maa and I were so happy to think we could travel from ashram to ashram and join in *pujas* and *yagyas* and share *satsangha* as we had for so many years in India.

How strange were the telephone conversations as we called ashram after ashram, asking if we could come to visit.

"No," came the invariable reply. "This ashram is open only to devotees of our guru. If you would like to take our course and pay the fees for our seminars, you will be welcome to come and join us in learning our techniques of meditation."

Traveling from community to community, we were dismayed to find so many religious businesses filled with so few spiritual people! We had no place to stay and were driving from place to place looking for a community where we could share until we could return to India.

It was in this condition that we came to Swami Shantidas' ashram in Northern California. I narrated to him the story of our travels and he very graciously allowed us to stay in his ashram for a few days and perform our *pujas* and chanting.

"What are you going to do next?" he asked me.

"I'm not really sure," came my reply. "Shree Maa wants to make worship in various places to inspire devotees, but there are very few ashrams that will give us accommodation."

"Take a look at this," he said, as he lifted up a copy of the *Common Ground Magazine* and handed it to me. "This is a magazine full of advertisements for people who want to do spiritual work. Unless you advertise, you won't be able to survive in America."

I poured through the index of spiritual masters, each claiming a greater degree of enlightenment and handed the magazine back to the Swami.

"I don't think this is appropriate for us."

"Suit yourself," said the Swami. "But if you want to survive in the West, you'll need a stream of income. All the yoga teachers in the West put their businesses first."

It was a great disappointment to view this spiritual materialism as we traveled from one place of refuge to another. And quite homeless, impoverished and dejected, we returned to Southern California, contemplating our next move.

We were staying with quite a worldly family, wondering where we should go next, when one day the telephone rang.

"It's for you, Swamiji."

"Hello, Swamiji. I heard that you used to live in cremation grounds. Is that true?"

"Yes, it is."

"Well, I have a great problem and I am hoping that you can help us find a solution."

"Please let me know how I can help."

"My mother was murdered over a year ago in her house in a small community of Northern California. The next-door neighbor's son was convicted of the crime. He is currently serving a long prison sentence. The house has been for sale for over a year and it is filled with such bad energy, no one has even made an offer. Furthermore, every time I go there, I get a terrible headache and my wife gets a stomachache that makes her want to vomit. Do you know any *puja* that could purify the area? You can stay in the house as long as you like. We'll provide all the food and everything you need for your worship. Whatever you can do to help us would be so greatly appreciated."

I replied, "We'll be there tomorrow."

First thing the next morning, we were on our way back to Northern California. We found the house and met the owner, Kashyap, and, indeed, the house was in terrible condition. Upon arrival, Shree Maa immediately converted the living room into a temple and having set up the altar, she went and began to clean the kitchen. By evening time, we were already absorbed in worship.

The owner was astounded. "I've never been able to spend even a few hours here and today, in your company, I enjoyed it very, very much. What will you need for your worship?"

Shree Maa's face lit up. "Do you mind if we dig in the garden?" she asked.

"No, of course not. Dig wherever you like."

"Then," said Shree Maa, "we will need some straw and some string."

"Straw?" asked the man with great curiosity.

"Yes," said Shree Maa, "straw and a ball of string."

"What are you going to do?"

"You'll see," came Maa's reply.

Early the next morning a bale of straw and a ball of string along with a pick and a shovel were left outside in the backyard. Shree Maa and I lost no time. After the morning worship, we began to make the life-sized earthen image of the Goddess Kali. The straw was bound with string and plastered by mud. By evening time, the first coat of her form was complete.

When Kashyap, the owner of the house, came to visit that evening, he was amazed to see the deity Kali ready to greet him in the living room. He saw the altar was covered with flowers, the walls were covered with pictures of divinity and the house was filled with song. His heart rejoiced.

"Tomorrow," said Shree Maa, "we will need some paint and some brushes. Bring some costume jewelry and cloth."

The next evening, Kashyap returned with his friend Gautam and his wife Aditi, and the music got louder. By the time the altar was erected, the house had become wall to wall with sleeping bags: Sarvananda and Maitri, Nirvanananda, Ramananda and Jyoti, Avadhut and Uma, all had heard about the visiting *sadhus*, and moved in immediately. The worship continued day and night so that it was difficult to find a parking place in the street where we now lived.

It was past midnight on the fourteenth day of the dark half of the lunar fortnight, when the police knocked on our door to request that we lower the volume of our chanting. The sacred fire rose from the back patio. Mother's children were filled with the delight of worship. The house had been filled with song. The appropriate offerings had been made to the departed soul and the joy of freedom filled the hearts of all who participated.

After the completion of that worship, we all knew it was

time to move on. About ten of us together pooled our resources and signed a one-year lease for a six-bedroom house on a twenty-acre estate in the hills of Moraga, with a swimming pool, tennis courts and sauna.

Moraga

No sooner had we moved into Moraga than it became obvious that we were destined to be in America for a much longer time than we had originally anticipated. The devotees brought their friends, and their friends brought their friends, and pretty soon the field in the lower ten acres of our property was filled with cars. We turned the living room into a temple and made a large ceremonial fireplace outside. Every Sunday we conducted *homa* and *satsangha*, and all throughout the day the regular *pujas* and recitations of scriptures continued.

Some devotees offered us an Apple II computer and we started to type the mantras and translations of the *Chandi Path*. Within a short time it became apparent that we needed a legal structure upon which to base our ashram, so we made the Devi Mandir a non-profit corporation exempt from taxes.

We purchased a small trailer to carry our instruments and created a traveling *satsangha*. There were a half a dozen of us as we headed east over the Sierras. Shree Maa poured water which she had brought from the Ganges into every river we crossed, and everywhere we went, we shared in *satsangha*. People would come and sit in the trailer until it overflowed. There would be as many as eighteen or twenty people sitting in the luggage racks, on the floor, on the tables or hanging from the sides, everyone making music by banging on whatever they could find to hit, joining in the rhythmic chants and reading along with the words which we had typed and printed out. Shree Maa could cook for a hundred people inside that trailer, and the group grew as we moved across America.

During the heat of the day, every time we crossed a river, we would stop our little caravan and get out to swim. As we traveled we remained singing and chanting and enjoying the fullest communion, rejoicing in our celebration with God, visiting churches, colleges, ashrams and various spiritual communities across the country, sharing our songs and love. We made numerous Shiva lingams and established clay *murtis* in peoples' homes and gave them our books of instruction on the meaning and method of worship. We were warmly received in Chicago and Detroit and made our way to Toronto, where we participated in *satsangha* at the Vishnu Temple of Richmond Hill and the Ramakrishna Mission in Missasagau, and visited many friends and devotees.

Kripalu Yoga Ashram

It was at the Kripalu Yoga Center in Lennox, Massachusetts where we were so generously received by Yogi Amrit Desai. His devotees had converted an entire college into an ashram, and had over four hundred people as permanent residents along with several guests who lived on the ashram premises. After escorting us on a tour of the grounds, Yogi Desai graciously invited us to attend the evening *satsangha*. One other swami, Swami Dayananda, was also to be a guest at the *satsangha*.

That evening at the appointed time we were escorted to the backstage of a large hall. Shree Maa and I entered from behind the curtain and were led to the side of the stage where a large easy chair was placed for Maa to sit. Shree Maa looked out upon the crowd of faces sitting on the floor. Lights were glaring in her eyes and video cameras were focused upon her. She looked at the attendant who invited her to sit in the chair. In the center of the stage two other large throne-like chairs were placed upon which the other two gurus would sit.

"Our guru has requested you to sit in this chair," said the attendant with great respect.

"But," Shree Maa said, "all these other people are sitting on the floor. Must I sit on a chair?"

"Yes, our guru has requested you to sit on this chair."

Again Shree Maa objected, "But all of these people are sitting on the floor."

Once again the attendant replied, "It is our guru's instructions that you should sit on the chair."

"All right," said Shree Maa sitting down gracefully into the chair. She sat for a moment and looked all around her and then stood up. "You can take it away now. Thank you," she said. The attendant was aghast, but had no alternative but to remove the chair. Placing an *asana* on the floor she allowed Shree Maa to take her seat.

Now the two gurus Yogi Desai and Dayananda Saraswati entered through the rear of the auditorium, walked through the crowd giving blessings and took their seats upon the thrones on the stage. Yogi Desai looked around the entire auditorium and ultimately his gaze fell upon Shree Maa, who was sitting upon the floor, already absorbed in meditation. He turned to the attendant and said, "I told you to put a chair for Shree Maa to sit upon."

"Yes," replied the attendant. "But Shree Maa refused, saying that she would like her *asana* to be on the floor with everyone else. She is a mother with her family."

Both of the gurus cringed as they sat upon their thrones. They began their discourses for the evening, sang some bhajans, told a story and then they brought the microphone to Shree Maa and asked her to please speak some enlightening words to the congregation of devotees. Shree Maa was totally lost in meditation. Although they introduced her at least four times, and placed the microphone in front of her and waited for her to speak, Shree Maa didn't show the slightest sign of recognition — she was lost in *samadhi*.

Harvard University

Another such experience occurred in a class of comparative religions at Harvard University, where Shree Maa and I were invited to conduct a lecture defining the principles of Hinduism. Before entering the lecture room, I turned to Shree Maa and said, "Maa, I will tell a story and lead a short meditation. After about five minutes, you please sing a song."

We entered the classroom and began our discourse. The eager students leaned forward with anticipation until I came to the point where we were to perform some meditation. I closed my eyes and drifted into that beautiful space and waited to hear Shree Maa's song calling us to waking consciousness with her harmonious melodies. I smiled within in such contentment, waiting to hear the song. And I sat and waited.

When I opened my eyes, the room was empty. A clock on the wall showed that a few hours had passed, and Shree Maa was still sitting with her eyes closed. All of the students and the professor herself had already moved on to other chores, and Shree Maa sat lost in her own internal reality!

Speaking English

During those first months in America Shree Maa said little in English. I was her translator, and most frequently she spoke to me in our own personal mixture of half a dozen languages which I would strive to interpret into English. One day she stood in front of an altar of Goddess Kali and in extremely clear English she said to the Goddess, "All right, are you going to speak or not?" We were all amazed to hear her utterance and even more impressed when she turned around and began to speak English so sweetly and clearly that there was no further need of a translator.

However, one day while I was engaged at the *hawan kunda* reciting the mantras of the *Chandi Path* and offering oblations to the sacred fire, a man named Swami Narayananda telephoned the ashram and talked to Parvati, Shree Maa's secretary. He said, "I'm coming to your ashram with a number of people and we would like to stay the night."

Parvati replied, "No one can stay the night without Shree Maa's permission."

"Don't give me that bullshit!" retorted the swami.

Parvati dropped the phone and began to cry. Shree Maa, seeing Parvati in tears, ran over to comfort her, "What is the matter, my child?"

A sobbing Parvati said, "He said to me, 'bullshit.'"

"What is bullshit?" asked Shree Maa.

Parvati stood there sobbing in tears. Shree Maa ran to her bedroom and took her dictionary and began to search. Ultimately she wrote a note to me and placed it on my chanting table where I was reading Sanskrit scripture in front of the fire: "What is bullshit?"

In the middle of my chanting, I couldn't imagine what she was talking about, and having taken the firm resolve to refrain from movement or speech until the completion of my text, I sat looking at her note: "What is bullshit?"

"What is bullshit?"

"What is bullshit?"

When at last the mantras were completed, I picked up Mother's note and went into the kitchen to comfort her, "Why are you asking me about bullshit? Where did you learn language like that?"

"From the swami, where else would I learn about bullshit? What does bullshit mean? Parvati won't explain to me. The swami used the expression 'bullshit' and she began to cry.

What is bullshit?"

"Shree Maa," I replied. "It is not a good word."

"Not a good word? An Indian *sadhu* will come to America and tell my devotee a bad word!? For this reason they came to America — to teach my disciples bad words? She immediately grabbed the telephone. "Get that swami on the telephone!" Parvati dialed his number.

Shree Maa's voice was raised, "Swami you have come to America to teach my disciples bad things? Swamis should be examples of goodness. Why would you teach my disciples bad things? You owe my disciple an apology." She hung up the telephone abruptly.

That evening, Swami Narayananda came to the ashram door. Parvati was surprised to see him when she opened the door and even more astounded when he bowed down and touched her feet and begged forgiveness. "I have done wrong," confessed the swami, "and your Shree Maa has set me straight. I will not use that kind of language again. Please excuse me."

Martinez

Having completed a tour of America and inspired a handful of sincere devotees, Shree Maa felt that it was time to sit for *tapasya*. She wanted to demonstrate the meaning of sincere spiritual discipline and teach the methods of worship.

In order to engage in her demanding effort, we required a very specific type of property. The building had to be suitable to live in. It had to have public usage zoning and parking so that a congregation could gather; and it had to have industrial zoning so that we could maintain the divine fire inside. The perfect facility was found in a nondescript warehouse in Martinez, California, immediately adjacent to the Shell Oil Refinery. It was here that Shree Maa and the Devi Mandir family undertook the vow to maintain the devotional fire and recite the entire *Chandi Path* for twenty-four hours a day for three years without going outside from the building.

The following article appeared in the local newspaper in 1991 describing those efforts:

The clay was culled from the muddy embankment of the Sacramento River; the straw came from rice fields in nearby Yuba City. Mixed together and dried in the sun, in a process as old as antiquity, they gave birth to an army of divine images, icons representing the Gods and Goddesses of the Hindu Pantheon, which are being worshiped regularly in the Devi Mandir according to classical tradition.

Amidst the factories and refineries of industrial Martinez, the Devi Mandir appears from the outside as a nondescript warehouse building. Even so, within it has become the "Home of the Gods," where purifying austerities of worship and devotional services are continuing day and night. "We take over the refining business from where Shell, across the street, leaves off," declares Swami Satyananda, an American renunciate who spent twenty years studying first hand the Sanskrit traditions of Indian spirituality. "Shell purifies petroleum. We purify the minds and hearts of men."

The Swami is among a group of spiritual seekers gathered from around the world, who have not been outside from the building since the vow of a sacred fire sacrifice began three years ago. "Every time one moves into the world, the senses experience numerous perceptions," said Shree Maa, the Reverend Mother, whose spiritual inclinations trace back to her childhood, when she had repeated experiences of divine vision and transcendent meditations. "One perception gives birth to numerous conceptions. If you want the mind to become quiet, the senses must be disciplined to a cloistered environment. You must bring your senses inside."

In pursuit of that objective, a group of aspirants initiated the Temple of the Divine Mother Goddess, Devi Mandir, a converted warehouse, which has become a storehouse of blessings. "We said to God: We know you are everywhere, in all things, places and times. But we can't remember you that much. Our minds are not disciplined. Please give us some special places, special times and special forms with which to remember," explained the Swami.

"God replied: With all of your devotion, take the natural clay from the river bank and mix it with straw and pray. If you are sincere, divinity will manifest in a perceivable form."

"That is just what we did. These are the forms that came from our hearts, fashioned with clay according to the descriptions of the scriptures, the manifestations of our own innermost Self. They came from Nature in order to receive our devotion; and we have made them a promise. When we will no longer give them regular devotion, then we must put them back into the river, the infinite expanse of Nature from which they have come."

Spiritual discipline in the Devi Mandir continues twenty-four hours, day and night. Around the clock devotees maintain vigil at the sacred fire before the altar of their divine inspiration. The fire is said to burn karma, to purify the actions of participants, so that they become free from the bonds of negativity. "All the bondage of thought, the dross of memories, fears and projections, it is all thrown into the fire, along with an assortment of grains mixed with clarified butter," reports Durga Krummer, who has lived at the center since it first opened in 1987.

Shree Maa and the Swami, leaders of the group, each sit from twelve to fourteen hours a day before the altar of the sacred fire, leading chanting recitations of Sanskrit scriptures and meditation exercises. "We have heard or read about complex and lengthy spiritual disciplines, the intricate practices which refine perception," said Farrell Dernbach, a construction foreman, one of a number of devotees who has moved into neighboring houses, in order to participate in the worship during his free time. "But this is the first time we actually have an example to see what it really means to perform austerities for the purpose of attaining God realization. Daily we sit, we chant and breathe the names of God, fixing our gaze in one-pointed attention upon the deities, or staring at the glowing embers of the fire, while chanting the texts of ancient mantras. There is so much more to spirituality than listening to entertaining lectures, or even memorizing religious precepts and history. Religious life is a current experience, rather than vicariously derived. It is not intellectual; it is intuitive."

When through the force of willpower, one can make consciousness become absorbed in attention, then the result will be efficiency. This type of concentration, of willing the absorption of consciousness, can be directed into any endeavor. Once one has learned the art of paying attention, awareness can be directed into any desired objective, and therefore, all actions can be performed efficiently without the unnecessary depletion of time or resources or an abundance of costly errors.

Classical Hindu scriptures speak at length about sadhus, masters of efficiency. Such attained ones have purified their minds through concentration on the experience of the present moment. By practicing various techniques of meditation, they have mastered the art of paying attention. Furthermore, by understanding how to pay attention, they have refined their skills of learning.

"Even after only three years, I can really feel the difference," declares the Swami. "I find no desire to go outside whatsoever, nothing needs to be seen, to be done or experienced. My life surrounded by symbols of divinity is so all-encompassingly beautiful and free from conflict. There is sus-

taining peace within."

The residents do not watch television or read newspapers. They have no news of the present world, except for the occasional visitor who asks some question of current events. "They live in another world," says Lall Ramrattan, a federal government economist and professor at San Francisco's Golden Gate University. Their concept of time is totally different from what others perceive. Through the practice of yoga, they can spend the entire day sitting in one posture contemplating scripture, communing with God, with no necessity even to move."

Now in the Devi Mandir, amongst the factories and warehouses of an industrial district, the tradition is continuing according to the ancient prescriptions for a peaceful way of life: simplify your life-style, be free from debt, appreciate what you do have, think about God, study scriptures, be diligent in your spiritual practices, seek a divine interpretation in all experience.

How warmly the community received the blessings of Shree Maa's *tapasya*! News of the expression of the pure devotion in the Devi Mandir traveled from Northern California to Southern California, and people began to come from all around America, even from India. As the local community began to congregate on a regular basis, many of the gurus and *sadhus* who came to America began to put the Devi Mandir as a necessary engagement on their itineraries. Many were the holy people who came to visit the Devi Mandir and show their respects to Shree Maa's *tapasya*.

Swami Mohananda Brahmachari came to visit and Swami Arjun Puri; Ammachi Amritananda came and so did Ma Yoga Shakti; Swami Shuddhananda Bramachari and Haridan Chakraborty, Pandit Rajmani Tigunait and Swami Shantananda and many others too numerous to mention.

Many of the Swamis from the various Ramakrishna Missions came to visit from Calcutta, New York, Toronto, Sacramento and Los Angeles.

In 1992 Shree Maa, Swamiji and a number of devotees returned to India for a short reunion. Devotees came from all over India to congregate in Calcutta. Thereafter Shree Maa led her family across the North of India to various pilgrimage centers, where the disciples joined in worship, *homa* and the celebration of divinity.

Returning to America, Shree Maa moved the Devi Mandir Ashram to Napa, California, on an eighteen-acre parcel of land in the mountains above Lake Berryessa, a little more than an hour's drive from San Francisco. Moving onto the rustic hillside which straddles both sides of a seasonal creek, Shree Maa, Swamiji and devotees began to make roads, and self-sufficient utilities, and the ashram community of the Devi Mandir family has been growing. The deities of the Cosmic Puja of the *Chandi* reside there, along with temples for Ram, Lakshman and Sita, Radha and Krishna, Hanuman, Durga, Santoshi Maa, and an ever-expanding number of devotees who reside in the sanctuary of Shree Maa's presence.

Today Shree Maa stays most frequently in the Napa Ashram, but travels throughout the world to share with devotees in the delight of worship and meditation. In addition to large families across America, Europe, South America, and Asia, she has uncountable devotees in places too numerous to mention. "All my life Ramakrishna has been my Guru," says Shree Maa. "I never go anywhere without Thakur's order. He has ordered me to share unselfish divine love, and so I am doing. The most important accomplishment of human life is self realization. It doesn't matter what we become, it doesn't matter what we attain, it doesn't matter what we possess. All of that is so temporary. It will all be left behind after only a moment's enjoyment. A well-lived life is one that is full of love and joy and peace and compassion. Visit the place of peace within and celebrate the gift of Life! Don't be a miser with life. Give her your best! She will love you and comfort you and elevate you to her most exalted being!"

Chapter Six

Recollections by Devotees

Recollections by Sarvananda

In 1992, Maitri and I joined eight other devotees for the trip of a lifetime to India with Maa and Swamiji. What a way to experience India! No tourist-bus rubbernecking for us! Maa's return to her homeland after an absence of a few years fulfilled the hopes and prayers of countless devotees. From the moment of our arrival at the airport, where we were all garlanded and welcomed as family, to the last tearful good-bye on leaving, we were shown why Indian hospitality is justly famous. The fact that we were traveling with the Divine Mother and a teacher of Swamiji's renown caused us to be treated as royalty ourselves. Everywhere we went there were crowds of devotees! We visited many ashrams, temples, sacred sites, and private homes.

So many wanted to see Maa that our time was full from morning to night. Once we arrived at a place they were reluctant to let us go so it was difficult to keep our schedule. And of course trying to make our way through the teeming streets of Calcutta added to our problem of being on time! Frequently we were held up for long traffic delays amid the confusion of cars, people, and sacred cows. Once we were two hours going a couple of miles in a crowded taxi. We were impressed that despite the traffic, the noise, and the heat, Maa was always calm and centered in the midst of the chaos around her. This is the way Maa teaches — not by commandments and strictures but by example. When we returned to the Mandir there was inevitably a crowd hoping for private *darshan* with Maa. These sessions continued until late at night. When the doors were opened in the morning there would already be another line patiently waiting for a chance to spend a moment with her. Somehow Maa and Swamiji kept up the pace without visible signs of tiring. It seemed obvious that their strength for the daily demands was gained through the two hours of worship and meditation which they did very early in the morning before beginning their busy day.

Our first stay was at the Mira Mandir in Calcutta. Anyone who has ever seen one of Swamiji's fire ceremonies and experienced the *bhava* he inspires can easily imagine how he was able to make the Mandir fairly "rock," in contrast to the regular *pujaris* and other visiting *sadhus* that we saw there. Several of our hosts, lifelong Hindus, told us how Swamiji's inspiration caused them to see the old ceremonies in a new light. The tendency in all religions over the years, it seems, is to have the living wine of God-intoxication that inspired the ancient ones become old wine in an old bottle that loses its savor and no longer quenches one's spiritual thirst. Swami's fire ceremony at the Mira Mandir was an example. The atmosphere was infectious as he became more and more transported in divine ecstasy. His example was inspiring and soon a throng was attracted. Together we offered the *masala* with a resounding *"Swaha!"* to the divine fire that burns away our impurities. We were young and old, Indians and North Americans, united in a bond beyond nationality and language, offering our common praise to the Divine Mother of us all.

The glow of total immersion that shone on the faces of those assembled was truly an unforgettable experience!

We were to see Swamiji electrify audiences again and again during our visit to India. Despite the rigors of his self-imposed austerities and a daily schedule which includes hours of recitation of the Cosmic Puja as well as a demanding writing and teaching schedule, we saw him find energetic renewal time and time again while worshiping in front of the altar of the Goddess or leading the fire ceremony. For hours he would sit without breaking his *asana*, his *bhava* infectiously radiating out to all. During one such time he called out joyously, "If we come to our worship with enough devotion and an open heart, all of the Goddesses will come down from the altar and dance with us!"

Once in the Mira Mandir in front of a packed assembly he and Mother both went into *samadhi* at the same time! It was some time before many realized the situation. But as it became apparent what was happening a respectful reverence descended on the audience. We sat for a long time as our teachers sat transfixed in their inner gaze, oblivious to the sights and sounds around them.

A similar thing happened to Swamiji while we were visiting a small temple near a village where we stayed for a few days. During a long meditation he went into *samadhi* and it was obvious to all that he was in no hurry to "return." It took all of Mother's force and power to bring him back. His dawning recognition of time and place and the look of sheer bliss on his face made a strong impression on all. As we were leaving the little temple the local *pujari* prostrated himself at Mother's feet and begged that she take him with her. For years he had devoted his whole life to living there in the utmost simplicity and austerity, worshiping at his altar and performing ceremonies. But after an hour spent with a living Divine Mother he was eager to forsake all he had known and follow Shree Maa. He prostrated himself before her. "Please, Mother, please take me with you!" he begged again and again. When Maa gently told him he would have to stay tears and lamentations wracked his body. She continued to soothe him until he reached some measure of acceptance. Her teaching was plain: we must all serve in the way that we are best suited. Only a fortunate few of us are able to be with Maa on a continuing basis. We counted our blessings anew!

Wherever we traveled it was always interesting to visit the homes of Maa's devotees who had been with her before her move to the States. Always the house was bedecked with flowers and offerings and we would be served a royal feast. We quickly learned to go easy on eating much before these visits! Usually the houses were overflowing with neighbors. After not having seen their Divine Mother for a few years they were reluctant to let her go and, as mentioned, we would have trouble adhering to a schedule! In the home of one of Maa's ardent devotees, Manju, we were humbled when she insisted on washing the feet of all of us traveling with Maa and not just the feet of Maa and Swamiji, which was frequently done as a sign of respect. She washed our feet to show her love to the visitors whom she considered family.

Most of the time outside Calcutta we spent in the home village of Tiwari, one of Maa's most fervent devotees in all of India. Tiwari is a very successful businessman and employer who owns a steel mill in Calcutta. He has access to all of the luxury and comforts that money can buy but several times he has walked the length and breadth of India carrying water from the holy Ganga which he shares with temples along the way. He takes these trips for the austerities that purify his own practice as well as to inspire by his example along the way. It is Tiwari's belief that Hinduism, like so many other religions, has become rigidified and insulated from modern life and that we need *tapas* to rediscover the treasure hidden within the teaching and in ourselves.

Some years before our visit Tiwari had built a temple in his native village but it had never been used as it had not been dedicated. But he would have no one but Maa dedicate it! And at last it would happen! The whole village was put on high alert and the visit of our entourage brought out the entire village and others for miles around. A giant feast was prepared after which a large amount of clothing and other gifts that we had brought from California were passed out.

The next day Swamiji led us in the most inspiring fire ceremony I have ever witnessed. A throng of villagers sat and stood around him during the hours of the ceremony. After this, the formal dedication ceremonies took place at the temple. As I listened to the *kirtans* of praise, and looked out over the level fields stretching out in all directions, I sensed the timelessness of the rituals we were doing, stretching back in an unbroken line through the mists of time and history. The celebrations lasted all day and it was night before the last guests reluctantly left.

As the crow flies, Tiwari's village is not that far from the hustle of the more modern world. But there was very little vehicular traffic. Bicycles were the preferred mode for the narrow dirt paths twisting through the humble mud and thatched houses. Wherever we walked we were followed by a clutch of wide-eyed children. One time I took a walk by myself and soon felt like the Pied Piper of Hamelin. When I walked, the children walked. When I stopped, they stopped and solemnly studied me. We were the first outsiders many of them had ever seen and doubtless my funny-colored white skin was a source of wonder. It was interesting to have the tables reversed on this and so many other things that we saw from a different perspective. The fact that I am six-foot, three-and-a-half made me a particularly strong source of fascination!

We, too, were astounded at what we were seeing, even if we did a better job of disguising it than the children. Families are typically large in India and the land can't support all who would like to stay close to the earth. It was typical for all of those who had gone to make their living in Calcutta and other cities to still identify with the region of their birth. In answer to the question, "Where are you from?" the typical city-dweller would give the name of his ancestral village, even though it might have been years since he had left. The measured and timeless ways of their ancestors and the rhythms of nature still called to them. Maa says it is in the same way that the spirit calls to all of us. We get dazzled and distracted by *maya*, but the call of something deeper and more fundamental beckons us and we long for our spiritual home.

This is one of the truly remarkable things one notices when spending time around Maa and Swamiji; they are not distracted by the world, by the latest "news," and by the tumult and shouting of the moment. Instead, theirs is an inner focus and like good helmsmen they steer straight for the inner target. One of Swamiji's main themes, which he returns to again and again in his teaching, is the importance of efficiency in all that we do. Whether it's a simple task or a life-calling, we must be efficient in order to reach our goal in the quickest way. The lives of our Divine Mother and Maharaj are their teaching in how to live in the world without being distracted by it.

And as anyone knows who has been there, India has a way of showing the world in all its bewildering variety! Even seasoned travelers agree that it is impossible to describe the welter of sheer sensory overload that is India. And, as mentioned, Maa was invariably an island of calm in the midst of the hurricane. She was like a mighty tree, giving shelter and shade to those around her. This was poignantly brought home in Varanasi. We had hired a boatman to row us down the Ganges, past the burning *ghats* where bodies were being burned and set afloat amid offerings into the sacred waters. I was feeling solemn and reflective and was surprised when Maa said, "Let's sing!" And sing we did! The throngs bathing in the water and along the shore must have been surprised to hear joyous hymns of praise to the Mother of the Universe as our boat passed by, celebrating the gift of life and the inherent joy in things behind the veils of suffering and death. I was reminded of the time that I had a physical problem and remarked to Maa that I was slowing down. Rather than commiserating with me Maa smiled sweetly and replied, "Your body is getting closer to God! One day we will all leave our bodies and be with God. Isn't that wonderful!" At that moment I found a new depth in our mantra, *"Om Aim Hrim Klim Camundayai Vicce* — One who can see birth, preservation, and destruction in all things is enlightened."

As all of us know, sometimes the greatest blessings come in the form of afflictions. My most memorable time in India was when I was sick! I was laid low by a high fever and aching body that caused me to miss some of the activities. It was at a time when we had gone to a small ashram belonging to one of Maa's devotees on the outskirts of Calcutta. It was a haven of green and quiet compared to the frenetic activities in the nearby streets. I was up in my room with my eyes closed when I heard a familiar voice. "Sarvananda! I have come to give you a massage! You'll feel better, OK?" I opened my eyes on Maa's smiling face! I was overwhelmed! There were disciples waiting to see Maa wherever she went. Some had been waiting for years for her to return to India. All wanted *darshan*. But Maa took time out to heal the sick. I floated away under her touch and am sure that her visit worked magic as the next day my temperature was normal and I was able to join the group activities. "Look for the teaching behind the illness" says the sage. In my case I found a blessing behind my illness!

In Calcutta a short time later I had the opportunity to work for a few days in the hospice of another Divine Mother, Mother Teresa. Her hospice is for those who are beyond medical treatment. The clients are most often homeless people who are dying on the streets. The caregiving consists in making them comfortable and respectfully helping them die with dignity. I was humbled by the experience and was grateful in a new way for my health and strength and tried to impart something of the love and care that Maa had shown me. I remembered something I had once read about Mother Teresa. Many of the guests who are there to die have open sores and various diseases. Someone had asked her how she could continue her work in the midst of such unending need and appalling conditions. Mother Teresa had replied, "Because no matter who it is or what the condition, I see the face of my beloved." And Mother Teresa also said something that seems to personify Maa. She said, "What we need is a spirituality that doesn't get tired."

This is what I see when I look at the spiritual work of Maa and Swamiji. They don't get tired! To be sure, like any of us their bodies run down and need rest. But their discipline is such that the next morning, usually around five a.m., they do their morning *puja* regardless of the hour they went to bed. They exemplify their teaching about the importance of efficiency. And anyone who has been around them very long knows that being efficient and one-pointed in one's life doesn't rule out joy and laughter! To the contrary! One of the things that first attracted Maitri and me to this path was the amount of laughter and delight in ordinary things that mark the spiritual odyssey of Maa and Swamiji. For example, at Varanasi we were staying in an ashram close to the Ganges. When some of our group asked Maa about swimming she said, "I'll come too!" She led us to the water and jumped right in, robes and all, and for a half-hour she laughed and played like a little girl, delighting in the moment. We have all seen temples and churches where the prevailing mood seems to associate spirituality with a long face and a sober disposition. The wine-cup of God-intoxication has become dusty. Not so with our Divine Mother!

One visiting seeker we know was struck by the lack of feeling during hymn-singing in one of the churches he visited. He commented that you could tell from the words that the author knew of the divine. However, the hymns were being sung, he said, as if the singers were reading the telephone directory! "Make a joyful noise unto the Lord" says the Psalmist. The joyous dancing, drumming, singing, and laughing that is experienced at the Mandir is an oasis in a too often dry desert of spiritless spirituality. At the Devi Mandir we celebrate the feast of life and the bounty of the Divine Mother for this incredible smorgasbord of sight and sound and sensual delight with our voices and every variety of western and eastern instruments.

As mentioned, Swamiji's enthusiasm is marvelously infectious at such times. It is not uncommon for everyone assembled to form a circle and go around and around in front of the altar celebrating the Goddess and the eternal mystery. At such times the Devis do seem to come down from the altar to lead the dance! During one *arati* a new devotee did a spontaneous and abandoned dance that had so much energy and creativity that he set the whole temple to dancing. Afterwards he was filled with wonder as he told us that it was the first time he had done anything like that. He wasn't a dancer, he said, and was astonished and in awe as he danced because it was as if someone else were dancing and he was just watching! In the long silent meditations following these celebrations the energy is palpable.

During those early years some of us who liked music formed the Jaya Maa Band. Anchored by the virtuoso guitar-playing of Nirvana and ably assisted by Gautam's sweet fiddling, the dazzling mandolin counter-melody picking of Mitra, and a few singers, we soon became a unit. We played at a number of temples and *satsanghas* in the Bay Area and enjoyed jamming together at the Mandir.

One of Maa and Swamiji's teachings is to honor all spiritual traditions and learn what we can from all. "God cares for the effort to get to the mountain top more than the route" is one of the ways Maa has expressed this idea. Some visitors have been surprised to find statues of Mother Mary and Buddha on the grounds of the Mandir and in the temple along with the more familiar Hindu deities. This ecumenical approach was reflected in the music of the Jaya Maa Band. To be sure, the majority of our music was the traditional Hindu *kirtans* but we also sang with equal feeling such songs as "Amazing Grace" and "Just a Closer Walk with Thee."

At Christmas time we sing carols. One of the songs from the West in the Devi Mandir Songbook, "Tis a Gift to be Simple" states well my own feeling about our music:

"When true simplicity is gained,

To bow and to bend we will not be ashamed,

To turn, to turn, it will be our delight

'Till by turning, turning, we come round right."

During the early years of our association with Maa and Swamiji I had written several songs for Maa that my heart had felt compelled to express. It somehow just seemed as if the songs wanted out! Typically the process would start with a line in my head that would eventually galvanize into a song over a period of time. One of those songs, which tries to describe the joy and *bhava* mentioned above is called, "Like No Other Mother at All." In absence of musical notations just imagine it lively and joyous!

"Why are we singing, and why are we dancing,

Why are we laughing, and why are we prancing?

'Cause we've got a mother like no other,

We've got a mother like no other,

We've got a mother like no other,

Like no other mother at all!

Why are we singing, our devotion bringing?

Why the bells ringing, why our hearts winging?
'Cause she's so amazing we can't keep from
praising!
She's so amazing we can't keep from praising,
We've got a mother like no other,
Like no other mother at all!

So come with your *bhakti*, receive Mother's *shakti*,
She'll open your heart right from the start,
Then you'll know why we're singing, our devotion
bringing,
You'll join in the singing, your heart will be winging,
'Cause we've got a mother like no other,
Like no other mother at all!"

So it was in this way that I wrote a number of songs — a seed would slowly germinate and an end-product would emerge somewhere down the line, perhaps a month later. So I wasn't prepared when Maa said to me one Sunday after *arati*, "Sarvananda, please write me two songs from these verses of the *Chandi*. Can you finish them by Tuesday?" I gasped inwardly as the time was so short and the ideas for the other songs had all come from inside. But if Maa wanted it, it would be done! So hoping the muse wouldn't desert me I looked at the verses and starting noodling around on the guitar. For better or worse I wrote both of them that night. The verses were in praise of the Goddess and following is one of them. The title is "Goddess, Oh Goddess!" Again, the tempo is lively and the beat strong!

"Goddess, oh Goddess, you're the ruler of the earth,
We take refuge in you from the moment of our birth,
The brilliance of your body is like sunlight in the morn
And from your energy, all the world is born.

For those devoted to you, you take away distress,
You take away discomfort and our life is blessed,
You slay all our thoughts, you slay meanness, too,
You slay all our passion and you give us rest,
So we bow to you, so we bow to you,
Mother of the universe we bow down to you!
(repeat first section)
You are the ever-pure one and we bow to you,
The energy of all, and we bow to you,
Exposer of consciousness, and we bow to you,
Wielder of the discus, and we bow to you,
Destroyer of all fear, and we bow to you,
Goddess, oh Goddess, we bow down to you!"
(repeat first section)

The songs were played that Sunday night and Maa, as she often does, accompanied the Jaya Maa Band on the drums. But what we really wait for are the times Maa sings. Maa's voice can only be described as angelic and when listening I close my eyes and am transported into another realm. How fortunate that there are now a number of cassettes and CD's of her singing! Some of these tapes were engineered by Angelika, one of Maa's devotees. Angelika has also produced a number of wonderful tapes of her own singing, and Maitri and I find that tapes of Maa or Angelika make the freeway miles fly by!

It was the *bhava* that was apparent in the music and the worship at the Devi Mandir, as well as the joy we felt just being in the presence of Maa, that attracted Maitri and me to this path. In the course of our own *sadhana* we had visited a number of other ashrams, spiritual centers, and churches. But we had never been "ashram hoppers." We are privileged to be among the very first devotees of Maa and Swamiji here in the states as we felt something very special at our first meeting back in 1985. It was a feeling that we didn't have to keep looking for a path, that we had come home.

During those first meetings when we visited them in a house where they were staying in Concord, California, shortly after they arrived, and later at their first ashram in nearby Moraga, we were treated as family right from the start. I have had a longtime interest in comparative religion and my initial interest was more intellectual than spiritual. I was teaching a course in Transpersonal Psychology at the nearby community college and had visited many other spiritual communities to experience different approaches to the transcendent. But, as mentioned, both Maitri and I felt a heart connection to Maa and Swamiji right away. They were something special!

This feeling of an immediate connection reminded me of something I had read in one of the Castaneda books. The reader might remember that Carlos Castaneda was a university professor who kept puzzling over why he wanted to make continued trips to Mexico to see a wise old Indian named Don Juan. He was a professor at a prestigious university while Don Juan appeared to be an uneducated simple man, out of touch with the main stream of world happenings and intellectual frontiers. After a time he shared his perplexity with Don Juan whose answer was to laugh uproariously and reply, "Your body likes it here!" Some might use the term "*shakti*." Whatever it was, it was a good feeling just to be in Maa's presence.

The temple in Moraga was over an hour's drive round trip from our home and late one afternoon I had a strong desire to see Maa. The trouble was I had a set of papers to grade that night and I had told my students I would return them the next day. So I decided not to go to Moraga but then rather suddenly changed my mind and decided to burn the midnight oil and go to the temple and do the papers when I returned. Maitri and

I dropped everything and drove out to the ashram and arrived just in time for *arati*. We were invited to stay for the evening meal during which time we found out from one of the devotees that Maa had said to prepare food for two more as we'd be coming.

And speaking of food! Never had we tasted such great Indian food! We quickly observed that when it came to *seva* that Maa taught by example. She did much of the cooking herself and instructed a long line of devotees, particularly Durga and Parvati, in the fine art of Indian cooking. I already had a rather famous appetite, but it got to be a source of amusement to watch me under the spell of Maa's cooking. Maa noticed that I had a particular fondness for *samosas* and rice pudding and would regularly include them in the *prasad* which she sent home with us. Now, ten years later, when we're preparing to drive to our home in Oregon from the Napa Ashram, Maa will still send these things with us. Often she makes them especially for us. As the song says, "We've got a mother like no other mother at all!"

This is something that also struck us right away about Maa and Swamiji. No generals and privates here! Both work alongside the rest of us during work times. Many times when the temple has been overflowing, particularly during special times on the Hindu calendar when the temple was heavily visited by people from the Bay Area Indian community, Maa would cook for the multitude. And day in and day out Swamiji dons his boots and drives the bulldozer or works on the water system or any of a thousand other jobs. Sometimes he seems more like Durga as he has so many projects going that he seems to have eight hands!

At the time of our initiation Maitri and I were given *mala* beads by Maa and Swamiji. I would remove them for bathing and most athletic exercise but the reader doubtless knows how they can become one's constant companion.

Imagine the shock one day when I couldn't find them! An intensive search was to no avail. At first I thought little of it, assuming they would eventually turn up. But after a few more days and a few more intensive searches I reluctantly concluded they were lost.

When we next went to the Devi Mandir I told Maa of my loss and asked if there were any extra that I could buy. Now, the Devi Mandir has never run a "store." The only thing they have for sale are some of the tapes and CD's of Maa's singing and copies of Swamiji's several books. But these things are just placed in the back of the temple with a posted price and a basket for payment. I had never seen *malas* there but thought some might be on hand for future initiations.

After hearing of my loss Maa wordlessly went to her own altar and removed the one set of *mala* beads there. She came back to me and with shining eyes placed them around my neck. Of course I was astonished! I started to mumble something about not wanting to borrow hers. But Maa stopped me. "I have another set I can put on the altar. Sarvananda, you take these beads!" What can one say in the face of such an overwhelming happening? I gratefully acknowledged the great gift while feeling bathed with love.

How very special my *mala* beads are to me now! And, oh yes! It has been some years now since this event and I still have them as I take very good care to know where they are!

During one of my earlier visits to another spiritual community I spent an evening with another Hindu group that was also in the tradition of venerating a Divine Mother. This mother, however, seemed to spend most of her time on a raised platform, sitting on special cushions. There was no physical interaction with her devotees. After a half-hour question and answer period she left. What a contrast to our "user-friendly" mother!

Being around Maa and Swamiji is very special. Maa has devoted her life to serving God since she was a little girl. And Swamiji has sought the "pearl of great price" ever since his travels took him to India as a young man. All of us love hearing of the way they connected and joined together as a team to serve God. But that is outside the scope of this narrative. However, they complement each other perfectly.

Swamiji has also given up his former life and now lives only to serve the Divine Mother. In his *sadhana* he has performed awesome austerities, including a number of forty-day fasts where he takes only a little water each day. With the same efficiency he has become one of the foremost Sanskrit translators in the world and the number of books he has authored is staggering. But he can find time to do this work only by sacrificing a normal sleep schedule and working far into the night. Swamiji speaks several Indian languages and on several occasions while we were in India I asked locals how his accent was and was invariably told it was flawless. And some of us still remember our surprise the first Christmas Eve we were together to have him do the traditional mass in Latin with a homily on the symbolism of the Christmas story and not looking for Christ (or Krishna) outside ourselves. All of us, he said, have a Christ-child waiting to be born inside us, a divine being that reflects who we really are. We concluded the service with a sip of wine to symbolize rebirth.

We are grateful to our two teachers for their example. Come to the Devi Mandir any morning and you will see the two of them, plus other of their devotees, reciting their *pujas*. You will see Swamiji's face beam with radiance as he contemplates the Devas and you will see the perfect *mudras* that characterize every movement that Maa makes. Maitri and I are blessed to share this path with them. They have not fled the world; they are very much involved in it. Here, as in India, they will frequently interrupt their busy lives to visit the sick or to assist those whose lives are in crisis. It might even be someone they don't know well as was true when they found out my brother Royce was dying of cancer. They traveled to Santa Clara to visit him and the next morning his picture was on the altar.

Maa is the refiner and the reliever of difficulties. It might not mean that the difficulties will go away but she inspires us to transmute life's leaden metal into gold. Once she sat at the crowded desk in our house to make a telephone call. Scattered about were some pages of a manuscript. Maa knew I was doing some writing and she left a note on the desk which is now on the wall where its message can inspire every day. It says, "With Saraswati's blessing, Sarvananda you go forward! — *Jaya Maa!*"

All of us want to go forward spiritually. In the tangled jungle of life it is easy to get lost. When we find someone who has traveled the path it becomes easier to find our way. Maa and Swamiji know the way and teach by their example. *Jaya Maa!* Victory to the Divine Mother!!

Recollections by Maitri

When we "happen" to meet someone who proves to be a significant figure in our lives, is it fate, synchronicity, serendipity — or pure chance? One of these, at least, was at work for us on Thursday, January 24, 1985.

I had gone to pick up my husband Bob at his office at Diablo Valley College after our day's work. His colleague Marcia, knowing of his interest in meditation, dropped in unexpectedly. She told us that two wandering *sadhus*, recently from India, were staying at their home in Concord, performing a Vedic fire ceremony and maintaining other spiritual practices. We should come soon if we wanted to meet them, because they might be leaving in a couple of weeks. We went that very evening.

A small house in a modest neighborhood was the place. We entered, having not the least idea what to expect. Swami Satyananda was articulate, witty, and enthusiastic. Shree Maa seemed a deeply mysterious being — the more so because she was just learning English, and spoke little. Working silently next to her in the small kitchen, I wondered what she might really be.

In the living room was the altar, with a nearly-life-sized figure, a *murti* of Kali, one manifestation of the Divine Mother. With her dark blue-black skin and her long necklace of skulls, she seemed terrifying indeed. Swamiji and Shree Maa had made her from straw and clay, had painted her, dressed her in a sari, and adorned her with jewelry and a crown. She stood atop the prostrate form of the God Shiva.

At the hour for evening devotions, or *arati*, Swamiji asked Bob to perform the ceremony, and handed him the articles of worship one by one. What an incongruous sight: Bob in his red plaid shirt, waving incense and lights and flowers before Kali, who emanated from a spiritual tradition over 2,500 years old! Wasn't leading worship, I wondered, reserved for people with years of training and experience? (As I learned later, one of the clear purposes of Shree Maa and Swamiji is to give everyone the opportunity to become a *pujari* or worshiper, and to make his or her home a temple where the Divine Mother is revered and honored with regular devotions. They teach us that all of us can experience directly the grace and love of the Divine Mother.)

Already, within a couple of weeks, five spiritual seekers, inspired by the single-minded devotion and deep commitment of Shree Maa and Swamiji, had come to live with them: Marcia (Moti) and her husband Kasyap, Gautam, Uma, and

Ramananda. They worked together under Shree Maa's and Swamiji's guidance, and at night all seven spread out their bedrolls in the living room and slept peacefully under the watchful eye of Kali.

This evening after *arati* and meditation a cloth was spread on the floor, and we sat around it, reciting before our meal the famous prayer of St. Francis: "Lord, make us instruments of thy peace. Where there is hatred, let us sow love, where there is injury, pardon; where there is doubt, faith; where there is despair, hope; where there is darkness, light; where there is sadness, joy. Oh Divine Master, let us not so much seek to be consoled as to console, to be understood as to understand, to be loved as to love. For it is in giving that we receive, it is in pardoning that we are pardoned, it is in dying that we are born to eternal life." (Though Maa and Swamiji follow traditions that grew out of Hinduism, they revere the great teachers of all spiritual paths. Just so, Maa's guru, Shree Ramakrishna, the 19th century Indian saint, studied and respected several religious traditions — although his principal devotion was to Kali.)

The food, so delicious, had been prepared by Shree Maa in her effortless, focused way. We spoke of the events which had brought these seven beings together, including Swamiji's trip overland from Europe to India many years before. He related also the ways in which Indian culture and traditions had seeped into the Middle East, even as far as Greece, helping to shape those civilizations more than two millennia ago.

We visited that little house in Concord numerous times in the next few weeks, intrigued by what we had discovered there, and drawn back by the warmth and energy and love we sensed. Just being there, participating in whatever might be taking place, felt peaceful and good and right — like being at home. One evening as we sat at dinner I looked around, and aware of the growing bond within the group, said, "It's a beautiful family you have here." Swamiji's immediate reply: "It's your family, too!" And I knew it was true.

One evening the fire ceremony took place at an informal fire pit in the back yard. Swamiji led us in chanting various mantras, and after each repetition we tossed a few grains of *masala* into the fire, with the word "*Swaha*" — I am one with God. We could throw into the fire, and rid ourselves of, anything we wanted to discard from our lives, purify ourselves, and reconnect with the Divine. Two of the devotees remained at the fire all evening, chanting a mantra as part of their initiation rites.

More people started to come to that little house as word got out of the remarkable beings who were staying there. One night was *Shiva Ratri* — Shiva's night. We would spend the entire night in devotions to Shiva, the Consciousness of Infinite Goodness and the source of the potential creative energy of the universe. Many miniature clay Shiva lingams had been prepared, candles were on hand, and the milk, yogurt, honey and ghee were ready to be offered to Shiva at the appropriate hours during the night. Chanting, singing, making the offerings, and meditating filled the entire night, and we breakfasted together at dawn. Driving home, I felt the traffic and stores around me were much less real than what I had experienced through the night!

We wanted to meditate at home too, and Shree Maa gave us a black-and-white picture of herself in meditation in India. Lighting a candle and incense in front of her picture and placing a flower there gave me the same peaceful feeling as actually being with her. She could be with me even when we were miles apart!

Soon it became clear that these two *sadhus* would not be moving on right away. There was talk of renting a house for a year so that these five devotees could continue to live with them. I know that none of us who had been spending time with them wanted to stop experiencing the power and joy of their presence.

In mid-February they all moved to a spacious two-story house in the country, near Moraga. Now a large downstairs room, with the altar all across one end, was the temple space. More *murtis* were constructed of straw and clay, and we saw them in various stages of completion. Shree Maa always was in charge of the details of shaping and painting the Goddesses, and she knew just how to clothe and adorn them to bring out their beautiful qualities.

Soon the altar was the home of Saraswati, the Goddess of learning and the arts, Lakshmi, the Goddess of true wealth, and the Goddess Durga, the remover of difficulties, as well as Kali. Swamiji explained that all these Goddesses, and the Gods as well, are various aspects of the one divine being, just as we have various roles in our lives; at different moments we may be a parent, teacher, tennis player, sister or brother, or friend, for example. Durga, riding majestically on her lion and brandishing her many weapons, one in each of her ten hands, held a central place on the altar. Below her was one of the *ashuras*, or demons, whom she vanquished in the story of the *Chandi*.

All the Goddesses were splendid in their red and white saris, with sparkling earrings and pendants and jewel-laden crowns. They seemed to have an energy and a presence all their own, enhanced by the candle light and the heady, musky incense. At the times when Maa requested that I perform *arati*, I felt flooded with peace and joy. In dancing before the altar, I knew without a doubt that I was celebrating all the beauty, all the goodness of the universe — and I felt humble and deeply grateful.

Evenings at the temple we began to read the *Chandi*, the story of how the Gods, relying on the power and wisdom of Durga, finally defeated their enemies, the Ego and Self-centered Thoughts. Swamiji a few years earlier had made a translation of this spiritual classic from Sanskrit into English. The oral traditions of this work stretch back possibly as far as 900 B.C. Being part of so ancient, yet so meaningful a spiritual tradition seemed amazing. Swamiji, with Shree Maa always sitting beside him, would explain how the tales of the *Chandi* hold truths that illuminate our everyday lives.

Shree Maa's graceful, serene presence was a constant inspiration. She somehow was always in the moment, giving her complete attention to the person or task before her. More and more people were coming to seek her advice about all areas of their lives. Even though she was still learning the ways of American culture, her common-sense, practical suggestions had the ring of truth.

Indeed, truth has always been one of her primary teachings: "Be true. Say what you mean and do what you say. If you are true, you will be without fear. If your conscience is clear, your heart will be silent. That is Peace, no matter what the result." Her example and her devotion to truth make me realize how often I hedge just a little, or leave out a bit of the truth, so as to please myself or someone else.

Another teaching I can't forget is, "Show respect to every atom." Her example was throwing her broom into the corner, as she once did when very young, rather than setting it gently in its place, as her guru then requested. Respect for every tool we use, every object we handle, every person or creature we meet, all are embodied in this concept. "Remember that the God you seek resides in every atom." This one teaching can embrace every moment of our lives!

Another revelation for us was Shree Maa's singing! Her

pure voice, floating high, then gracefully dipping down and soaring up with the melody, seemed the most beautiful sound I'd ever heard. My eyes always closed, so that every speck of attention could focus on those divine vibrations. Traditional Bengali songs, English translations, newly-written melodies — all were transforming and captivated us. We started bringing our tape recorder to the temple, wanting to preserve some of her songs.

Swamiji was teaching us too, giving instruction in the beginner's Shiva Puja, teaching some mantras, and showing us how to count on our fingers the prescribed 108 repetitions of a mantra, so that we don't always need a *mala*. His fund of knowledge seemed to embrace every topic, and his enthusiasm and delight in his subject were contagious. Knowing just how to relate to every imaginable kind of person is one of his many admirable qualities. I've long felt that he may be most in his element when he is teaching, whether one person or a hundred.

Around this time several of us who loved to sing and play music formed the Jaya Maa Band (not to be confused with the professional group of that name, under the direction of Bob Kindler). Under the leadership of Nirvana and his great guitar we had a wonderful time practicing songs of the Devi Mandir. Dressed in red and white, we traveled to participate in *satsanghas* at Fremont and Livermore. It was a privilege to share in this way the love and enthusiasm we found at the Devi Mandir.

That winter Bob and I signed up for a short trip to Nicaragua, with a group of observers of the civil war there. Before we left, Swamiji and Shree Maa gave us a special blessing for a safe journey. They also gave us this mantra from the Devi Suktam, The Tantric Praise of the Goddess: "*Ya devi sarva bhutesu shakti rupena samsthita, namastasyai, namastasyai, namastasyai namo namah.* To the Divine Goddess who resides in all existence in the form of energy, we bow to Her; we bow to Her; we bow to Her, continually we bow, we bow." This mantra proved a real source of comfort and strength to me when we found ourselves in a highly trying situation. The love and blessings of Shree Maa and Swamiji know no geographical bounds!

At the October Durga Puja, a nine-day period of special ceremonies and worship, all the Gods and Goddesses on the altar are dressed in new saris or other raiment. The cloth they had worn may be given to some of the devotees. Shree Maa presented to me the red, white and gold sari which had adorned the Goddess Durga. I felt overcome by this gesture. Wearing it truly makes me feel humble and grateful to have the oppor-tunity to follow the example of the Divine Mother in her myriad forms — particularly the example of Shree Maa, the Divine Mother who lives among us.

As the year in Moraga drew to an end, Shree Maa and Swamiji announced that they would spend a few months touring the U.S. in their small travel trailer. They would be wandering *sadhus* of the 20th century! They needed to find new homes for the Goddesses on the altar, for once created and instilled with the breath of life, the deities must be worshiped faithfully. Bob and I felt honored to be given the Goddess Durga. She would be installed in our home, and that room would be our temple. (Shree Maa always says that Durga has been her favorite since early childhood, and she tells of spending long hours with the Gods and Goddesses at the temple near her home in India while her grandmother cleaned the temple each day.)

Our teachers are always carrying out their idea of enabling every home to be a place of worship. They show us that it is possible to know God directly through worship, meditation, study of sacred texts, and through serving others. They demonstrate through their lives that spirituality is not limited, but can guide our every action when we give of ourselves. Maa says, "If we are gentle, loving, kind and honest in our dealings, that is spiritual." She teaches us that true spirituality does not come wrapped in exotic experiences, but in the fabric of everyday deeds and ordinary actions.

In a special ceremony Swamiji withdrew the breath of life from Durga, in preparation for the move. She came to our home riding royally in a pick-up truck, and was moved carefully into place. Many of the Devi Mandir devotees were there to help, and Shree Maa personally supervised the move and the decoration of our new altar. Now we had the Goddess right under our own roof!

A day was set for Durga's inspiration, the breathing of life into her. The ceremony took several hours, with chanting, meditation, recitation of scripture by Swamiji, and of course his blowing the living breath into Durga's mouth. *Arati* followed, and Durga truly seemed to radiate life and joy, and to be watching every move with her dark eyes. The candlelight reflected   everywhere on her shining ornaments, and the incense made us breathe deeply.

This was the first of a great many *satsanghas* in our temple — always with singing, dancing, meditation, and usually a talk by Shree Maa or Swamiji. Especially wonderful were the times when Maa would sing, with her pure, clear voice truly the sound of the Divine Mother. Last would be supper, with all of us sitting around the tablecloth on the floor, basking in the warmth and camaraderie of a meal with these divine beings — our much-loved teachers and our fellow devotees. Often Swamiji and Maa talked of their experiences in India — how they met, and other memorable events along their spiritual paths. We felt so appreciative of their presence in our lives.

The trailer was readied for their journey. The last time we

went to Moraga before they departed, I looked around inside it and wondered how it would be for wandering *sadhus* who were used to walking from village to village in India, now and then spending a few days with ardent devotees. What kind of reception would they find in the towns and cities of the U.S.?

Before we left them, Maa handed me a package. Inside was a beautiful white skirt, with a red border and heavy lace edging, which she herself had made for me. I felt over-whelmed by her blessings and love. I wanted to serve her — and she had made this lovely garment for me! I still treasure it, and love to wear it for *satsangha* or *puja*.

After a few months word came that Maa and Swamiji were returning to the Bay Area and needed a house to rent. Gautam and Nirvana found one in the hills beyond Concord, along a road in the open country. A creek bed, dry in the hot season, ran just behind the house. Soon they were settled, and Maa began to create new *murtis* of the Goddesses. More people made the long drive to attend nightly *satsangha*.

Maa continued her teachings as we gathered at her feet. Before falling asleep, she shared her nightly routine of feeling herself cradled in the lap of Vishnu, He who sustains and pre-serves all. On awakening in the morning, she instructed us, that we were to bow to ourselves in the mirror, while acknowl-edging the divine energy which resides in each of us, and ask the Goddess to make our eyes her eyes, our hands her hands, and our feet her feet throughout the day. What a shine and sense of purpose this gives to the day!

At this time Swamiji took a three-month vow of silence, at Maa's direction. His small chalkboard was always near him and he would write just one or a few words to communicate an important idea. I marveled at his consistent self-discipline, and even without many words this articulate master of expression and explanation was amazingly effective. We discovered that teaching doesn't always require many words; in fact, perhaps the fewer words that are spoken, the more we remember!

Of course, Maa was always teaching us by her actions and her example — as well as verbally, now that she knew more and more English. Her caring concern and affection for everyone, welcoming every seeker and visitor with the same warmth and attention, were a constant reminder and inspiration for us all.

Another move took the Devi Mandir to a residential area of Concord, and the most important task was moving the *murtis* — oh, so carefully. Soon they were in place in the new temple room, and in the next few months the Gods Shiva, Brahma and Vishnu took shape and joined the Goddesses on the altar. Those commanding, colorful figures now took up the entire side of the room.

Bob and I asked Maa and Swamiji for initiation, as we were feeling a deep desire to follow the example of our teachers. We prepared new white clothing for the ceremony, and the day was set in accordance with auspicious times on the Hindu calendar.

The temple was adorned with flowers and candles and incense, as usual. We put on our new clothes, ready to become our new selves. While waiting in the temple for the ceremony to begin, I suddenly felt completely overcome by Maa's love and caring; it was almost too much to fathom, and I felt tears running down my cheeks. "What happened?" Maa anxiously inquired, and I did my best to explain that they were tears only of joy and gratitude.

Toward the end of the ritual, Maa and Swamiji gave us our spiritual names: Bob was to be Sarvananda, "All Bliss", and I was Maitrinanda, "The Bliss of Friendship, or Loving Kindness." We finished the evening sitting at the fire pit, chanting our mantra as we tossed a bit of *masala* into the flames with each repetition, saying "*Swaha,*" I am one with God. It truly felt like a new beginning.

Our first Mother's Day with our Divine Mother Shree Maa was a real festival, with devotees coming from all parts of the Bay Area, bearing flowers and food, and most important, lots of devotion. Now Mother's Day had a completely new meaning — a celebration of divine motherly love and caring, and an opportunity to return that love in rich measure.

Sarvananda and I were honored to host Shree Maa and Swamiji a few times at the vacation home we owned on the Mendocino Coast. It was wonderful to see the Divine Mother at play and at rest: walking along the beach, dipping her feet into the water, or just relaxing deeply on the deck. No matter what her situation, Maa gives the same undivided attention to each individual or circumstance — no reliving the past or worrying about the future for her. What a lesson for us all, in being in the moment!

At Thanksgiving that year, the entire Devi Mandir made the trek to Mendocino. The divine family was gathered together for some intensive time with Maa and Swamiji — and for some feasting, featuring Tofu Turkey, complete with carrot drumsticks! Maa engineered the dinner in her usual effortless style, helped by many eager hands. We truly had much to be thankful for.

On another visit to Mendocino, Maa was relaxing after dinner in the evening light, when she was inspired to sing. Song after song, mostly in Bengali, came from her lips. The sound, as always, transported us to another realm. Sarvananda and Swamiji, ever the enthusiastic dishwashers, stopped their work to listen. Fortunately we had the tape recorder ready and that evening's songs are now on a cassette, professionally recorded, for all of us to enjoy as "Shree Maa Sings in Mendocino."

As 1987 came to an end Shree Maa, Swamiji, and a few devotees moved the Devi Mandir to a commercial building on the edge of Martinez. The new home was scrubbed and painted inside and out and soon was ready for the Gods and Goddesses to dwell in. They were carefully transported, one by one, and installed on their new, even larger altar. Maa always knows just how to decorate an altar, with metallic paper, flowers, sparkling swags and tiny Christmas lights and beautiful fabrics. This temple was the most beautiful yet!

The space for the sacred fire, the *hawan kunda*, was in the center of the temple, a square fire-pit surrounded by a low brick enclosure. A great many *yagyas* were performed here by Swamiji with Shree Maa always at his side, sanctifying the ceremonies with her calm presence. One of my favorite times was the annual New Year's Eve *yagya*.

What better way could there possibly be to begin a new year, than to be sitting at the sacred fire with our spiritual guides and perhaps a hundred and fifty fellow devotees? We literally tossed into the divine flames embodying Shiva, the Consciousness of Infinite Goodness, all our attachments, disappointments, frustrations and desires which belonged to the dying year. Finished with them, we could begin the new year at midnight with freshness and serenity and joy, thanks to the grace of the Divine Mother. Special sweets, prepared under Shree Maa's direction and served after the ceremony, gladdened our mouths as well as our hearts!

After the Martinez temple was well-established, Shree Maa and Swamiji took a *sankalpa* — a vow to perform specific spiritual practices — to chant the *Chandi* every day, to keep the sacred fire going day and night, and not to leave the premises of the Devi Mandir, for three years! The idea of these stringent self-imposed limits was completely new to me. It deepened even further my respect and admiration for these divine beings and their devotion to their own spiritual path, and for their eloquent example, for each of us to follow according to his or her situation. This vow enabled them to concentrate fully on the world of the spirit, without the distractions of dealing with life outside. They encourage us all to gradually reduce outside stimulation and activities, concentrating our time and energy on meditation, chanting and study. As Shree Maa says: "Take refuge in God. Neither your friends, relations or others will take you to heaven. Only Wisdom will be our salvation."

It is so true that the drama and meaning of the stories of the Gods and Goddesses (especially when retold in Maa's simple, clear manner or when related by Swamiji with his characteristic enthusiasm and energy) far outshine the momentary attraction of a movie or a play. The Devi Mandir offers lessons in life — how to find full, satisfying, purposeful living, and how to support others in their search, and how to use our lives to express our devotion for our teachers and guides.

In some ways the kitchen seemed the heart of the Devi Mandir, for here we worked with Shree Maa, slicing, chopping, stirring, frying to make the utterly delicious meals which were offered to all who came. Never looking at a recipe, she added a pinch of this, a sprinkle of that, creating the most flavorful Indian food one can imagine — as well as such American favorites as lasagna and enchiladas! I've learned so much in Maa's kitchen — not only the preparation of rice, samosas, dahl, chapatis, and rice pudding, but also the importance of a pure heart and a focused mind while one is cooking.

Idle chatter has no place in Maa's kitchen. Instead, reciting a mantra either aloud or inwardly is the way to prepare food. Tasting food, or even inhaling the aroma, is out because we are cooking for God. After the finished dishes are offered at the altar, they provide a superb meal for the divine family which always gathers around Maa and Swamiji.

What delightful times those meals are, nourishing the soul as well as the body. If visitors were not present at the Martinez temple, we would spread out the cloth on the floor in the kitchen, squeezing together to make room for everyone around the table. Joy and laughter, so much a part of the Devi Mandir scene, surfaced especially at dinner or lunch time. Puns, jokes, and good-natured banter floated back and forth across the table. Or the conversation might be quite serious, with questions about Shree Maa's and Swamiji's time in India, or a discussion of some point of philosophy or spiritual development. Always our teachers have been so generous in sharing their insights and experience. How lucky we are to be members of this divine family!

Maa's teachings continued always, showing us how to deal with the events of daily life with composure and centeredness. If an honored guest were expected, or a special ceremony or festival day required extra preparation, she never grew tense or pressured. As all our fingers were flying to complete the many tasks, Maa would exclaim, "We are dancing!" and would immediately make us feel joyous and exhilarated, and our work did become a dance!

Another of her guidelines for living is, no judgment of others. She continues, "If you want peace, see no fault in anyone. Find all mistakes within yourself." Of course this doesn't mean we should fall into self-deprecation; we must remember that we and everyone else are beloved children of the Divine Mother — and as such we must humbly try to do our best in every situation.

Maa also says, "Learn to make the entire universe your own." I've heard her say many times, "I am at home everywhere," and it's perfectly true. She has no attachment to any certain place; she enjoys her surroundings wherever she may be. Furthermore she makes the entire human family her own, welcoming every person with warmth and attention. She seems as completely comfortable and relaxed in a new place, surrounded by hundreds of new people, as she is in her home temple with just a few devotees around her. Wherever she is, she's always herself, the same loving and serene Mother whose joy is her devotion to God and giving of herself to those around her. Her example helps us to be more patient and attentive to everyone who touches our lives.

"If you call upon God in a true and simple manner, you will know that all you are performing is divine work," Maa teaches. So many times this has reminded me that the most humble task, whether cleaning a room, washing dishes or doing laundry, truly is divine action, because I am serving my family members or my fellow devotees — all children of the Divine Mother. Working in my home, I am caring for the temple in which I'm privileged to live. Whatever promotes the health and happiness of those around us can be seen as a sacred act. Not with a sense of heavy obligation or duty, but with the joy of expressing our love and gratitude for this divine universe — this is the way to carry out our daily tasks.

Maa says, "God is eternal; the world is temporary." This simple statement gives one perspective on the ups and downs of daily life. The problem or difficulty which looms so large today may seem insignificant, or be forgotten entirely, by next week or next month. Just doing our best each moment, and completing our tasks so that we don't leave a mess or a problem for someone else to deal with, is the way to live each day fully. Worries about yesterday or tomorrow drop away, and we can respond with serenity and joy to the demands of each moment as it arrives.

Maa and Swamiji have many pointers and suggestions for developing our inner lives. They say regular practice is important for the growth of our spiritual selves — there are no short-cuts! Spirituality is, very simply, giving more than we take. The feeling of devotion is what fosters our spiritual development; such things as reading books are not enough. When we do *puja* or other forms of worship, it's best to sing loudly and enthusiastically so the Gods will hear us! Furthermore, our worship is even more meaningful when we feel gratitude that we have the impulse and the opportunity to perform these devotions.

Some of Shree Maa's most potent teachings are the things she doesn't say! I've never heard her complain about her situation, her health, or things she doesn't have. In our materialistic society, many people want things that they think will make them happier. Maa's way is to live in complete simplicity. Her whole life is a statement that the important elements of life are the spiritual ones.

Occasionally, when pressed, she will admit that she doesn't feel completely well, or that she slept very little the previous night. Yet she never volunteers that information, and she breezes through her daily schedule with all her usual energy and attention. I blush to think how many of us lament the loss of an hour or two of sleep, or relate the details of a headache or backache to any listening ears.

Some of our most dramatic moments of learning from Maa and Swamiji came during our trip to India with them and eight other devotees in 1992. Maa's poise and serenity never wavered in spite of the crowds, noise, and the unexpected delays that are an integral part of being there.

For one thing, I discovered that singing the sacred songs can make any moment sublime and charged with love and beauty. One precious memory that stands out was our crossing the Ganges from Dakshineswar to the temple at Belur Math at dusk. It could have been just any boat ride in a lovely spot, soon to be forgotten. However, we sang "*Jaya Maa!*" the entire way and felt that our love for the Divine Mother was rippling out on those vibrations to the farthest point we could see, and even beyond.

One morning after breakfast in Calcutta Maa shared with us several bits of her wisdom: "We all should teach by our example. We must work on ourselves, and change society by influencing those around us. We must always be dedicated to the truth, even if this upsets or angers other people. We are all God, don't look far away from yourselves to find God. We can make heaven here on earth. We can learn from many people," said Maa. She also commented that Swamiji is her guru as she is guru to him.

One of Swamiji's teachings came early in our trip, from a lecture he had given in Hindi: "The cement for this building had water as an essential ingredient — but you can't see the water. The walls couldn't stand up without the addition of the water. Just so, your divinity, though it can't be seen, is an essential part of you." This was a beautiful expression of Maa's admonition not to look far from ourselves to find God!

Another unforgettable moment with Maa came in the railroad station at the city of Gaya. We had slept a few hours on the train but had to wake up at 2:00 a.m. to prepare to get off. (Trains in India may arrive at one's destination at any hour of the day or night, perhaps pausing for only a few moments. One must be ready to jump off after tossing down one's luggage, or risk missing one's stop!) We walked down a long platform past sleeping figures shrouded in tattered blankets. The main waiting room and nearby stairway had many more sleepers — presumably passengers waiting to depart. We finally settled ourselves in a smaller waiting room, sitting on the floor or on our bags. We would need to spend a couple of hours here, until the ashram where we were to stay opened for the day. Some of us tried to sleep a bit more, while others chatted or looked around in amazement at the ancient, unwashed walls with peeling paint. We were overtired and short of sleep, and perhaps it seemed the low point of the trip to some of us. But Maa saw the perfect time to remind us of something important. "Isn't this fun?" she exclaimed. "We can always have fun, wherever we are!" I'll never forget that moment. Whether we have fun, or enjoy our lives, ultimately depends on what is inside us, not what is outside us.

The crowds of people in India, especially those living on the sidewalks in deepest poverty, aroused real concern among the members of our group. I knew that even if I were a benevolent dictator, I'd have no idea where to begin to solve the social problems we saw around us every day. Maa responded to our questions one afternoon. She told us that we must work on ourselves — that the desire to "fix things" or help people is part of our attachment to the idea that we have the answers and the solutions — our ego. God is always working through us, and we have to be prepared. When the time for action comes we will not think, "I am helping this person" or "I am doing a good deed," but what happens will just be the natural order of things. We and our actions will just be part of the flow of life. This made me realize how much we Westerners view life as a series of problems to be solved, and how important it is for many of us to feel that things are OK. Some situations just have to be accepted — even while we strive to serve and care for all those we come in contact with.

How to balance our lives was another area of Maa's teaching. "Spend eight hours of the day," she said, "doing your work in the world — fulfilling your obligations or job responsibilities. Devote eight hours to the acts you desire to do: *seva*, *tapasya*, meditation, *puja*, and singing, for example. The remaining eight hours are for yourself, for sleep, cooking, cleaning, and so forth." This division of the day would be difficult for many of us, but it gives me a sense of what a balanced devotional life would be.

One way that Maa and Swamiji expanded our horizons in India was through meeting a series of remarkable people. One was Vashishta, a white-haired priest whose devotion to Maa runs very deep. I felt much moved by his commitment to the spiritual life. The majority of his time is devoted to worship and ceremonies in his temple, and at night he returns to his small, humble room, containing only a bed, some pictures on the wall, a few pots, a burner for cooking, and a change of clothes.

Another unique person we met was Tiwari, the owner of a steel factory in Calcutta. His adoration of Maa and Swamiji was obvious, and he could not do enough for us all. He put his jeep at our disposal many times, and he and his wife and younger children traveled with us to Gaya and Varanasi. He did so many things to smooth our journey. Tiwari brought along the young man who became our cook, and we had many delicious lunches and dinners that he prepared. When Tiwari did *arati* to Maa and Swamiji on one occasion, his devotion and love were written all over his face, and he was singing his heart out. All of us were deeply touched.

While we were spending several days in the home village of Tiwari, in the state of Bihar, we all walked one morning to a neighboring village, to meet a *sadhu* who was living there. He was peaceful and serene, and he shared some of his wisdom with us:

* Sing the name of God, and all philosophical questions will be taken care of — that is, they will no longer be important.

* Truth, consciousness, bliss — duality and ego keep us from realizing these states. Unite yourself with the earth and

worship every conceivable form of the earth in order to overcome duality.

* Make sure your car remains connected to the train engine (God) or your life won't go anywhere!

* The earth is our mother, and we are all Gods and Goddesses.

Another special being was Sushil, who at the age of sixteen or so began to work and study with Swamiji, an association that lasted ten or twelve years. Sushil told me that the two of them roomed together while studying Sanskrit at the university. Part of the time only one of them had the money to actually enroll, so that one taught the other whatever he learned. They taught each other English and Bengali through translating scriptures as they chanted. Sushil's devotion to Swamiji cannot be better expressed than in his own words: "When I heard that Swamiji was coming to India, every drop of my blood was dancing!"

Ganapati is a longtime devotee of Maa and Swamiji, and also a great-nephew of Sarada Devi, the wife and disciple of Shree Ramakrishna. Ganapati guided us to his home when we visited Jayrambati, his village and also the birthplace of Sarada Devi. He welcomed us wholeheartedly and gave us sweets. His radiant face showed him to be in complete harmony with the universe.

Malati is another most devout disciple. She and many others welcomed us with smiles and flowers at the airport when we arrived in Calcutta, and she went out to the market and bought clothes for us, when it seemed that our luggage had been delayed, or possibly lost! Malati frequently brought beautifully prepared food to the temple where we stayed. She took all our group to spend a few days at the ashram where she worships at the village of Rajpur, in the jungle on the outskirts of Calcutta. We were welcomed with such warmth, care and attention, and everything was done to make us comfortable.

Other names could be mentioned, but this sampling of the family of devotees in India illustrates the joy, dedication and selflessness of those who gathered around Maa and Swamiji during the years they worked together and traveled there. The devotion of these disciples spilled over onto all of us, simply because we had come to India with Maa. Their actions of respect and love made us feel humble and grateful, and deeply blessed. As Swamiji remarked to us during the trip, "What feelings do you have when people bow down to you, or even try to touch your feet, because you are with Maa? Imagine what the state of her consciousness might be!"

Being in the company of Maa and Swamiji for an extended period, having the special privilege of receiving their *darshan* and teachings, and experiencing every day their way of being, made this introduction to India unlike any other. We counted ourselves fortunate beyond measure to be able to share these weeks with our loved and respected teachers. What a blessing it was to feel their sweet and enveloping love, and to see others blossoming in that love!

Every day we are still in the company of Shree Maa and Swamiji, whether we are in the same room with them, or miles away. We know that they carry us in their hearts, and we carry them in ours. Their love, devotion, and purity of heart inspire us and will continue to as we walk further together with our spiritual family into this mystery called life.

Recollections by Parvati

Swamiji has always said that you can tell the value of a spiritual experience if your life changes as a result of the experience. Meeting Shree Maa changed my life completely. Rare it is to come into the presence of a saintly soul and rare indeed it is to find such a jewel among saints as the beloved Shree

Maa from Kamakhya, Assam, which is described in the Devi Gita as "the jewel of all places on the earth and there is no other place superior to this on the face of the earth." Wherever Shree Maa resides, that place is superior. So why not make a seat for her in your heart? Once in a while a great soul comes along whose pure light has the power to change another soul's course of action. Shree Maa is like a beacon of light illuminating the path for all those who strive for truth, peace, and wisdom within this worldly existence.

There is a Sanskrit phrase which reminds me of Shree Maa's purpose. It translates as, "Whenever the forces of *dharma* become weak, in order to put down the forces of unrighteousness, My soul takes birth in creation." Shree Maa has taken birth to help us fight the battle for righteousness against unrighteousness, for light against darkness, for love against hatred.

As I reflect back upon my life I regard each event, whether good or bad, as a blessing because each one of these events led me to the Divine Mother's doorstep. Swamiji says, "When you find a soul of wisdom, let your foot wear out his or her doorstep." Shree Maa is such a soul whose doorstep I seek to wear out!

When I was growing up I always felt that there must be another way of life, a way of life based on real harmony and peace. As I passed from childhood to adulthood I searched for answers. I wondered if it was possible to always be happy, even in times of difficulty. I wondered why people suffered, including myself. As I traveled around the world I never realized that what I was searching for existed within until I met Maa. And that was where one journey ended and a new one began.

During my college days I prayed to God to direct me toward truth and to reveal my purpose since many of my questions were not answered in school, at home, or in Sunday school. My religious upbringing was slight and attending services a few times a year and Sunday school once a week did not bring soul satisfaction. It is unfortunate that at the time I was not able to appreciate my religious upbringing. It was not until after meeting Shree Maa that I came to a deeper understanding and a respect for all religions and a much greater love for all that I had learned, but at the time had rejected due to ignorance.

Shree Maa teaches that God accepts all people as his or her child. God does not make division; man does. And more specifically, the great ego within each person creates disharmony. When a soul leaves its body, God does not say, "You have a Christian soul and you go over here. You have a Jewish soul and you go over there and you have a Hindu soul..." etc. On various occasions I have seen Shree Maa light Chanukah candles, sing a Christmas hymn, offer a flower to Guru Nanak, or chant Buddha's mantra. For Maa, all is divine and there is only one energy pervading this whole universe that runs through every atom of existence even though God exists in infinite forms. We are all interconnected. Only the ego makes us forget our true divinity, but Shree Maa reminds us, wakes us up, and teaches us how to live as human beings again.

This reminds me of a song that Maa recently wrote called "Mother of the Universe". It goes like this:

Mother of the Universe,
Wake up wake up us
To your Divine Grace.
You are Divine Being,
We are your Being.
Mother you are Great Goddess
You give us true nature.
We bow to your true wealth.

Mother, Mother, you are endless grace
We bow to you.
Give to us forgiveness.

How the Divine Mother woke me up was really a blessing. When I graduated from high school the idea came to me to attend college 3,000 miles away from home. The decision to leave home was difficult, but I did it anyway. As it turned out, my roommate in college had a friend who was a free spirit who traveled around the world like a *sadhu*. He often told of his many adventures and of the unique people he had met. On one occasion he had just returned from California, wild-eyed and full of energy. He had just accidently met Shree Maa on top of Mount Shasta. As he related this story to us I immediately said, "I want to meet her." Now I knew nothing of gurus, saints, or spirituality, but I wanted to know all about this holy Mother that he so eagerly described.

He described her red and white sari, long black hair, and divine qualities of peace and pure love which exuded from her every pore. Sean continued to narrate his experience of how Shree Maa and Swamiji had taken him home with them and clothed and fed him for several days.

He carried with him a little blue book about the Saint Ramakrishna which Shree Maa had given him and some sacred ash which had come from their special fire sacrifice on top of Mount Shasta. After putting a little ash on my forehead I eagerly thumbed through the little blue book and for the first time became very inspired upon reading of Shree Ramakrishna's experiences with the Divine Mother Kali. His intensity of devotion and joy overflowed the small pages of the book and resounded brilliantly in my heart.

There I was, in the middle of *maya*, like a small fish swimming aimlessly around, when all of a sudden the Divine Mother cast her bait, and I got hooked. At the time I did not realize that she was slowly reeling in her catch but this fish was also hungry.

After graduating from college, I moved to Northern California to look for a job. Soon after I landed a part-time job and moved into a small house with some friends. I continued to think about the Divine Mother and how I could meet her. My roommate from college and her friend Sean came out to visit. It was during this time that I asked if we could visit the Divine Mother.

One Saturday we ventured to Moraga and traveled along a narrow and winding road through the hills towards the house that Sean remembered staying at for a few days. Dark clouds loomed overhead and some big black ravens swooped over and around the car. This did not seem like a good sign but we kept on driving. It was late afternoon when we arrived at a rather big, isolated house situated amidst the rolling hills. There was no sign of life. Everything was boarded up. Only a small note on the door said that Shree Maa and Swamiji had moved to Clayton. There was a phone number on the bottom. Feeling disappointed we returned home since it was getting late.

The next day Sean called the Divine Mother and asked if it was okay to visit the next weekend. Of course I was extremely nervous as Saturday came by and we headed on our journey once again. This time I brought flowers to offer. We arrived in the early afternoon at a small, peaceful cottage nestled among the pines. I could not even imagine that I was going to come face to face with the Divine Mother. How should I act? What should I say? My heart pounded so hard and fast it was hard to walk.

As soon as I stepped out of the car the smell of incense lifted my thoughts to a Divine realm. The smell of a burning fire, and singing voices led us toward the back of the cottage. Ever so slowly and cautiously I peered around the corner of the house. Through the rising flames, I lifted my eyes toward the Divine Mother, Shree Maa, who was sitting so still, her eyes closed in deep contemplation of the Divine. She appeared as a young girl, ageless and extremely beautiful. Her long black hair flowed like silk down her red and white sari to her waist. In the middle of her forehead a red dot shone brilliantly signifying a mark of truth and pure love.

Immediately upon our arrival, Swamiji, who was leading the fire ceremony, motioned for us to join in. There was one other person there who was also participating. We sat down in front of two bowls of rice which had already been placed there as if we had been expected to join in the ceremony. With my eyes locked on the fire, all my thoughts dissolved. There was only the present moment. In that moment my attention was completely focused. Swamiji was enthusiastically chanting a mantra while throwing small amounts of rice into the fire. (Later I learned that the rice was mixed with five other ingredients common to the fire ceremony). Of course I knew nothing of mantras but I could at least offer the rice mixture into the fire and say "*Swaha*" which means "I am one with God." Shree Maa remained with her eyes closed in meditation throughout the ceremony. Soon after we sat down, Swamiji began ringing a bell and his voice became louder and louder, creating a crescendo of divine energy aimed towards the heavens.

When the worship was completed, all was still and silent. Never before had I experienced such peace let alone known what inner peace was but I was eager to learn more. We circumambulated around the fire pit and Swamiji raised his hands to give blessings of twelve lifetimes of peace for the seven generations of our families before and after us for each grain of rice that went into the fire. What a blessing to be able to partake in such a ceremony that benefits one's family members as well as the whole universe! Afterwards Swamiji put a little sacred ash from the fire on our foreheads. Incidentally, this was just like the ash I had been given the year before.

The next event centered around the evening *arati* which is a dance of praise to the Divine Mother and happens three times a day. As we wandered into the temple a few more devotees dressed in red and white were sitting quietly in meditation in front of the altar which housed twelve life-sized *murtis*. Shree Maa sat down in front of a drum and Swamiji played the harmonium to the tune of *Jaya Maa! Jaya Maa!* This was easy for me to remember and I could join in without difficulty. Someone handed me a tambourine which I lightly beat against the floor. Jyoti, one of the devotees, waved some lights, incense, and other articles in front of the altar as well as in front of Shree Maa and Swamiji and danced around gleefully. At the end of the *arati*, all was silent and still again while a silent meditation time ensued. Afterwards Swamiji sprinkled *shanti* water on our heads while Jyoti passed out a white substance in our hands. Swamiji explained that this was a special offering from the Divine Mother's feet. Literally, I thought that he washed Shree Maa's feet with this sweet tasting yogurt offering every day. He told me to taste it. This first taste of divine nectar blessed with hundreds of mantras began to transform my thoughts although at the time I did not realize it.

After *arati* Shree Maa stood up to retire to another room but first she sweetly asked my name and where I lived. Shree Maa has since told me that in India she never asked people their name. Sometimes she explained that a name would just come to her lips and she would call that person by that name. Feeling shy and in awe I could barely answer. After that she left the temple.

Swamiji immediately sat us down on the floor in a circle

and began talking as if we were old friends. He wanted to know where I had been, what I was doing now, and where I was going. Of course I told him that all of this was very new to me and I didn't know anything. He proceeded to describe spiritual life and outlined his and Maa's daily *sadhana*. He gave me a *rudraksha* bead to wear around my neck and explained that Rudra takes away the tears or suffering. Swamiji then excused himself. To this day Shree Maa still reminds me that I told Swamiji that I would return within a couple of weeks to help him with the Ananda Bazaar newsletter, which I never did.

After Swamiji left we sat down on the floor with Gautam, Jyoti, Ramananda, and Govindananda for dinner. There was a light meal served of rice, dahl, and chapati. Everyone ate with their fingers. Once again, this was a new experience for me but it was fun. After dinner the only thing I remember was taking the dishes into the kitchen and seeing Shree Maa by the sink. The only words that came out of my mouth were "How can I serve you?" I had a very good feeling after leaving the ashram that night. A warm glow filled my heart.

Stepping outside the ashram is like stepping into *maya*. If you are not rooted in truth you never know where she will lead you. In the Kashyapa Sutras translated by Swamiji, one of the sutras describes how every soul is on its own individual *yatra*. Perhaps that is why I did not return to the Divine Mother's doorstep for at least a year and why some people never come back or why some people stay immediately or why some come and go continuously.

During that year I often thought of Shree Maa and secretly envisioned living in the temple yet my *yatra* led me back into *maya* following old habits and patterns and I made no effort to contact the temple again. Coincidentally a few months later I wandered into the Indian Fabrics Store on

University Avenue in Berkeley. To my amazement there was a poster of Shree Maa and underneath was her message. It read:

Be true. Say what you mean and do what you say. If you are true you will be without fault. If your conscience is clear, your heart will be silent. That is peace, no matter what the result. Be simple. Many words are a burden to the soul. The real message of your heart will be communicated by your actions. The words will only explain the actions. But they must agree, lest we become hypocrites who preach what we ourselves do not practice. Be free. Leave your selfishness behind. The people whose opinions are valued will love us for what we are, not for what we have. The respect which can be bought is as useless as a tree which bears neither flowers nor fruits. When the leaves will fall and the trunk wither, none will come again. Take refuge in God. Neither your friends, relations or others will take you to heaven. Only wisdom will be our salvation. Cultivate wisdom. Learn from everyone, everywhere. Then use that knowledge which will bring you into harmony with the universe. Develop discrimination. Pursue only those desires which will make you free. Leave the ones which will get you into trouble. Know the difference and remind yourselves daily. Remember that the God you seek resides in every atom. You can offer respect to every atom, even while you maintain your own discipline inside. That you are a spiritual seeker is not something that you need to show outside. It will manifest in your behavior, without your having to try. If we are gentle, loving, kind and honest in our dealings, that is spiritual. Your spirituality cannot be hidden. Similarly, if one is full of fears and trying to hide his inner emotions such a person is not full of spirit. That is only ego. Let all our actions manifest our love. Work is visible love, the expression of love that we can see. People want realization, liberation, to become enlightened. Do not think it is something different from doing for oth-

ers as you would have them do for you. Spirituality is very simple. "I am everywhere," says the sage. "I exist in every form of creation. If I hurt any form, I hurt myself. If I raise any form to a higher level, I myself find progress." It is easy.

These simple words of wisdom inspired me not only to meditate upon them and incorporate them into my own life but also to share them with everyone I met as well. I asked Rama Sachadev, the owner of the store, if she had another poster like this. She did not but kindly removed the poster from the wall and gave it to me. I thanked her profusely.

A few months passed and I went to visit a friend who happened to have a recent issue of India Currents Magazine on her kitchen table. While I was nonchalantly thumbing through the pages a small ad in the back caught my attention. It read, "Opening Ceremonies for the Devi Mandir Temple in Martinez, California." There was also a listing of the times various *pujas* and *homas* were to be performed with a phone number at the bottom along with Shree Maa and Swamiji's name. This intrigued me and I proceeded to call the number listed. A very joyful voice answered the phone and gave me directions to the temple. On the following Saturday I began a journey that was to change my life forever.

Swamiji has often compared the soul's spiritual journey to that of a road map. At first you have to read all of the signs in order to get to your destination. Eventually you memorize the path and don't need the map anymore. And of course on that day that I headed to Martinez I had to follow the road map very carefully. I arrived at a small, unobtrusive white and red building that looked like a warehouse. It was directly across from a huge oil refinery. Maa jokingly said she was also a refinery, but a refinery of thoughts. The second I got out of the car the familiar smell of incense reminded me that I was on sacred ground. Once again I was greeted by a symphony of

Sanskrit mantras that cascaded out of the front door and up into the heavens purifying all on its path. The heavens must have sent down blessings upon hearing the beautiful Vedic verses.

Immediately upon entering I was greeted by an older woman with white hair, Vijaya. She was very friendly and helped calm my jittery nerves. Swamiji was sitting in front of the same altar that I had seen in Clayton. He was actively engaged in performing a special *prana pratishta* ceremony to establish life in the twelve life sized *murtis*. All that was visible was the back of his head and Shree Maa was not in sight. A fire was burning in the center of the temple in the *hawan kunda*. I sat in the back against the wall, content to be an observer, yet nervous to see the Divine Mother again.

For the next couple of hours I did not move from where I was sitting until someone asked me if I wanted to eat. Actually the thought of food had not crossed my mind, but I accepted the invitation gratefully. Mother always takes care of her children and she knows their desires better than they do.

In the evening there was a Kumari Puja which is the worship of a young girl as the Divine Mother. She represents the Goddess in her purest form. The Mandir was filled wall to wall with Indian families and friends. The entire evening was transformed into a joyous festival of singing, dancing, chanting, praying, and meditating. The pure vibration inside the temple was so great that I ended up staying awake all night partaking in the continuous *satsangha*.

In the morning the whole festive scene started all over again. Both Swamiji and Shree Maa were up at the crack of dawn performing their daily worship. Later I found out that this was an auspicious nine days devoted to the Goddess Durga to remove all difficulties. And the festivities continued on like this for nine more days! In actuality, every day is like a festival around Shree Maa. In the *Devi Gita* the Divine Mother says that, "Every moment is the time of my vow. Festivals are at every time, because I am the form of all."

During the next nine days I remained at the temple as long as I could. I remember sitting for several hours at a time at the *homa* offering Sanskrit prayers into the fire along with Swamiji, Shree Maa and other devotees. One particular evening stands out in my mind most and that was when I sat at the fire with Shree Maa while she chanted some mantras from about 2 a.m. until 5 a.m. When I could barely keep my eyes open any longer I realized it was okay to lay my head down at the feet of the Divine Mother, at home like a child once again. And Maa, in her powerfully quiet divinity, was always giving blessings, no matter what.

For the next few days I remained at the temple engaging in *pujas*, *homas*, meditation, chanting, singing, and dancing. The energy generated within the four small walls of this old warehouse was so full of love and devotion that it was difficult to pull myself away until I absolutely had to in order to return to work. It was not until stepping outside of the door of the Mandir that I realized a gift had been given to me. It was not a material gift, but a gift of transformation. I felt different. My way of perceiving the world around me had changed. Even familiar interactions no longer held the same importance.

Maa explains that as the mind becomes more absorbed in mantras and one pointed attention that the world naturally leaves you. You do not renounce the world, but the world renounces you. Old patterns knock on the door and you are not home because your mind is currently focused on God. As I began spending more and more time at the Mandir, the world eventually left me. That does not mean I was going to go sit in a cave and meditate alone for twenty years. Rather I began to learn how to be a part of the world and yet not of the world.

Maa's recipe for success is that with one hand you hold on to God and with the other hand do the work of the world.

Over the next few months I spent more and more time at the temple until I eventually lost the desire to be a part of that worldly existence which brought pain and confusion. Rather I sought to learn how to extricate myself from this attachment to the world of objects and relationships and to incorporate peace and harmony. Shree Maa was a pure example of a soul who embodied those qualities I was searching for. The opportunity to learn true wisdom from a saint was certainly an opportunity not to be passed up. This time I was ready to sit on her doorstep and wear out the mat.

It just so happened that I lost my part-time job so there was nothing holding me back from moving to the Mandir. I remembered that several times Maa had asked me on different occasions if I still lived in the same place. The answer was always the same. At the time I did not realize why she kept asking me this question but later understood that she was dissolving my worldly attachment.

During the next couple of months I would come and go, often spending the weekend at the temple or a few days during the week. During this time Swamiji asked me to come to the temple for *Shiva Ratri*. Little did I know that this was one of the biggest if not the biggest celebration in India. The whole day and night was spent in devotional worship to Lord Shiva — the Consciousness of Infinite Goodness. The day started out by each person making 108 small clay *lingams*, symbols of Lord Shiva. These were placed all around the temple. During this day I learned that many people do not take one drop of water until the last *puja* is finished because it is said that Lord Shiva is most pleased when no food or water is taken. Maa said that from her childhood she fell in love with Shiva. By evening time the entire Mandir was filled with song, chanting, and *puja*. There was so much joy and inspiration that it was easy to fast all day and night without a second thought. Once again the atmosphere was charged with a festival-like feeling full of love and devotion. And once again when it is all over one feels somehow different from the experience. Problems and difficulties which once plagued you are less bothersome. You feel stronger, lighter, and more capable of dealing with life's continuous changes.

After *Shiva Ratri*, full of excitement, I moved into the temple, into a new way of life, a new way of thinking, a new way of being. This change did not come about overnight and even to this day changes are taking place very rapidly and that is the blessing of being around a living saint whose pure light illuminates the darkness a lot quicker than knowledge from a book. In the *Ramayana* it says that there is nothing to compare to the peace of being around a saint.

One of the first things that Maa told me when I moved into the temple was to organize my life. That is the first step of yoga because you cannot sit in meditation if you have to get up to get more or get rid of too much. In order not to be a burden to anyone and to give more than I take I had to become efficient. One cannot hide anything around a saint and any loose ends or unattended *karma* always gets tied up.

So it happened that one morning after I had just moved to the Mandir I was driving Shree Maa and Swamiji to a hospital to visit a sick patient. We had not driven more than a few blocks when all of a sudden a police car pulled up behind us with flashing lights. I felt highly embarrassed and nervous. The policeman proceeded to explain that the registration on my car was overdue and needed to be paid. He then continued to report that I had two outstanding tickets that also needed to be paid. Luckily he did not ticket me and sternly suggested that I take care of the situation very soon. Politely I thanked

the police officer and off we drove. The next day Swamiji paid
off all of my arrears and took care of my payments until I was
self-sufficient.

It is rare to find souls like Shree Maa and Swamiji who are
only interested in the upliftment of humanity without selfish
desire. They seek to help other people become free from the
bonds of attachment rather than to bind them. Therefore Maa
never puts a price on spirituality. She leaves it all up to the
individual. If one likes to give that is fine; if one does not like
to give that is fine, too. But grace comes about by what you do.
Kripa means grace. *Kri* means to do and *pa* means to get.

Kripa means to do and get. Just so much as you sow, just
so much will you reap. Grace is not something that magically
descends upon an individual. Remembering *kripa* and one of
the first rules of spirituality which is to not be a burden to anyone, to pay off your debts, and to give more than you take, I
set about becoming more efficient.

Maa always says that a *sadhu* is one who is efficient, who
pays attention to every action, and who offers the highest
respect to all atoms of creation. She tells us that it does not
matter what job you are performing, whether it be cleaning,
cooking, chopping wood, negotiating a business deal, or sitting in meditation, efficiency is desired. The most important
point to remember is to be aware and awake.

Basically when I moved into the temple I was emotionally
a near-basket case that would cry at the drop of a pin. For the
first couple of months that is what I did on more than several
occasions. As I reflect back upon these earlier months around
Maa I realize that all of the tears were a result of the ego getting purified. But Maa with her gentleness, pure motherly
love, and sword of wisdom nurtured and helped me grow in
strength, divinity, and independence. Maa still reminds me
occasionally that when I first came to her I looked about forty-

five years old rather than my actual age of twenty-four. Now I just laugh inside about it.

The life I had been living was without direction or understanding of life's continuous changes. The nature of life is change and when one identifies with the changes suffering comes about. In a sense I was like a leaf in the wind, being tossed about wherever the wind would blow.

Now Maa has taught me that it is very important to watch the changes, and take a firm stance upon the wheel of life so as not to get blown carelessly about and suffer the consequences of each turn. Maa has shown through her shining example how it is possible to remain joyous amidst the ever changing tides of duality. Therefore, during my first month of living in the Mandir I was given a new discipline, new clothes, a small Shiva *lingam*, and taught how to do beginner Shiva Puja. This was a golden opportunity to strive toward divinity and give up old habits and patterns which led nowhere.

Now it was not my habit to wake up early and pray but it was more embarrassing to wake up at 9:00 a.m. and find that Maa had already chanted the *Chandi*, performed Shiva Puja, and had fixed breakfast. As the old saying goes, "When in Rome do as the Romans do," so I began to wake up earlier and do *puja*. Swamiji used to say that this was the same way that he started and now he has inherited the Cosmic Puja, an altar of twelve life-sized *murtis*. Besides being around Maa, performing *puja* in the morning helped to bring a quality of peace and joy into my life that previously did not exist.

Before meeting Shree Maa I had attended a ten day silent meditation retreat where we meditated all day and night. Although after the retreat I felt calm and peaceful, my life did not change nor was I inspired enough to continue meditating on my own. But after meeting Maa my inspiration grew and I began to practice a disciplined way of life, for I had the privilege of seeing how a true saint lived. Since I really wanted to make changes in my life, I was going to practice living like Shree Maa.

In order to make changes Maa says that you first have to have inspiration. Next comes learning and then practice. After practice comes refinement which gives birth to divinity and purity which cause the surrender of selfishness and egotistical thoughts. Then comes wisdom and finally perfection. And so it goes with any kind of endeavor. Since Maa was my inspiration I started to learn, study, and practice. This is the path of the nine Durgas or the path of perfecting divinity accessible to all.

Not long after I moved in, Swamiji told me that he and Maa were going to partake in a three-year *Chandi Yagya* where they would both recite the *Chandi* every day for three years without leaving the property. I eagerly responded, "Can I do it too!" Although Swamiji thanked me for being so inspired and enthusiastic, he explained that it was necessary to have your life organized first before taking such a vow of worship.

I remember waking up countless times at 3:00 in the morning hearing the most beautiful chanting imaginable. Maa tells that she got everything from chanting the *Chandi* and when she was in India she would chant the *Chandi* every day. People would come from all over to hear her chant. Swamiji says that when he was in Jayrambati at the monastery, and Maa was staying at the convent, he would climb up on the wall every day to listen to Maa sing the *Chandi*. She did not know he was listening but by the time she had finished many of the other ladies would be looking at him and smiling. He said that Maa sang the *Chandi* like an angel and still does.

Singing the *Chandi* is only a small part of Maa's daily rhythm at the temple. She also cooks, cleans, sews, gardens, sings, draws, counsels, doctors, and performs many more things as well. Every action she performs is done with the highest efficiency. I have seen her cook for fifty people in about twenty minutes with no dirty dishes left in the sink. When I hear other people complaining about how tired they are because they had to cook for five or six people I tell them about Shree Maa.

How does Shree Maa give so tirelessly and effortlessly all day and night? There is one simple answer: that is God. Every action she performs is for God. She does not think that she is doing the action. She does not have one selfish bone in her body and relies completely on God. That is why she came to America she tells us. She received an order from her guru to come to America to unite the Fatherland and the Motherland. Currently all over America divinity is taking birth.

It always amazes me to think that when Maa first came to this country thirteen years ago she came only with the clothes on her back, not knowing a single soul except for Swamiji and not knowing any English. And now Maa has her own successful ashram in Napa, and has built countless ashrams in this country and in thousands of peoples' hearts. Her divinity is spreading like wildfire igniting the spark of divinity which lies within each and every soul. Maa says, "It is time to wake up!"

The temple in Martinez remained open 24 hours a day for a while until stragglers began to drop by in the wee hours of the morning looking for something other than divinity. Any time a visitor came Maa would serve that person with the highest respect. It did not matter their caste, creed, or color. She saw divinity in all. She told us to treat each person as if God was at the door.

Maa grew up with this kind of practice. From her childhood she tells us that she always served everyone in her family first and prepared the house whenever any saint would come to visit. Her goal was to bring harmony and peace to every situation. That is why even when she was very young people would come to her seeking her advice and wisdom. Her essence radiated peace and tranquility from a very early age. She told us that she never even cried when she was little or when she was born.

When Maa gives advice to people she looks at the individual and knows intuitively where they are, where they have been, and where they are going. She gives them precisely what their soul needs at the time in order to progress toward the light. Many people come looking for miracles. What people call miracles, Maa calls natural.

One night, it was Trailinga Swami's birthday and several devotees were gathered around Maa as Swamiji read stories about the life of this great saint. Swamiji quoted Trailinga Swami when he said that most people forget their true nature and are always looking for a miracle rather than looking for the power within. No sooner had these words come out of Swamiji's mouth when Maa started clapping gleefully and said, "See. See. I am so happy." She was so happy because this is exactly what she has been saying. When you are living in a pure and true way the miracles are natural. Maa says, "Nowadays, human life is not natural."

Then Swamiji said, "Maa, you are a miracle." She humbly replied, "I am not." But there are many of us who consider her presence a miracle. What more do people need to have faith in God? Miracles?

With one word or glance Shree Maa can calm a troubled mind and heart. That is also a kind of miracle. One time a lady who had lost her daughter came to the temple for a special *puja*. She was totally distressed and sobbing very loudly. Within a few seconds, Maa took a handful of *shanti* water from the morning *puja* and slapped that water into her face several times. Instantly the lady stopped crying. To this day that lady has thanked Maa for taking away her grief.

When one devotee was telling Maa that he felt a special connection with a certain mantra, and was seeking an explanation from her about its meaning she told him to first try to keep that heart connection by reciting the mantra and then the meaning would become clear. Maa has said that many people seek intellectual understanding first, forgetting about the heart's intuitive wisdom.

Another time when Maa was at a big *satsangha* a devotee asked about the meaning of the *Chandi* and Maa said, "The *Chandi* is my life. I am there." This simple answer so much pleased the devotee that he started to cry. He later told Maa that her few simple words had touched his heart.

Life at the Mandir was like one big festival after another and the joy spilled over into daily life interactions. Day by day my life became more centered and rooted in divine service. After I had taken up two different part-time jobs, Maa inspired me to go back to school. During that time, Maa carefully and lovingly made a whole new wardrobe for me to wear. Every stitch she made was with a mantra. It is no wonder that the highest mark I received on my evaluation was for my professional appearance.

Soon after, I landed a full-time job close to the Mandir. What a blessing it was to return at lunch only to be served the finest *prasad* cooked by Maa herself. Her extremely tasty *prasad* cooked with pure love inspired me for the rest of the day. Little did my co-workers know that my actions were an extension of Shree Maa's divine blessings of peace and pure love!

And that is how it is possible for peace to spread in this world. It starts with one pure soul, like Shree Maa, who is without selfish desires, who ignites other souls ablaze with the same inspiration, *shakti*, and sincere longing to serve this creation with pure devotion. Maa has said on many occasions that when the women of the world become like Divine Mothers, the world will be at peace.

Life around Maa speeds up at the same time that being in her presence removes the concept of time. Although life around Maa is like a festival there have been times when she has been displeased because of an action performed inefficiently or without consciousness. Those times are the times that are the most difficult to bear because she illuminates your darkness and forces you to look within at parts of yourself that you might not ordinarily have a chance to see. How you deal with it is what is most important.

Maa teaches by example. One of the first rules she taught me was that cleanliness is next to Godliness. When I was growing up, this rule was not enforced in my house so I was not accustomed to living with the high standards that Maa was accustomed to. I used to read the ten Golden Rules when I was little but it did not sink in the way it did being around Maa. And there were several occasions when she would be very displeased with me because I did not clean well enough for God. Those were the times that I had to gather the most inner strength to combat self-deprecation and a whole host of other armies. Being in the middle of the battle is the most difficult because it is hard to see the victory which lies at the end of the battle which always ends up in your favor, provided you do not "chicken out" and run away from yourself.

You see, Maa is not attached to her anger. One moment she will appear to be upset, and the next moment she blesses you with her sweet smile and laugh. In my case, Maa has told me that she has to get angry with me in order to teach me. In all honesty, as hard as those times are, when they are over I am always so thankful to have had the opportunity for the transformation of thoughts. This is Maa's purpose: to reveal the depths of your soul so you may in turn present the core of your very being to God with truth.

Although I have made countless mistakes, Maa's teaching is to remain in equilibrium through difficulties or good times, criticism or praise. Sometimes it feels to me, if Maa is upset, that not even the sun could brighten my day. If I perform an action without proper consciousness, if my mind is thinking of something else other than the action I am performing, then I get into trouble. And being around the Divine Mother, performing inefficient actions always brings the sword of illumination.

Maa often breaks out spontaneously into song and I am reminded of a tune she made up:

Love is the ocean.
I am a boat.
One paddle is devotion.
The other paddle is wisdom.
It is easy to cross the ocean.

With Shree Maa navigating the boat it is easy. May all beings experience an easy crossing across the shores of difficulties.

Recollections by Durga

It was in 1984 when I scratched some innocuous lines into a plate creating an etching of two people sitting quietly upon a blanket in a land unknown. They were two forms drawn without detail in their faces, but their silent stare reached a deep inner place beyond the horizon. The etching showed one woman and a man bearing a cloth surrounding their bodies and protecting their heads. The blanket wore tassels and zigzags so fair. The ground beneath them was soft and the wind blew gently.

I smiled with peace when in 1989 or 1990 it dawned on me that the two people I had drawn years before were the same incredible and holy saints that I was residing with. Amazing! A profound assurance rang within my consciousness, my heart sang. It was a clear moment of knowing that I was in the right place at the right time. I had been searching for these two beings even prior to actually knowing it in my mind. A couple of years after this insight, I found a photograph on someone's wall, similar to my etching, of Shree Maa and Swamiji sitting in the wilderness side by side with the wind whispering around them.

Each one of us has a unique story of how we met Shree Maa and Swamiji and I was deeply touched when I met those two mysterious figures who came to life in the etching with red ink. I recall printing in red and blue tones and finishing one in burgundy ink to display in an exhibit. I was attracted by the characters who portrayed a powerful call. I was miraculously introduced to Shree Maa and Swamiji in 1986. I had no previous experience with "gurus" from India, or the Eastern philosophies aside from collegiate studies. Naturally, the textbooks are far from the living truth. Nothing prepares you to walk up and meet Jesus even if you have worshiped Him your entire life.

It was a friend of a friend who introduced me to Shree Maa and Swamiji and I soon found myself walking into their door quite often. I remember feeling very comfortable in the small temple house in Concord. The love was divine and the rice pudding famous; both called everyone to return for more. I lived four miles from the temple and worked just around the corner. At 6:30 a.m. before work, I would sit in the back of the temple and listen to Mother and Swamiji pray. Sometimes I went there during my lunch hour. One can never exactly pinpoint what it is that magnetically captivates one into returning day after day but I was so happy. I felt very welcome and was mesmerized by Mother's stories of how she could no longer refuse God's calling and finally left her home at an early age.

Minute details of stories didn't seem to matter, but Mother's presence and the power in her words were impressed on my heart. Sometimes her softness of voice made it seem as if a girl of five was speaking. Sweetly, she would convey stories that would ordinarily cause the listener to quiver with fright. In each story, she surpassed obstacles which seemed foreign and insurmountable to my own reality. And as I listened with amazement the hours turned into days and the days into nights.

One day, as I observed from my seat in the rear of the temple, Mother said something in Bengali. Swami translated her invitation for me to do *arati*. My body froze instantly with delightful hesitation. Would my legs hold my trembling shell of a body? Just dance and wave around some articles which I had seen before but did not understand. Inside, one realizes that Mother's invitation resembles the call of God.

How does one respond to God? Well, of course, one begins the dance; the privilege of worship unfolds. I was dressed in white, and the sweat was bathing my body as I intently waved each article. Music filled my ears as we sang *Jaya Maa! Jaya Maa!* The ringing seemed to cause the small congregation to disappear and the deities became my reality. Any worry of making a mistake vanished from my consciousness as I melted deeper into the carpet. Time stood still, my pores breathed silence. I stood in front of the faces, the arms, the weapons. I had little idea of what was happening to my life. I knelt down after finishing and bowed for a long time. My heart pounded, causing me to tremble. I held that moment to absorb the vibrations of the swaying surrounding bliss. I grasped the swirl within as I caught up with my heart.

I felt as if I had changed colors and wondered at the marvelous transformation inside. These graces were only apparent to the two great beings seated behind me. In these moments between seconds no words can be spoken. Somewhere inside, beneath the silence, "Yes, this is," vibrated. And yet, after this short glimpse of God, of entering His kingdom briefly, we would return to a regular routine and probably wash dishes together. This is how to live your religion — to pass from the depths of His kingdom into the vestibule, blessing yourself with the holy waters. Each action becomes one.

Some mornings at around ten o'clock, we would share potatoes and chapatis, and at night Mother would lovingly set up a bed on the floor for me. The days turned into nights. We shared in Kali Puja in the Fremont Temple. We went to Mount Shasta together. Mother sewed a unique skirt from a tiger print material to give me at Christmas time. It was delightful.

People have knowledge about many things, but there is no explaining how Mother "knows" certain things. Shree Maa and Swamiji even located me in a hotel in Lake Tahoe to invite me on a trip to Los Angeles. I was reeled in without a doubt; it was becoming ever more difficult to be away from their loving presence. I recall memories of cutting Swami's hair and beard in the backyard in Concord. We would also use the yard to host a fire ceremony where we burned our *karma*. On visits to the Concord Temple, Jyoti would delight us with peanut butter on Hi-Hos. Mother always knew when I was hungry.

I remember when I was diagnosed with strep throat and I went to visit Maa and Swamiji. They were in the living room of the house discussing some camping trip. I was resting in the garage which had been converted into a temple as I heard from the other room in a strong voice, "Oh she's not sick, she doesn't have a bad throat! This is a perfect time to go on a vacation." It was Swamiji. So about half an hour later, I was driving home to collect my sleeping bag and clothes. I was on my way to Mount Shasta for a five day camping trip!

I recall the seating arrangements in the Jaya Maa station wagon. Swami drove, I sat in the middle and Maa was in the passenger seat. Mother seemed so petite and out of deep unspoken respect, I recall trying not to even bump my leg onto Maa's pure white cloth. After driving 50 miles or so, Maa told me to relax. After 100 miles she pulled my legs from their stiffened position and said it was OK.

At our campsite we shared five glorious days of chanting, walking and bathing in the cool streams. We cooked kichuri, a one-pot meal of rice, dahl and vegetables and spices, over makeshift fire stoves we built. Swamiji sat in a long *asana* one day at the fire and repeated the entire *Chandi* five times forward and backwards.

After being captivated and absorbed into this new, strange life-style with the Indian *sadhus*, all preconceptions were shattered on an exit off a Northern California highway. While driving home Mother wanted french fries. Where in the world would we find french fries on this highway I thought? We pulled off an exit with one gas station, one store and one restaurant. Of course, we needed our french fries fried in vegetable oil free from garlic, onion or meat. What are the odds of this happening between Mount Shasta and Redding? I thought it was impossible. They sent me into the restaurant to ask all the questions. The folks thought I was nuts for asking such nonsensical questions, but I got a positive reply to them all. I ran to the car to give my report. Maa said, "Buy five orders!" A french fry never tasted so good!

Mother is always healing people and it is amazing that we get a conscious glimpse of even a small part of what is happening before our very eyes. After I met Mother and Swamiji, I was enabled to stop all of my medications for my back problems and I could run and jump again. It became easy to gain employment and simple to change to better job opportunities. Mother simply says, "Why don't you do this?" and suddenly you find yourself with that job!

It later came time to move to another facility as the worship was getting too loud for the neighbors. The Martinez place was found and the process began. How does one pack up twelve life-size *murtis*? Do you just drive them across town? You bet! After receiving keys to the building, rearranging walls and painting until very late at night, we packed up. We were all elevated by the exercises and satiated by Maa's famous sandwiches that she baked in a tiny toaster oven. We were ready to open the new Temple after a few renovations and many sandwiches.

Even though I lived about twenty minutes from the new temple, I visited often and found myself there more and more. Swamiji always invited me to stay and eventually I did move in. We were a happy family with a new way of life to experience. I learned the meaning of *puja* and we all prayed before going to work each day. Swamiji and Maa shared an incredible vow of one thousand days of reciting the *Chandi homa*. The temple was open 24 hours a day and I believe it was a special place of purity.

Recollections by Seema

Being on the road with Shree Maa as we headed up the Pacific Northwest for *satsangha* programs in Seattle, Issaquah and Vancouver was a unique experience to observe the Divine Mother in action. Most impressive about Maa is her compassion and care for her devotees. Swiftly, without any hesitation she will march to help her ailing child with boundless love. On the return home from an exhaustive performance of *homa* and *bhajans*, in a temple in the suburbs of Vancouver, Canada, we stopped for the night in Everett, Washington, and headed early the next morning south to Portland, Oregon, in our caravan of four cars and vans packed tightly with luggage, musical instruments and *homa* supplies and equipment. Short on sleep and rest, we had just arrived at a devotee's house when Maa inquired about Vicki Seward who had been fighting cancer for the last four years. Her condition was deteriorating rapidly as the malignant growth of cells invaded the tissues of her brain. Vicki and her husband Charlie had been in contact with Shree Maa for only a short time, but had already won her heart.

Without even making a phone call Shree Maa headed straight for the car to go to Carson to visit Vicki. Hurriedly, we tried to keep up with Maa's pace. We grabbed a large white marble Shiva *lingam*, some flowers, a few prayer books, a couple of incense sticks and a candle and jumped into the car. It was hard for me to believe that in her own ailing and fatigued condition here was Shree Maa running to bless her sick disciple. Maa herself was taking medication to fight an infection and was also suffering from a headache, but she took no care for her own pain and selflessly, as a true Mother, ran to the care of Vicki.

As we drove up the highway in the mid-afternoon, Maa recited mantras silently on her *rudraksha* rosary — of course she was praying for Vicki. Durga and I recited Shiva mantras while Joanna drove the divine entourage to Vicki's home in a remote cabin near the Columbia River. We parked the car a little ways from the cabin, crossed the railroad tracks, then hiked down a hill to the house. We spotted Vicki resting outside on a blanket with her eyes closed. Maa broke the silence of the forest with a warm greeting, "Hey! Vicki, my baby. How you are?"

Vicki awoke from her slumber looking at Maa in sheer disbelief. With her eyes wide open and a big smile on her face she cried, "I can't believe you are here! This is a dream! I love you Maa!"

Lovingly Maa hugged her and blessed her with mantras. Playfully, Maa cheered her on, "See, I didn't forget you — you are my divine child. I love you!"

"Where's your temple, Vicki?" Maa inquired, wanting to get right down to business. "Let's go worship so Shiva can bless you! I've brought a beautiful marble Shiva *lingam* for your altar."

Vicki led the way to a small green tent staked by the bank of the lake where monolithic water-carved boulders lined the shoreline. Tall evergreens perched over the outdoor temple and sweet chirping birds sang the song of Mother Nature, who was now present, incarnate as Shree Maa. Mother shone like a bright light amidst the forest green and blue water, draped in her colorful, red-bordered, gold-yellow silk sari. For a moment, the chatter of the forest and the splashing waters wanted to pay their respect to Maa by gently quieting their timeless motion. For Vicki, Maa's light was her beacon of hope and refuge.

Respectfully we all removed our shoes and stepped inside the simple but neatly-organized dome temple.

"Don't mind Vicki, I will move some things here on your altar, OK?"

Durga and I smiled, laughing inside since we knew well how Maa would visit people's homes, take their altars out of dark dusty closets, shift them to a central location in their living room and decorate them with bright red cloth, fresh flowers, and brass candle and incense holders. Within a few moments Vicki's altar also took a new shape and form — the Gods and Goddesses had new seating arrangements, a tea candle was lit in front of the marble *lingam* while heavenly sandalwood burning incense filled the air. The altar breathed new life with Maa's touch! Now content with the new look, Maa sang with her heart to God reciting Sanskrit mantras which produced purifying sound vibrations as did the ringing bell and clapping sounds of *mudras*. God smiled back from the altar adorned with red, white and pink carnation petals and scented with perfumed incense. Together we meditated in the silence of the forest, closing the worship.

After a quick break for *chai*, Indian tea served with spices and milk, Maa was back to work. She showed Vicki and her husband Charles, who had just arrived carrying a *hawan kunda* of heavy metal and cement construction, how to perform *homa*, or fire ceremony. Sitting outside the cabin on a wooden stool with Vicki and Charles to her left and right, Maa placed her faxed notes on the mushroom shaped wooden table. Setting her red-trimmed eye glasses on top of her head, she took a black felt pen and made quick notes on the instruction sheets. Looking more like a prime minister of a country than a saint, Maa instructed, "There is a system of worship that needs to be followed: arrange the kindlings in a triangle, place camphor in the center while reciting the Gayatri mantra...."

Dusk was on the horizon as we retraced our way to the car. Both Charles' and Vicki's eyes gleamed with hope and faith as they waved good-bye. This was just another little glimpse of a divine life on the road back to Napa Valley, to the ashram of the *rishis*, the temple of the Divine Mother.

Recollections by Savitri

"SHREE MAA DOES NOT DO ANYTHING"
Shree Maa

Sewing
Shree Maa sews original design creations for all the chil-

dren of her ashrams. Often, she recites mantras and puts a mantra in every stitch of the garments her children wear. Her designs are practical, comfortable, fashionable and reflect the spiritual values which she exemplifies. Using an assortment of fabric paints, she creates individual art designs, writes mantras across the clothes, and sews pieces of reflective mirror and glitter in such a way that each piece is a unique expression of her creative talents.

Like her cooking and her music, her fashion design also reflects the fusion of the practical needs of the Western world with the spiritual values of the East. The ladies of her ashram are often seen to be wearing white saris with red borders, neatly pleated and draped with elastic bands secured at their waist. She sews *kurtas* and *pajama* pants for the men, petticoats and blouses for the women, and in the holiday season often distributes 300-500 originally designed t-shirts and sweatshirts to members of her congregation.

Every article of clothing that any individual wears conducts a special vibration which is appropriate to the function which they intend to perform. Everyone who wears clothing sewn by Shree Maa immediately assumes attitudes of tremendous tranquility and intensities of respect and peace.

Sculpting

Shree Maa prepares all of the images of worship from clay in the soil dug from the side of a flowing body of water. Using freehand tools, a razor blade, a knife, and a small spoon, she handcrafts each of the images into the perfect depiction described by the scriptures she reads. The fingers are each shaped into the *mudra* described and every detail is attended to. She mixes the mud with straw, fashions the straw with string and sunbakes the image attached to a wooden frame. She strengthens the cracked areas with strips of cloth and further applies mud in a continuous process as the deities take birth. Thereafter, she applies paint and ornaments, the various accoutrements such as hair and eyelashes, and then drapes the image in the finest cloths.

Through many centuries this tradition has evolved from man's longing to experience a personal relationship with God. The individual says to God, "We know you are one God, infinite and omnipresent. We are not capable of remembering you all the time in every circumstance. Please give us a special time, a special place, and a special form with which to remember you." With that objective in mind, the infinite deity is scooped up from the infinite expanse of nature, and fashioned into the image of divinity by the devotion of the spiritual seeker. Images created by Shree Maa have been installed in homes from California to New York and in temples from Bombay to Calcutta.

Her creations convey a certain delicacy which makes it impossible to conceive the images are made of merely mud and straw. The fineness of her lines and the beauty of their expressions make the faces come alive so that, truly, meditators can feel the immediate presence of that form of divinity. The images are invariably draped in exquisite silks and brocades from India and adorned by ornaments collected from jewelry stores around the world.

Philosophy

Shree Maa is not a historian of philosophy but her grasp of the various attitudes of philosophy give her the capacity to define the subtle nuances of philosophical thought. She cannot tell the names and the dates of the great philosophers, but she can convey perfect understanding of their philosophical mind.

Shree Maa's philosophy conveys a passion for unity and from her holistic perception she cannot accept division.

Therefore, the various attitudes of philosophy and theological dispute are all reconciled as threads in the weaving of her spiritual tapestry. Shree Maa does not promote philosophical disputation, but rather invites all the various philosophies into the path of union with the Supreme. Every attitude from the most gross materialism to the most subtle idealism has a place of respect in the harmony of Shree Maa.

Priestess

Shree Maa's relationship to divinity is a harmony in the oneness of universality. What are described as various religions are merely translations of the one eternal truth into language and cultural symbols of the people surrounding them. The physical exercises and manipulations of life-styles of people may differ according to circumstances, but the underlying truth in pursuit of divinity remains consistent no matter how many ways it is expressed. Shree Maa's worship is communion with that oneness. She personally practices in the Sanskrit traditions of yoga and Vedanta and yet she encourages people of all faiths to maintain the discipline of their faith.

In many festivals of worship, she passes out copies of the *Bible*, the *Koran*, the *Dhamapada* in addition to the Hindu scriptures of the *Chandi Path* and the *Bhagavad Gita*, while she requests all participants to pray together in their own language and culture.

Shree Maa sits for meditation exercises with great regularity several times throughout the day and observes all of the customs and traditions of a temple priestess living in a temple of God. Sitting in one *asana* appropriate for meditation, she uses mantras and the offering of flowers, fruits, sweets, and various other objects in order to guide her awareness into the presence of God where she sits in total silence for long periods of time. She explains the worship as the process of inviting

God into our lives.

What will you do if God comes?" she asks.

What would you do if a highly respected human guest were to come to your home? You prepare, offer them appropriate refreshments and when they are comfortable, you tell them how happy you are that they came. In the same way, worship is a guided meditation with your chosen form of divinity as the chief guest. As you call on the Lord or the Divine Mother to come into your lives, rejoice in the opportunity to serve them and to offer to them the best that you have, including your very own self.

Shree Maa performs worship at the sacred fire. Residing in the hearts of devotees, the flame of devotion is burning. In the *agnya chakra*, the light of meditation is shining. The fire outside is the objective measurement of the light within. *Yagya* comes from the Sanskrit word to unite and the fire ceremony is the union of the fire within with the fire outside.

Sitting before the sacred fire, Shree Maa regularly recites scriptures and for each mantra, makes an offering comprised of rice, barley, sesame seeds, milk, honey, sugar, and clarified butter. Just as the humans inhale oxygen and exhale carbon dioxide, and the plants inhale the carbon dioxide and produce oxygen into the atmosphere, in the same way, in the sacred fire ceremony, devotees surrender all negativities and receive the blessing of Divine illumination. All thoughts of duality are sacrificed in the sacred fire and the joyous love of unity takes birth in the hearts of the participants. When Shree Maa sits for worship, the silence creates such a stillness, that all observers are conducted to her vibration.

Gardener

Shree Maa cultivates her garden with an attunement to the harmony between the soil and all life. She communes with the spirits of nature within the seeds which she wishes to nourish. In the same way she finds the harmony of nutrients of the food she serves to others, she promotes the nurturing spirit of the earth to germinate her seeds.

Shree Maa sings in her garden regularly and is especially fond of the Gayatri mantra which is the root of the eternal ideal of perfection.

"I am with them," she proclaims as she prays for the increase of wisdom and understanding in every circumstance of life. Her capacity for feeling this at-one-ness between the plants and nutrients inspires a vitality within all that she cultivates so as to produce abundance.

Just as her human crop of devotees are inspired to success from her cultivating skills, just so her garden thrives with a variety of seasonal vegetables, flowers, and assorted fruits. She uses no artificial or chemically induced products. Using an ancient technique practiced by the Indian *sadhus* who protect the exposed parts of their skin from pests by rubbing ashes on it, Shree Maa sprays her crops with a combination of ash, lime water, and products made from *neem* which have no effect on the toxicity of the harvest, nor upon the natural flavors of her produce.

Shree Maa is very attentive to conservation and uses a system of gravity-fed drip irrigation.

Musician

Shree Maa has studied various forms of classical Indian *ragas* and has mastered the scales of the music she brings to life. She always has perfect pitch in any key, although one is never certain of the key in which she will sing. She has the perfect rhythm for every song, yet it is a different rhythm each time. Shree Maa does not sing with musicians. Rather, musicians are privileged to play with her. She demands the freedom to do her own music each time she performs, not willing to be confined to any prearranged structure.

Cook

Shree Maa is truly the personification of Annapurna, the Divine Mother of Nourishment. For Shree Maa cooking is not work, but rather a practice of meditation or *puja* performed with pure devotion, exceptional creativity, and the highest efficiency. Pure love is the main ingredient in all of her cooking which she always performs with the recitation of mantras for purification. "I cook for God," she is often heard saying. Her food is so vitalizing, pure and delicious that anyone consuming her culinary delights knows that it was prepared by divine hands — the spices are just in the right proportions, the texture and consistency perfect and the presentation artistic.

Divine food prepared by Shree Maa is always made with the freshest ingredients. Even in a small cooking area, she can easily prepare four or five tasty dishes to feed from fifty to one hundred people within a span of thirty to forty minutes, while still having the counters clean and the sink free of dishes. To keep in harmony with the bounties of Mother Nature, all of her vegetarian cooking is made with the freshest vegetables that are in season.

Remarkably, Shree Maa has mastered the art of cooking without having any prior knowledge of Western cuisine. She has created so many original recipes of Indian, American, Italian, Chinese and Mexican dishes that devotees cannot keep up with recording her creations. Included in her soon to be published cook book are recipes for delicacies like baked eggplant parmesan, Chinese noodles with fresh snow-peas and cabbage in plum sauce, tofu-bean enchiladas, cinnamon spiced pumpkin squash, cashew-raisin rice pilau and jackfruit with tofu and potatoes in tomato sauce.

All of her recipes follow the principles of Ayurveda, the ancient Vedic Wisdom of harmony for life. Therefore, she combines appropriate spices with specific vegetables, and groups the foods that convey the maximum vitality and are most conducive to conducting positive energies. Living the life of meditation as she does, she refrains from cooking with ingredients that create heat or anxiety in the body or mind. She does not use onions, garlic, meat, fish, poultry or eggs.

Healer

Although Shree Maa advocates prayer for healing, she also respects the value of medicine in treating diseases, firm in the belief that they too are another tool which God has given for healing. Employing both modern and ancient medicines, Shree Maa has synthesized her vast knowledge of conventional Western medicine with Ayurvedic, homeopathic and folk remedies. She can quickly prescribe treatment for many common illnesses, and researches more specific problems in depth before she gives counsel. Shree Maa regularly studies books on Ayurvedic medicine and has knowledge of treating maladies ranging from mental disease, high cholesterol, low blood pressure or gingivitis. She often prescribes remedies such as *brahmi powder* for clinical depression or the use of *neem soap* for minor skin infections.

Many of Shree Maa's remedies are home-grown. In her front porch garden, she grows aloe vera to treat cuts or burned skin and gotakola plants for increasing brain power. With her large dispensary of medicines she has healed countless devotees of maladies of the body and mind, not to mention how much she does to heal the spirit. Often times her one touch gives patients such comfort that they forget all about their complaints.

Author

Shree Maa has written hundreds of songs in Assamese, Bengali, English and Hindi. She writes beautiful poetry in a number of languages describing her spiritual longing as well as her communion. She has written several translations of Sanskrit mantras in many languages, and her work is highly regarded in Europe, North America, South America and Africa as well as throughout Asia.

Her books have been translated into Portuguese, and her Ashram Center in Rio de Janiero distributes her teachings throughout South America.

Recollections by Kalika

The first time I saw Shree Maa, she was sitting in front of the *homa* fire beside Swamiji, on a rainy day in January 1995 in Napa. I was afraid to look at her face, and so my eyes rested mostly on her hands, which have long graceful fingers which picked up the rice between the thumb, middle and ring fingers and drew it to her heart, and then flung it into the fire. I fell in love with her dark hands, and the face I was afraid to look into. Mostly her gaze was down and calm. But I was afraid that if I stared at her, she would feel it, and look back at me.

We sat beside Swamiji later... Hayley, my daughter, and Richard, my husband, and I, and he said, "Your home isn't far away, not considering what you will receive from Shree Maa."

The next day I took the ferry into San Francisco and was struggling to learn the Durga mantra. And when I was standing on the outside of the San Francisco trolley, holding onto the railing, I finally got it right. I watched an old man push a woman in a wheelchair; and another old woman pushing a shopping cart up the steep San Francisco hills. What was it that was different? I really saw them with my head and my heart and my soul. There was an outpouring and an inpouring, a vividness, which made my previous life feel like a black-and-white movie. The sky was blue, there was a cool wind and the air was clear. There was so much busyness with the traffic and the pedestrians and tourists, the steep narrow streets, Chinatown with the crowded shops, and the tourist sections with long lines of tourists waiting to see new things. And I hung onto the side of the trolley, reciting a mantra, saying the syllables all wrong and I, myself, was part of it.

But the mantra was as still and ancient as history, like a crystal the size of the sea. For a moment my feet were wet by its waters, and my eyes hung onto the scenes of people on the city streets — sad lives, hard lives, in wheelchairs and shopping carts, in little dusty shops. I had been on the earth for forty-six years, but it was as though I was seeing life for the first time. How trite to say that. The crystal sea had eyes in my heart. My heart took roots in the sea. I was in love.

I had brushed up against it by the grace of forces I knew little of, and so for a moment, the clarity of the crystal shone upon the city scene. My eyes saw in a new way I can't describe. Rather, I was leaning against a crystal clarity for the first time and it was using me.

Later, when walking off the ferry, the travel bag that I was carrying in my hand slipped unnoticed from my fingers, landing in the path of other passengers. I walked on without it, but a young man ran up.

"Your bag..." he said.

"Oh, thank you," I said. "I didn't notice..."

Richard, my husband, stood outside the gates, watching the scene and laughing. "I'm a little concerned about your attachment to the material plane," he said.

"I am so happy!" I remember saying to him a few weeks later, "I love being with her, but what I can't imagine is standing beside her in a kitchen just doing ordinary things. That would be too much." Oh, if I only knew that a year later she would spend ten days at our house, standing beside me in the kitchen and teaching me to cook as meditation.

Recollections by Divyananda

I have been blessed with two wonderful mothers this incarnation. My physical mother took very good care of her children, and prepared us well for the physical world. Then when I was ready to progress along my spiritual path, Shree Maa came into my life. She is like my graduate school Mother. She prepares devotees for our adventure in the spiritual world. Her love is every bit as real as my first mother's, and her teaching is even more important as we make our way along our spiritual journey.

Shree Maa teaches us mostly by example, using few words. Many teachers are inspired lecturers. They seem filled with beautiful words. Their talks make sense, and make us feel good. But in a few hours or days, we fall back into our old patterns and habits and nothing really has changed. Like the old saying about Chinese food, you soon find yourself hungry again. To internalize subtle spiritual teaching, I needed the powerful example of someone who had attained.

Mother changes my life on a day to day basis. She changes how I view life and how I live it. She does this in two ways. First she gives me unlimited unconditional love. Imagine for a minute love that is limited only by my openness to receive it. Have you ever received unlimited love in this life — love that is not conditioned by your being in the same family, by your appearance, by your ability to give something to the "lover"? Mother loves each one of her devotees (and all others) unconditionally because she sees God in all of us, and treats us accordingly.

Unconditional love is addictive. It is not possible to experience it without craving more, and eventually you must love what brings you pleasure. I found myself loving Shree Maa more and more, as she showered more and more love upon me. I learned something of unconditional love and was able to offer some back to her. Eventually, I was able to offer some resemblance of it to my family members and friends. Maybe someday I will be able to offer some small version of Mother's love to all others, as she does.

Mother's love helps you realize that it is not the words that are important but the actions. When Mother does teach, her words become that much more valuable.

On one of my first visits to see Shree Maa, I was involved in a complex concern, and had worked up a long monologue geared toward steering the "question" toward the outcome I favored. I hoped to get Mother's approval for my actions. I remember Mother listening to a short bit of this self-serving monologue, and saying simply, "Oh, confusion!" As she said it, it was as if a bell went off in my head, and I realized that, yes, confusion was the problem, and none of the minutia in my prepared questions mattered a bit. All of a sudden the issue became very clear, and I was suddenly able to see the forest instead of just the trees. Since that time, I have often found myself remembering that lesson — keep your life simple!

Though Mother is an expert in the nuances of the sometimes complex Hindu theology, her teachings are simplicity itself — keep your life simple, always be truthful, and give pure love to all, recognizing all as God.

Secondly, Mother teaches us the time-tested methods used by the successful sages to organize our lives so that we may progress rapidly on the spiritual path. She teaches us how to perform our daily duties as an offering to God, whether we are working, cooking, eating, bathing, singing, or worshiping.

Mother is an avatar. She was born with the ability to go into the spiritual state of *samadhi*, or as she would say "Going beyond." She told me one time that she was really sorrowful as a child to learn that other people did not possess this power also.

Perhaps that is why she has devoted her whole life to serving others. I remember one time when I had just started visiting the ashram, I was on a juice fast. Mother's custom was to cook meals for all the devotees that showed up for each program. This particular night she had cooked for about thirty devotees, and everyone had just sat down to eat. Mother noticed I was not eating and asked why not. When I explained that I was on a juice fast, mother dropped everything to find some oranges to squeeze for me. She would not allow one of her children to be without.

When you spend time with Mother, you soon see that her whole life is serving others. She has little concern for her own welfare. She is very thin and weighs less than eighty pounds. So little thought does she give to her own welfare, that she often has to be reminded on occasion to eat and take care of her own body. One time Swami noted that she stayed in *samadhi* for three days without any movement.

Another time I especially remember, was when Mother and Swamiji married Diptananda and me. Mother sewed both sets of wedding clothes for us and even thought to sew us pillow covers and sheets for our bed. The marriage ceremony took over four hours.

I mention these acts of Mother's kindness not as special acts. In fact they are typical examples of her kindness to all. Any long term devotee would have many similar examples to share.

Mother's Love is equally there for all depending on your ability to receive it. She is the perfect example, the highest example of the human life form. Incidentally, Mother never asked that I love her personally. She wants us to learn to love all Mothers, all family members, all friends, and all sentient beings as God.

Recollections by Diptananda

It happened on a pilgrimage in Europe while waiting for a train in Zurich, Switzerland to be exact. There I learned of a saintly woman who lived north of the Bay Area about an hour and a half from my home in California. This was Divine Mother Shree Maa. I was traveling around the U.S., Europe, and soon to India to bask in the peaceful presence of God in human form. Little did I know this presence was nearly in my own front yard back home.

Upon returning from Europe, an acquaintance I met while traveling called and asked me to join her for a *kirtan* in Martinez where Divine Mother Shree Maa resided. There I met Shree Maa for the first time. Shree Maa looked at me and said "Haven't we met before?" I said, "No, this is the first time."

Two weeks later another telephone call came for me to join the *kirtan*. Though it was the evening before my departure to India, I ventured out to see Shree Maa for the second time, a visit which proved to be very favorable indeed. Shree Maa approached me after the *kirtan* and I mentioned briefly about going to India the next evening for three months. In a peaceful reassuring voice Shree Maa said, "Every step you take will be blessed." Then very authoritatively but calmly she pointed to a devotee who was an Indian gentleman visiting from Calcutta, Dr. Rai, and said, "You'll stay with him."

So indeed it was made manifest, and it came to pass that I was cared for lovingly while in Calcutta. The navigation of India had its many trials and tests, but the sweet voice of the

Divine Mother saying "every step you take will be blessed" remained indelibly etched in my consciousness. It surrounded me with tranquillity and peace amongst the chaos and confusion.

The temple in Martinez was a small commercial cinderblock building with rooms on the periphery and the temple in the middle surrounding the *hawan kunda* or sacrificial fire pit. After the work week disciples and devotees would come to the temple for the weekend partaking in *sadhana* and *seva*, basking in the presence of the Mother. We'd all sleep on the floor of the temple, rising early for morning *sadhana*. For meals we'd place a tablecloth on the floor of a small kitchen, circle around and partake, breaking bread in the presence of the Mother.

Years later the temple moved to a quiet private rural setting in Napa County. A large metal warehouse was converted into the temple. There was no plumbing or electricity, so much work had to be done. The land needed additional clearing and on every weekend outdoor projects would abound with Shree Maa leading us in worship.

In the early 1990's Shree Maa went to visit her disciples and devotees in the Calcutta area of India. Shree Maa, Swamiji, and nine of us traveled together visiting and performing worship with the local disciples and devotees in their homes, at their factories, and in other ashrams.

One of Shree Maa's disciples had a factory in Calcutta and the family lived nearby. Yet the extended family lived in their birth place in the State of Bihar in the countryside, farming the land. Luggage and all, we piled into a jeep to make the arduous journey by road from Calcutta to Bihar fulfilling a request that Shree Maa bless the new village temple.

Compared to the noise and over population of Calcutta, Bihar painted a very stark yet serene picture with its expansive fields that seemed to extend infinitely into the heavens. The villagers in their quiet, benign simplicity gathered around us in great curiosity as if we were from outer space. To them we were, since it was the first time they'd seen foreigners travel through their land.

To celebrate the blessing of the new village temple and the presence of Shree Maa, the village and surrounding villages were invited to a worship ceremony led by Swamiji. We prepared a meal that fed over three hundred villagers.

It was very impressive to learn of and witness the unity of the extended family. Though some family members live and work in Calcutta, all income is sent home to Bihar and placed in a pot along with everyone else's income. Then the elder of the family doles out the resources according to the needs of each individual. Everyone helps everyone according to their capacity. There is no resentment or shame of contributing more or less financially, emotionally, or spiritually. The family works in unity and all are lovingly cared for by each other.

Shree Maa has been a guiding light in my life ever since our first meeting. Lovingly counseling my husband and me one year before our marriage, Mother performed and blessed the union.

Through Mother's example of unconditional love, she continually demonstrates the divine attributes of compassion, forgiveness, and detachment.

Shree Maa has entered my heart. No matter where I am or what I do, Mother's presence is forever with me.

Recollections by Charles Seward

"I was sure it was time to leave my body. Hundreds of devotees had gathered around me and Swamiji. I was going up and beyond when suddenly I began coming down, back into my body. When I opened my eyes, Swamiji's head was in my lap and all the devotees were crying. I said, 'Swami, why have you brought me back?' He said, 'I want a boon!' 'What boon do you want?' 'Just say yes.' 'OK, I will grant your boon. What is it?' Swamiji said, 'Mother please don't go, please stay.' And I told him, 'I will stay. . .'"

The beauty of the American country side, slipping by silently outside of the van windows, is somehow heightened by Shree Maa's presence. Even while traveling by van Maa's primary focus is on God. Time is passed reading scripture, singing devotional songs and discussing spiritual issues. Gossip is always discouraged. Mother has definitely mastered the art of economizing words. It is amazing how the most complex questions can be answered profoundly with a few words. Many people have seen her loving and joyful character but traveling with her affords an inside view of her truly playful nature. In this case she reminds me of the goddess Lalita - the Beautiful, Playful, Beloved One.

I met Shree Maa in the Spring of 1996, when my wife asked me to accompany her to a friend's house where the saint was visiting. When we arrived everyone was singing, ringing bells and dancing about the room. I thought: "Is this a wild party, or a spiritual gathering?" Trying not to feel out of place, I sat in the back of the room and watched. There were song sheets but I could not pronounce the words which were in Sanskrit. The atmosphere was alive with a kind of infectious loving, joyful feeling. Slightly out of character for me, my hands started to slap my crossed legs, and before long my knees were bouncing, my head waving and my hands clapping. My heart started to open, as the boundaries that separated me from others faded. The whole experience contained a great sense of elation.

A line of seated aspirants had formed about ten feet in front of Shree Maa and Swami Satyananda. The air was charged

with energy and everyone was anxiously waiting to meet the
Divine Mother and to receive her blessings. As my wife and I
moved closer in the line the intensity of good feeling began to
increase. It became clear that the small thin Bengali woman in
front of us was at the source of the wake up calls.

A year later, in the Spring of 1997, while touring the
United States with Shree Maa, I had the opportunity to see
hundreds of people undergo an experience similar to mine.
They would simply come to see Mother and their hearts would
begin to soar. Almost without exception they would leave with
a greater inspiration to pursue divine life. Even the tightest,
most in-the-head people would melt after two or three meetings.

While Swamiji piloted the van, Maa, from the passenger
seat, continued to speak:

"I am glad I stayed, it is a beautiful world God has created. My life is completely different now from then. Then I
knew nothing of this world."

I leaned forward from the back seat and asked, "Because
you spent most of your time beyond?"

"Yes."

"Mother, when you are beyond do you have any sense of
individuality?"

"No."

"You're not in another realm or another loka?"

"No, I am beyond all individual things. It is very, very
beautiful."

Maa smiled and chuckled. I was awe-struck with the casu-
alness with which she spoke about her life in the infinite. She
is so kind, so beautiful, so loving, so Divine and yet so very
human. No ego, just love and truth.

Maa explained that a person cannot stay in *samadhi* more
than twenty-one days without losing their physical body. They

must come out, even if only briefly. Holy men often expressed concern over the lengthy periods of time that Shree Maa would stay "beyond"; they were concerned that she would not come back. Maa often refers to *samadhi* as the "beyond" or as "my home".

Once my wife was talking to her about a period in Mother's earlier life, where she had spent most of a seven year period in *samadhi*. In that conversation Maa made the comment, "when I came back from my home," referring to when she came out of that total immersion in Supreme Divinity. My wife immediately responded with the question: "Mother isn't this your home?"

Shree Maa, with a beautiful smile and a little laugh, said: "I will have to tell you about that when we are in India."

I asked her if it is difficult to come back from the "beyond" to this world?

She said, "It is difficult to feel the sensations of this world."

"Do you mean it is difficult to distinguish in from out, or yourself from the outer world?"

"Yes," she replied, "they are the same to me." (I imagine that enough of a self must get established by the body, so that she can experience a faint shade of individuality — prior to that she is so unbounded that she sees only infinite consciousness.) "Recently a chiropractor asked me if I had hit my head hard, about twenty years ago. I answered, 'Yes, many times.' 'How did you hit your head so many times?' he asked. 'I would go into *samadhi* while standing and collapse on the floor—hitting my head.'"

Joking I said, "Going into *samadhi* is hazardous. Couldn't you control it?"

She replied, "I can now, but then there were times when I could not distinguish the body from my self."

"When did that change?"

"When I came to the West."

We all laughed and Maa commented that in the past she really had no interest in the affairs of this world.

I told Shree Maa that I knew many people that had been meditating two or three hours a day for twenty or thirty years and they were not having clear experiences of *samadhi*.

She said, "If they do *tapas* (deliberate action to overcome selfish ego based action) they will get *samadhi*. The meditation you do is very restful, but it is difficult to go beyond in the West. There is so much to draw you out. The influence of *maya* is so strong — always pulling you out. *Tapasya*, purifying austerities, are very necessary."

I assume she meant they are necessary to break the influence that *maya* has — pulling us out. They are necessary to stop the attraction the senses and mind have to go out, which prevents the mind from staying in a quiet state.

I asked if it was more difficult for her to go beyond in the West.

She said, "No, it makes no difference to me — I go like that," she snapped her fingers.

The talk stopped here, and Maa turned her head to look out of the window. There was a copy of Linda Johnsen's book, *Daughters of the Goddess*, on the seat beside me. I picked it up and opened it to a beautiful picture of Anandamayi Maa. Immediately out came the question."

"Swamiji, did you ever meet Anandamayi Maa?"

Swami replied, "Yes, many times, her ashram was just across town from me."

I then turned to Shree Maa and asked if she had visited Anandamayi Maa. Mother turned away from the window and in her usual selfless manner answered:

"Normally I do not go to see other saints; they have always

come to me. Anandamayi Maa came to me once in a vision about a week after she had left her body. She gave me a white lotus, and said: 'the responsibility is yours now.'"

"Responsibility Maa? What responsibility?"

Shree Maa turned to gaze out the window once again. The deep silence that followed made it clear that no more would be said, and no more should be asked. I sat back in my seat to think about the many extraordinary events that revolve around the lives of God-realized people. At least they seem extraordinary to those of us who do not share their level of spiritual attainment. I recalled an experience that happened in the United States which Swamiji had told me about. Shree Maa and Swamiji, along with about a dozen devotees, were celebrating *Vijaya Dashami Puja*, the day of victory after the Nine Day Festival, in Moraga, California. The celebration began in the morning with *puja*, and was followed by a *yagya* and singing. It was already night time, and Shree Maa had prepared a pot of rice and lentils with which to feed the group. They were all just sitting for dinner, when a number of cars began to fill the parking lot.

A large membership of the Bay Area Bengali Association, about one hundred fifty people, arrived unexpectedly just as they were blessing the food. As usual, Shree Maa immediately arose, welcomed everyone with great delight, and then invited them all to be seated in rows upon the floor. She instructed all the disciples not to touch any of the food, that she would like to serve the guests herself.

"With what?" exclaimed the disciples in dismay. "The pot is not big enough to give even a spoonfull to half the people!"

It was a regular household type stainless steel pot, with enough food to feed the original group of about fifteen people. Maa picked up the pot herself and chanted mantras. Without cooking more food or refilling the pot, she walked around the room and served all the guests a delicious dinner. Almost everyone had a second helping.

I asked Swamiji if he had ever witnessed this phenomenon before. He replied, "I cannot count the number of times."

Recollections by Linda Johnsen

Learning that my husband had a deadly form of bone cancer was a horrible shock. For nearly a year the doctors had been telling us the pain in Johnathan's leg was just a torn muscle. Now at least we knew the truth: it had been a malignant tumor all along, a particularly virulent form of cancer that is nearly impossible to treat.

As the grim diagnosis sank in, I thought of Kali, the Hindu Goddess who destroys everything that is less than divine. Suffering and death are two of the tools She uses to drive us back to God. There was a mantra to this Goddess which Shree Maa repeated constantly while we traveled with her in India. I asked Johnathan if he remembered it and he spoke the mantra out loud. Before he reached the last syllable the phone started ringing.

It was Shree Maa.

The last we heard, Shree Maa was still in India and was not expected back to the United States for several more weeks. It turned out two days previously she had abruptly changed her plans, flown back to her Ashram in California, picked up the phone, and called Johnathan.

We explained what was happening and the next day we had an extraordinary blessing of having Shree Maa, one of the most beloved saints of North India, visit our home in Sonoma. She and Swami Satyananda sat with Johnathan for hours, singing hymns to the Divine Mother, recommending protective mantras for us to chant and healing rituals we should perform. Placing her hand on Johnathan's head, she gave him her blessing.

Two days later we received an emergency call from Johnathan's doctor. He explained that he had just received the results of Johnathan's last biopsy and it completely contradicted the results of all the previous tests they had run. It turned out Johnathan did not have incurable bone cancer after all, but another type of cancer that could be treated easily. (To this day Dr. O'Donnell insists he and the team of oncologists he was working with were certain Johnathan had bone cancer, and the fact that it turned out to be a different type of malignancy came as a total shock to him.)

Johnathan is fine now, though we continue doing our protective mantras and healing *pujas* daily just in case. Johnathan did have to go through chemotherapy and radiation treatment (which he sailed through effortlessly) because it was our *karma* to experience this medical crisis. Yet somehow Shree Maa shifted the course of reality so that the full impact of our *karma* was blunted, and the awful outcome the doctors originally predicted never happened.

"She rearranged the stars for you," Swami Satyananda smilingly told Johnathan after the tumor disappeared. How amazing that in these dark and cynical times, saints like Shree Maa still walk among us. How utterly amazing.

Recollections by Carol and Charlie Hopkins

As Carol and I walked into the Devi Mandir in Martinez, a delicate and graceful woman approached us. I could feel a divine force as tangible as wind. I knew I was in the presence of a great soul. The humble surroundings magnified the greatness of Maa.

After welcoming us, the first thing Maa did was to offer us something to eat. The respectful way I saw her attend to everyone and everything around her was a teaching that books with thousands of pages could not have imparted.

Every action was a display of deep wisdom. I came away knowing that the greatness of God is manifested through simple acts of kindness. To this day I feel the effects of having been greeted so warmly and with such a Mother's care. My heart will never forget Maa.

Meeting Shree Maa was like coming into another plane of consciousness. Outside the Devi Mandir, the sky was literally on fire over the oil refineries in Martinez. Inside was a cave in God's heart — a heaven.

The first time I saw her, Maa was teaching scripture to Parvati and a young neighbor girl while they sat at her feet. My feeling was that right there in front of me is a great being, and that she knows me. Without even asking my name, Maa invited me to take a shower and spend the night at the temple. Then she went to prepare food which she served me with her own hands. While we ate, she talked to me as if I were important to her, not a stranger who knocked on her door and came in without asking.

That evening Swami Satyananda Saraswati performed the fire ceremony and chanted the *Chandi Path*. I closed my eyes and tried to meditate. After some time I began to feel as if a vacuum hose were attached to my heart area. I could feel a real suction taking place, something leaving my heart and flying into the altar fire. It went on for a long time and when I opened my eyes, Maa was across the room looking at me.

I feel she is always there looking at me in that way. When I think of Maa, I think of Truth. She is what Truth is, powerful and absolute, but Maa is also gentle and kind. I was a stranger and she took me in. I was hungry and she fed me.

And when I think of Maa, I think of Swamiji, the greatest example of devotion I have ever known. Swamiji gives form to my highest aspirations. But anything I could say about Maa or Swamiji would be too much or too little. I just want to go on knowing them and loving them.

Shree Maa often teaches in the most entertaining styles. In addition to her singing being filled with joy and love, her cooking, her poetry, etcetera, etcetera, she also tells wonderful stor-ies about spiritual life. Swamiji, in a playful manner, translates into modern Americanese, and the stories fill devotees with inspiration, joy and often times very important precepts which seekers will want to incorporate into the practices of our daily lives.

Shree Maa requested that we share some of her favorite *sadhu* teaching stories.

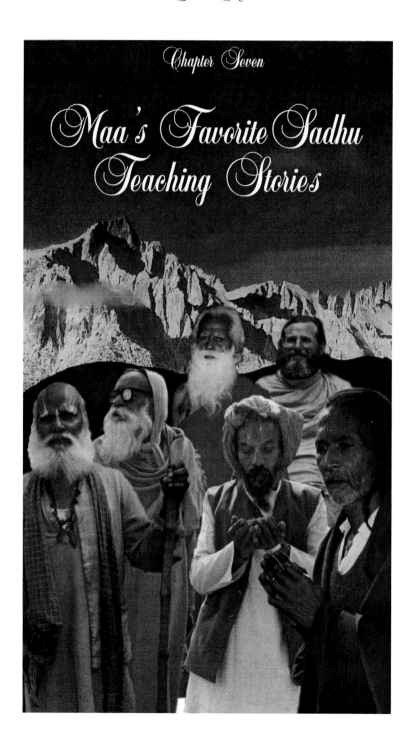

Chapter Seven

Maa's Favorite Sadhu Teaching Stories

Empty Your Cup

The first time Brahmachari Govinda went to see Swami Asheshakripananda he was really amazed. The swami invited him to tea. The brahmachari sat there as the swami lifted the tea pot and poured tea into his cup. The cup filled and filled until it was overflowing, and the tea was flowing onto the saucer, then spilling over on to the table.

Finally the brahmachari could watch in silence no further, and said, "Swamiji, stop! The cup is full. No more will go in."

Swami Asheshakripananda looked at him directly and said, "Like this cup, you have come here with so many of your own preconceptions of what is spiritual life, that no more will go in. First empty your cup. Prepare yourself for learning. Then you can assimilate the essence of spiritual teachings."

The Businessman's Three Sons

Once upon a time there was a very wealthy businessman who had three sons. He thought, "If I divide my estate into three equal portions, after some time they will no longer remain equal. One of the sons will be successful, another mediocre, and still the third may find decrease. Then surely jealousy will arise among the three, one thinking his brothers got the better shares or the like, and it is quite possible that after arguing over wealth, the boys will go their own ways, and the unity of my family will dissolve. Let me devise an examination by which I will see which is the most clever of the three, and I will make him the manager of the estate on behalf of the entire family."

Thus reasoning, he called his three young sons together and said, "Boys, I am giving to each of you one dollar. I want you to go the market and purchase enough goods to fill up your room from the floor to the ceiling and out to the four walls. For one dollar purchase whatever you like with which to fill your room."

Taking each his dollar, the three boys ran off in the direction of the market.

That evening the father came home, and immediately went to the oldest son's room. "Well, what did you purchase?" he inquired.

"Father," replied the oldest son, "on the way to the market I found a gardener with a truck full of grass. For one dollar he delivered the entire load here, and you see, I have filled my room from the floor to the ceiling and out to the four walls with grass."

Opening the door to his room, the father peered in to see that the room was indeed filled with grass. He thought for a moment, and then said, "Perhaps we can get a goat or a cow to come and eat all of that grass. I will reserve my decision until I see what the other boys have brought."

He moved over towards the second son's room. "What did you purchase?" he asked.

"Father," came the eager reply. "I went into the market place and negotiated with the cotton-seller, and after an intense negotiation, I succeeded in purchasing an entire room full of cotton. You see, Father," he said opening up the door to his room, "I have filled my room from the floor to the ceiling and out to the four walls with cotton."

The father thought for a moment, and then said, "We'll be able to make some pillows and new comforters, quilts and mattresses. But let me reserve my decision until I see what your other brother has brought."

Thus speaking, he moved off to the youngest son's room. "What have you brought?" he asked.

"Father," called the youngest son. "Here is ninety cents, your change," he said offering a fistful of coins to the amazement of his elder.

His father looked at the shining coins in the palm of his hand, and again requested, "How did you spend the money? What did you buy?"

"Father," replied the youngest. "I gave five cents for a small clay bowl, two cents for a piece of string, and another three cents for a little oil, and see, Father! I made a lamp, and filled my room from the floor to the ceiling and out to the four walls with light!"

Opening up the door to the room, the father saw that his room was most certainly filled with light, and with the greatest of joy he hugged his youngest son and proclaimed him the winner. "Where there is light, there is wisdom as well. And with that wisdom you will manage the wealth of our family."

Darkness and the Sun

One day Darkness went to the Lord. He said, "Lord, I know you have created all existence with purpose and meaning. Everything upon the earth and in the heavens has a reason. The waves that wash upon the shore, the sun that rises every morning, the stars that shine every night, the living beings and people who go about their functions upon the earth, all are acting in support of your purpose. Without your order no one does anything, nor is there anyone who can prevent himself from acting once you have ordered him to act. But Lord, I have one question for you, which I sincerely want to understand. Why is it that the Sun is always chasing me around the earth? Sometimes I get tired and want to sit down. Even then the Sun comes and chases me away. Please Lord, explain to me why the Sun is always chasing me?"

The Lord replied, "Let me ask the Sun about this." He called the Sun, "Sun, you come here."

Darkness departed.

The Lord continued, "Sun, I have fashioned this creation

with the ultimate of harmony. Everything has a purpose, a reason which can be understood in the divine plan of things. I want to know why it is that you are always chasing your brother, Darkness, around the earth? You never give him a chance to rest. Every time he sits down and wants to rest, you come along and chase him away. What is the meaning of this behavior?"

The Sun said, "Lord, please excuse me! I have never seen Darkness. Please bring him here and show him to me, and I promise not to chase him away."

The Sadhus and the Bear

Two *sadhu*s went off to meditate on a mountain, and as they were climbing, they met some people from the village coming down. The people warned them, "You better be careful up there. There is a very ferocious bear who is causing all kinds of havoc."

The *sadhu*s said, "Well, let's just go anyway. God will protect us." And so they camped out on the side of the hill.

That night they ate their food and climbed into their bedding and went to sleep. In the middle of the night they heard a noise. "It's the bear!" Both of them turned pale with fright.

One of them got an illumination and immediately started putting on his running shoes. The other *sadhu* looked at him incredulously and said, "Do you think you are actually going to out run that bear?"

The *sadhu* replied, "No, I really don't. But I have analyzed the situation. I only have to run faster than you."

The Sannyasin and the Prostitute

There was once a lady of questionable repute who lived across the street from a temple. A sannyasin who lived in the temple came to that lady one day and said, "You are living a contemptible life. I want to show you the heaps of your sins. For every visitor that comes to see you, I am going to put down a stone." And he did. He sat on the temple steps and he watched who came in and out of that lady's house. Every time a visitor came, he put a stone there.

That woman said, "Oh my God, will you ever forgive me? What else can I do with my life? I don't know any other way to make a living. Look at all of those stones there."

Meanwhile, the sannyasin sat in the temple and said, "That damnable woman. Look at the heaps of sins that she is piling up."

Through the years they continued this behavior until there was virtually a mountain of stones and sins piled up in front of the temple. The poor woman was totally distraught and constantly in prayer, "Dear Lord, please forgive me, but show me any other way and I will be glad to follow it."

One day a carriage came racing down the street, ran over the woman, and she died. All of the citizens proclaimed, "What a relief! All of that sin is gone from our community."

It just so happened that the *sannyasin* died on that same day. They threw the lady's body out beyond the gates, where it was torn apart and devoured by dogs. They took the *sadhu* on a silk stretcher, covered with flowers. With a brass band they marched all around the city and took his body to the burning *ghats*, the stairs leading to the river where religious ceremonies are performed, and they cremated his body with sandlewood. His soul went up to heaven and God said, "What are you doing here? You do not belong here."

The *sannyasin* said, "What do you mean, I do not belong here? I lived in the temple."

God said, "Oh no. Your body lived in the temple, but your mind was constantly across the street with the prostitute. You go to hell. She is coming to heaven. Even though her body was engaged in those irreligious acts, her mind was constantly begging for forgiveness. Therefore she deserves a place in heaven. You go."

The Swami Carries a Lady

Since several years both Swami Gambirananda and Swami Mahananda had been sannyasins, initiated in the very strict Natha Sampradaya, an order of monks descended from the ten groups of renunciates created by the Adi Shankaracharya more than twelve hundred years ago. They wandered as monks throughout the countryside, observing the rituals and customs of their order.

One day they were walking down a country path. It was such a beautiful scene: the lush greenery of the forest was highlighted by a myriad of flowers. The brilliant green of the parrots, who were chirping in the trees, reflected from the shadows of the dense foliage. All around was an atmosphere of freshness, a certain joy reflected in the nature.

When the two Swamis approached the river, they saw a lovely young lady dressed in a beautiful sari standing peering at the river with a look of distress on her face. Swami Mahananda asked her, "Dear Me, what is the matter? You appear to be in great distress. What can we do to assist you?"

The young lady replied, "Oh Swamiji, I am to be an attendant to my friend at her wedding, but I don't know how I shall cross this river without getting my clothes soaking wet. I don't see any bridge in sight, and if I will wade across the water, I will be a mess for the wedding ceremony."

Swami Mahananda replied nothing. He merely picked her up in his arms, and began to carry her across the river. Crossing the waters to the other shore, he set the lady gently down upon the opposite bank, bowed to her, and took his leave. The Swamis continued on their way in silence.

But after some time, having walked a few miles in deep contemplation, Swami Gambirananda began the conversation. "Swamiji, I have one question to ask of you. We have taken the vows of monastic life, and ours is a most restrictive order. We are forbidden to touch a woman, or to have any association with the opposite sex whatsoever. How could you take it upon yourself, in defiance of our monastic traditions, to take a young beautiful lady into your arms, holding her touching to your chest in close embrace, to carry her for some distance, and still have no thoughts of remorse? Is it not a sin to break your monastic vows, to hold a woman in your arms, and still you appear totally unperturbed?"

Swami Mahananda replied, "Swamiji, I put that lady down three miles ago. You are still carrying her!"

The Three Thieves and the Traveler

Three thieves came upon a traveler on a lonely road. The first thief said, "This guy is of no use to us. Let's just kill him and take all of his valuables." The second thief said, "Well, there is really no reason to kill him. Let's just tie him up securely, throw him in a ditch and take all of his valuables." That is what they decided to do. They tied him up securely, hit him over the head, and threw him into the ditch. They stole everything he had and ran off.

They had gone some distance away, when the third thief began to feel badly about their actions. He said to the two others, "You guys go on ahead. I have to go back." He did. He returned to the victim of the crime and found him all bound up, lying in a ditch by the side of the road. He untied him, bandaged his wounds, put him on his own horse, and led him to the highway.

The victim said, "You have been so kind to me. My house is just down the road. Why don't you come to my house and let me entertain you."

The thief replied, "I can't go there. The police will ask me why I was with the thieves in the first place. I will surely be arrested."

The first thief is the quality of darkness, who causes injury to others. The second thief is the character of activity who binds all of life with attachment to their actions. The third thief is the attitude of truth, which can show us the way home, but cannot enter into the house. To enter into the house of God we must be in complete peace, without any quality at all.

The King's Cut Finger

Once upon a time there reigned in the Kingdom of Pataliputra, a very righteous King by the name of Chandrasena, who governed his subjects with the loving and gentle guidance of a father to his children. That King had a very devoted and enlightened minister, who was also his best friend and confidant. His name was Uttam. No matter what happened, in the functions of government, in the personal lives of the King or his family, even in that minister's own life — no matter what course events would take, that minister used to say, "God performs all works for the best. It is God's will."

Occasionally, when things would go very wrong in the kingdom, and the worst results came to pass, that minister, Uttam, would say, "Don't worry, it's for the best. God has a plan, and He designs all for the best possible results."

This used to irritate King Chandrasena. He was frequently perplexed by numerous problems: enemies, finance, treasury, spies sowing seeds of dissension, the potential of drought and famine. For the ruler of a kingdom almost anything and every-thing can go wrong at any time. And then in the midst of havoc, while trying to deal with all of these difficulties, his minister would say, "Don't worry. God does everything for the best. Protect your *dharma*. Do what is right."

"Do I have to listen to this!" thought the King. "What nonsense this man offers. Again and again when we have problems he tells me not to worry. It's all God's will! How can I run a kingdom like that?"

One day the King was eating from a basket of fruit. He selected a fresh juicy red apple from the basket, and taking his knife, he began to peel it. As he was peeling it, his knife slipped.

"Owe!" he shouted, and he licked the wound where a slight trace of blood began to appear. "Darn it, that hurt!" cried the King.

The passive minister, when he saw the King's predicament, calmly replied, "Don't worry, it's all right. God has a plan. Everything is for the best."

"What do you mean it's for the best!" cried the King. "That's my finger that's bleeding! Everything is not for the best! What is so good about the King cutting his finger? Guards! Throw this idiot in jail!"

Immediately the guards came and arrested the minister and took him to jail.

King Chandrasena was very fond of hunting. He and his friend, Uttam, the minister, used to go out every afternoon into the forest to shoot at game, to enjoy the freshness of the outdoors, and to get away from the stuffiness and the considerations of the kingdom. This day Chandrasena's mind would not sit still. Being so agitated, he went off into the forest by himself. He started to shoot at some of the animals, but because of his lack of concentration, he could not hit anything.

Just then, a giant wild boar came running before his path. The King pursued the boar on horseback, following him into the denseness of the forest. The boar went on, darting in and out between the thickets with deceitful trickery, and he led the

King far into the dense forest, away from every area which the King had previously visited.

Suddenly in a thick part of the forest, a band of tribal natives surrounded Chandrasena. With weapons aimed at him, they made him stop in a clearing. "Dismount from your horse!" they commanded.

The King got down from his horse, surrendered his arms, and was taken captive. The warriors brought their prisoner to their High Priest.

"Ah!" he exclaimed. "An excellent victim for our sacrifice! Wash him. Give him food. Tonight the Goddess of Death will be pleased! We can sacrifice this noble head before our Goddess!"

The King was led away, bathed, dressed in the finest cloth, fed a scrumptious meal, and then bound to the sacrificial post. The Priest began to recite the sacrificial texts, while the members of the tribe gathered round. Chanting in the ecstasy of worship, the executioner raised the blade of the sword over the King's head.

"Stop!" said the High Priest. "What is that on his thumb?"

"It's a cut."

"This victim is not whole. He cannot be sacrificed. He has an imperfection, and our Goddess will not accept him. Release him."

The King was released, and immediately he made his way home back to his kingdom. After taking some refreshment and rest, he sent for the minister, Uttam. "Bring the minister from the jail."

When the minister was brought before the King, Chandrasena related what had happened to him during his adventure in the forest. The King said, "Now I understand what you said to be true, that God works everything for the best. I can see that the cut on my thumb in fact saved my life from being sacrificed before the Goddess of those natives in the forest. But now please clarify for me one point, just for my understanding. If God has a plan for everything, and everything is for the best in accordance with *dharma*, then tell me how was it for the best for you to spend the day in jail?"

Uttam, the minister, gave his reply. "Your Highness, you know you are very fond of hunting in the afternoons, of wandering in the forest to shoot game, and to seek refuge from the considerations of the kingdom. Regularly I accompany you on those hunting expeditions. On this particular day, when you were caught by native tribesmen, who were ready to offer you in sacrifice to their Goddess, you were saved by the cut on your finger. Well, Your Highness, I had no such cut on my finger! Had I accompanied you into the forest, I might very well have been required to leave my head in that very same place! So you see, Your Highness, God works everything for the best. He has a plan for all. Let us surrender to God's Will, and then we can see how His plan will unfold in bringing us to the ultimate realization of our *dharma*."

A Temple Can't be Built with Money

There was once a very wealthy King who was a great devotee of Lord Shiva. He spent millions building a huge temple, and he was preparing for the inauguration ceremonies. In a nearby village there was a *sadhu*, who had only one loin cloth and his *bhikshapatra*, his begging bowl. He went around the whole village and said, "I want to build a temple to Lord Shiva. Please help me. Give me something."

The people looked at him and said, "You are a crazy old *sadhu*. You are a beggar. You don't have anything. How are you going to build a temple to Lord Shiva? What a waste of money." They didn't give him anything.

That *sadhu* felt very badly, and he went down to the bank

of the river and sat down under a tree. He said, "Shiva, I really want to express my deepest devotion to you. I want you to know how much I love you. But nobody will help me build a temple to you and I can't do it by myself." He closed his eyes and said, "Shiva, if you would let me build a temple to you I would first perform *bhumi shuddhi*, the ceremony of purification for the land. I would make a *yagya* and a *puja* and I would make *hawan*. With the greatest intensity of devotion I would chant your mantra hundreds and thousands of times. Then I would make the foundation and I would write the name of Shiva on every brick. I would put those bricks in place singing your songs. I would make the walls rise very high as a monument to my love for Lord Shiva. I would make a roof and put a *trishula* or trident on top and install a Shiva *lingam* inside. I would meditate on Shiva's eternal presence."

That night Shiva came to the King in a dream and he said, "King, please postpone the installation ceremony for your temple."

The King said, "Shiva, I have spent millions to build this temple. It is the biggest temple in all of the land. I have priests coming from every corner and all the arrangements have been made. They say that according to astrology tomorrow is the day the installation must be performed. What do you mean, postpone the installation ceremony?"

Shiva said, "Just what I said. Postpone the opening installation ceremonies. I will not be there. I have other business to attend to tomorrow."

The King asked in the dream, "What else are you going to do?" Shiva said, "I am going to the installation ceremony at another temple."

"Where?" asked the King. Shiva told the name of the village, "The Devi Mandir in Napa." The King woke up from his dream and he called the priest and told him to cancel the installation ceremony.

The priest said, "What? You have spent so much money and time. Thousands of people have been working on this temple. We have got everything ready. We won't have an astrological configuration like this for the next twenty years."

The King said, "Cancel the ceremonies. Call the Captain of the Guard. Get my retinue ready. Get my army ready. We are going to the Devi Mandir to have the darshana of Lord Shiva."

The whole army got ready and the King proceeded in his chariot. The retinue came to the Devi Mandir and said, "Where is the temple where Lord Shiva is going to be present?"

All of the villagers said, "There is no temple here. We do not know what you are talking about."

The King said, "No, I know there is a temple. Where is it?"

The village people said, "King, you must be mistaken. There is no temple here."

The King said, "I can't be wrong. There must be a temple. Did anyone ever want to build a temple here?"

The villagers said, "There was one crazy old *sadhu* who came around begging to make a temple, but no one gave him anything."

The King said, "Where is that *sadhu*?"

The villagers said, "He is meditating under that tree over there outside the village."

The King went to the tree and saw the *sadhu* performing the installation ceremony for Lord Shiva in his heart. And the King felt very sorry for his own spiritual poverty and understood that he could not build a temple only with money. One can build a monument with money, but a temple can only be built with devotion.

Narad Becomes a Woman

One time Narad Muni asked Vishnu, "What is *Maya?*" And Vishnu said, "Come here and I'll show you."

So they went down to the earth. It was very hot. Vishnu said, "Let's take a bath." Narad went into the river and ducked his head under the water. When he came up, he had the body of a woman, and he didn't remember anything.

Just then the King of Kanauja came with his army and see-ing such a beautiful young girl said, "Who are you? Where is your father or your husband? What are you doing here all alone?"

The girl answered, "I don't know who my father or my husband is, and I can't even tell you from where I have come."

"Well, then, come with me," said the King.

So they got married and had children. Their children had children, and they all grew up to be beautiful princes and princesses. That queen thought she was the most fortunate per-son among women. She had a husband who loved her very much, many servants, wealth, children and grandchildren, and no difficulties of any kind.

One day an enemy King came and attacked the city. Her husband went out with his army, and was slain in battle. Her sons also were killed in the battle, and the city was sacked and burned.

The queen ran out into the battlefield, took up her sons in her arms, and began to cry in grief and anguish. Everything she had was gone. At that moment, a *brahmin* came and said, "You can't stay in this battlefield with all these rotting corpses carrying on like this. Go home, perform the funeral rites, and do what is proper. Now go take a bath, and then proceed with your *karma*."

The queen went to the lake and ducked under the water. When she rose up again she found she had the body of Narad

Muni. Narad looked behind him to find Vishnu standing.

"Vishnu," asked Narad. "How is it that when I was a queen I could remember nothing of the life of Narad Muni? But now that I am Narad again, I remember everything about my life as a queen?"

"That is Maya!" replied Vishnu.

The Teachings of the Gods and Ashuras

An *ashura* and Indra both went to study in the home of Brihaspati, the Guru of the Gods. They asked, "Guruji, what is the Self?"

He replied, "Go look at your reflection in the water. What you see in the water, that is the Self."

They both went and looked in the waters of the lake and saw their own reflection. They said, "Gee, Guruji meant that this body is the Self."

Then they returned to their respective places. The *ashura* went back to teach all of the other *ashuras*. "*Ashuras*, this body is the Self. This body is divine. Look for divinity by pleasing your body."

Indra was on his way back to heaven with the same teaching, when he started to think, "Sometimes the body gets sick. Sometimes the body is happy and sometimes the body is sad. Why is God sometimes happy and sometimes sad? God can't be the subject of all of the emotions of the body. I better go back to the guru and ask him what he meant by this."

Indra went back to Brihaspati. He said, "Guruji, please teach me more about the Self."

And Guruji said, "Do more meditation. Perform *tapasya*, your spiritual discipline. Then go back to the waters and see what you see."

Indra performed his discipline, and then he went to look in the water. He saw that the one who looks into the water is the

Self, not the reflection. And Indra went back to all the Gods in heaven and said, "Gods of Heaven, the reflection is not the Self, because the reflection is always changing. The Seer is the Self, because it is always the same. The Self is the consciousness which perceives the reflections."

The Sadhu's Daughter Marries

Once upon a time, a great hawk picked up a little baby mouse in its beak and flew up into the sky. As the bird rose up into the air, a gust of wind startled him, and the little baby mouse fell from his mouth.

Just then, a *sadhu* was standing by the bank of the river, praying before taking his bath. The palms of his hands were open, signifying acceptance of God's grace through prayer. As he was reciting his mantras, the little mouse fell right into his hands.

"If I leave this little mouse on the bank of the river," he thought, "then that hawk might return and take her again. I have an idea. I'll turn this mouse into a little girl, and take her home for my wife to raise."

Thinking thus, he transformed the little mouse into a baby girl by his yogic powers, and brought her home to his wife. His wife was so pleased to have a child, and she fed the child and raised her as a daughter.

When the child grew up to be of marriageable age, the wife said, "Husband, our daughter is going to be of marriageable age, and it is time we find her a suitable spouse."

The *sadhu* agreed, and taking his daughter, went off to find the bridegroom of her choice. First they went to the Sun. "Would you like to have the Sun as your husband?" asked the father.

"No, Father, he is too hot. Isn't there someone greater than him?"

"Yes," said the Sun. "The Cloud can hide me whenever he likes. He is superior."

They went to the Cloud. "Would you like to marry the Cloud?"

"No, Father. He is dark and cold. Please find someone else for me."

"Oh Cloud," asked the *sadhu*. "Is there someone better than you?"

"Yes there is," replied the Cloud. "The Wind. He blows me about as he pleases."

"Daughter, will you marry the Wind?"

"Oh Father, he is so restless. Please choose someone else."

"Wind," asked the *sadhu*. "Is there someone who is more steady than you?"

"Certainly," the Wind replied. "The Mountain. He never moves. Try as I might, I can never push him around."

"Daughter, would you like to marry the Mountain?"

"Father, please no. He is so coarse and lifeless. Please find someone more lively."

"Oh Mountain, can you suggest someone more suitable to be the husband of my daughter?"

"Of course, I can. The King of the Mice. He is the liveliest creature I've ever seen."

Seeing the King of Mice, the daughter exclaimed with delight, "Father, he's the one I want to marry. Please turn me into a mouse so I can be with my beloved."

Then using his yogic power, he turned his daughter into a little mouse, and with the greatest satisfaction witnessed her marriage to the man of her dreams.

The Sparrow Caught a Fish

Once a sparrow swooped down and plucked a little fish from the water, and rose up with his trophy into the sky. That sparrow was so happy, he immediately set his course towards home, where he would share the prize with his family.

As he rose up into the sky, he was spotted by a gang of crows. The crows saw the little sparrow with that beautiful fish in his mouth, and they resolved to capture that fish at all costs. Immediately they attacked.

The little sparrow flew to the north, but the crows were in hot pursuit. They pecked at him from above and below, and caused all manner of harassment.

The little sparrow flew to the south, but the crows did not leave his trail. They continually pecked at him and in the greatest of consternation, he dropped the fish from his mouth.

As God had planned it, another little sparrow who was flying below, caught the fish in his mouth, and with great delight began to fly towards his home. The crows, seeing that the fish was now in another's possession, went off in pursuit of the fish. They harassed that other little sparrow to the greatest degree. The little sparrow flew to the north, but the crows were in hot pursuit.

The little sparrow flew to the south, but the crows did not leave his trail. They continually pecked at him and harassed him in every manner.

Now the first little sparrow sat in a tree and witnessed the plight of the second sparrow, who now had possession of the fish. And he thought, "Am I glad I got rid of that fish! Anyone who has the fish will never know a moment of peace. Always the crows will be after him. Life becomes so simple once we drop our fish!"

Brahma, Vishnu and the Ketaki Flower

One day Brahma, the Creator, was walking down a path, when he met Lord Vishnu, the Protector, along the way. Not recognizing the Divine Lord, he enquired, "Who are you?"

"What do you mean, "Who am I?" responded Vishnu indignantly. "I am Vishnu, the Sustainer of All. Who are you who is asking?"

Brahma got angry and replied, "I am Brahma, the Creator of the Universe. You must show respect to me because I create everything that is."

And quite foolishly Brahma and Vishnu started to argue.Brahma said, "Unless I create, there will be nothing for you to preserve. You will have no work without me. You are totally dependent upon me."

Vishnu retorted, "You sprang from my navel, you ungrateful old man. If I cut your umbilical cord, you will be finished."

Right there where they were arguing, all of a sudden, up came a Shiva *lingam*, just there between them. And it kept growing from out of the ground and growing until it went out of sight.

"What is this?" they were both surprised. "It appears to be a Shiva *lingam*."

"All right," said Vishnu. "I'll tell you how we can settle this. Whoever can find the end of this Shiva *lingam* first, is the superior. Brahma, you go to the top, and I'll go to the bottom. The first one to reach the end will return to give the news. He will be the winner."

Vishnu became a boar and started down, following the Shiva *lingam*, burrowing down underneath the earth. He continued going down further and further and further.

"This *lingam* doesn't have an end," he thought. "It just keeps going and going. I'm tired, and I've had enough. I'm going back."

Brahma, on the other hand, got on his swan, and went up and up and up. He passed through the clouds and continued on towards the other end of infinity. As he was still going, he said in desperation, "When is this going to stop? Where is the end of this Shiva *lingam*?"

Just as he was getting near to what he thought must be the top, a flower fell down from Lord Shiva's head. As the flower fell, Brahma caught it, grabbed it in mid-air, and said, "Oh little flower, from where have you come?"

"I came from the head of Lord Shiva, replied the flower. "A devotee put me there as a token of worship, and a gust of wind came and knocked me off. I came from Shiva's head."

"Well," said Brahma, "I was just going up there to Shiva's head to get a flower, and it's so nice of you to come down here. Let me ask a little favor of you. Would you tell Vishnu that I took you off from the top of the Shiva *lingam*?"

"Well, that's not quite true," replied the little flower. "Actually, I fell off from the top of the Shiva *lingam* in a gust of wind."

Brahma said, "Do you know that I am Brahma, the Creator of the universe? If you just do this little thing for me, I will make sure that you are honored among all flowers."

He put the flower in his pocket, and went back down.

"Hello, Vishnu!" greeted Brahma. "Did you find the end of the Shiva *lingam*?"

"No, I didn't." I traveled on and on, but I couldn't find the end, so I returned here. Did you find the end?"

"Well, yes, in fact, I did. I went right up to the top of the Shiva *lingam*, where I took the darshana of the divine Lord Shiva, and then I came back down to tell you."

"What kind of story are you telling me?" replied Vishnu in disbelief. How could you find the end of the Shiva *lingam*? There was no end down below. How could there be an end on top? What proof do you have?"

Brahma said, "I thought you might not believe me, so I brought this little flower from the top of the Shiva *lingam* to testify on my behalf. Ask this flower. I brought him down from

Lord Shiva's head just to show you."

Vishnu looked at the flower and asked, "Flower, is that correct? Did you really come from the head of Lord Shiva?"

"Oh yes, Vishnu," replied the little flower. "I really came from the top of Lord Shiva's head."

"Did Brahma take you from the top of Lord Shiva's head?" Vishnu questioned again.

The poor little flower began to shake. "Ye-ye-ye-yes, Vishnu. Brahma took me from the top of Shiva's head just to show you that he was there."

Suddenly the earth began to shake. The clouds broke apart, and through the regions of heaven came the roaring sound, "LIAR!"

Shiva came down and said, "No one came to the top of that *lingam*, and nobody took that flower off from my head. Brahma, you are a LIAR! And this flower is lying. It is not possible to reach to the summit of infinity without my grace. Knowledge of the Self is not an attainment. It is a realization of being in the present reality. Realization comes about through intuitive awareness, not through egotistical action. If you want to earn that grace, then refine and purify your awareness through selfless actions. Perform the worship of my Shiva *lingam*, the eternal symbol of the Consciousness of Infinite Goodness, and being pleased I will grant to you that vision. There is no other way to attainment."

The Pundit and the Boatman

Shree Lochana Das Mishra was the most respected pundit of Prayaga. After defeating every opponent in debate, he was unanimously acclaimed the most learned man of the area. Now, after receiving such high honors and prestige, he was returning to his village across the Ganges, content in the pride that he was the most knowledgeable man in his district.

"Probably," he thought in his conceit, "the most intelligent in the entire country."

With considerable pomp and grandeur he walked up to the small boat which would ferry him across the river, took his seat, and motioned to the boatman to proceed. The boatman pushed off from the beach, and within a few minutes they were gently gliding over the water towards the other shore. It was quite a distance to the other bank, and after some time the pundit condescended to engage the boatman in conversation.

He said, "Boatman, do you know anything about meditation?" He paused a moment taking in the magnanimity of his question, and then proceeded. "Do you not know that it is an individual's spiritual search which distinguishes character. Those who have faith and study and practice, move beyond the realms of human experience, into those divine spiritual mansions of Godliness and the subtleties of Nature's expression. Developing intuition, they cease to react to worldly causes and effects, and through the processes of purification, they become masters of their own destiny. Meditation focuses attention, and it is by paying attention that learning takes place. Hence growth, increase and improvement — the evolution of consciousness beyond the mere necessities of the body. Boatman, do know anything about meditation?"

The Boatman replied, "No, Punditji. I don't have any idea of what is meditation, or how it is practiced."

The pundit thought a moment and said, "Without the capacity to focus attention, one cannot proceed in spiritual life. Without a spiritual life, there is but little to distinguish man from an animal. Without moral foundation or spiritual vision, there is absolutely nothing to separate you from the mediocrity of humanity. Boatman, at least twenty-five percent of your life is gone, wasted, for want of spiritual insight."

The pundit sat back in his seat and became lost in reflection. But after a few minutes of silence he asked, "Boatman, do you know anything about philosophy? Do you know that an individual's philosophy determines one's values, establishes the criteria by which one discriminates right from wrong? Certainly if there is one thing which distinguishes man from the animals, it is the capacity of reason. Without philosophy humanity would remain among the other brute animals, quite possibly in the jungles without any sense of civilization whatsoever. It is philosophy which establishes purpose in life, and thereafter paths to the attainment of one's goals. Boatman, do you know anything about philosophy?"

The Boatman replied, "No, Punditji. I don't have any idea of philosophy whatsoever. In fact this is the first time I have heard the word."

The pundit thought a moment and said, "Boatman, without the spirit of philosophy it is impossible for one to rise above his animalistic nature. What kind of existence could one hope to lead in the absence of all the graces of life. Boatman, at least another twenty-five percent of your life is gone, wasted, for want of philosophy. A life without philosophy is not even entitled to be called human."

The pundit sat back in his seat and again drifted off in his own contemplation. But after a few minutes he again asked, "Boatman, do you know anything about grammar? Do you not realize that humanity thinks with words, and that when one puts words together in a certain juxtaposition, the meanings become coherent only because of grammar? For example, if one were to read a list of nouns, it would be impossible to understand the relationships intended. Other parts of speech are also required, particularly a predicate.

Then we can readily observe that knowledge of grammar is mandatory for clear thinking, as well as effective communication. Without an understanding of the relationships among the objects of creation, it is not possible to reason. Without grammar how can we possibly understand? Boatman, do you know anything about grammar?"

The boatman replied, "No, Punditji. I don't know anything about grammar."

The pundit thought a moment and said, "Boatman, without the knowledge of grammar it is impossible for one to think clearly or communicate effectively. Boatman, at least another twenty-five percent of your life is gone, wasted, for want of grammar. Seventy-five percent is gone. You are living a life which is at most twenty-five percent of the potential of a human being."

The pundit sat back in his seat and again drifted off in his own thoughts. The boatman began to feel extremely badly about the course his life had taken. Here was the most learned pundit in the area telling him that his life was worth, even at the most, twenty-five percent of human potential. How worthless, how despicable, must his life be.

As he was thinking about the truth of the pundit's words, suddenly the pundit said to him, "Boatman, I feel my shoe is getting wet. See where this water is coming from."

The boatman put down his oars and walked over the bench to where the pundit was seated. Looking down underneath the seat he said, "There seems to be a hole in the bottom of the boat which is letting in water."

"Well, fix it!" cried the pundit.

"I can't fix it here," replied the boatman.

The water was coming in faster and the boat was filling up. "What are we going to do?" cried the pundit.

"Punditji," asked the boatman. "Do you know anything about swimming?"

"No," replied the pundit.

"Well, Punditji, one hundred percent of your life is gone,

wasted, for want of knowledge!"

The boatman jumped over the side and swam to the far shore.

The Brahmin and the Butcher

Once there was an aged *brahmin* couple who had only one son, and his name was Kaushika. One day Kaushika came to his mother and said, "Mother, I wish to advance on the spiritual path, and I have decided to go off into the forest and devote myself exclusively to the practice of *sadhana*, study and various forms of spiritual discipline.

His mother replied, "Son, your father and I are very old. He can hardly move, and I, myself, am quite feeble. What will become of us if you go away? Who will take care of us? Who will get our food and attend to our needs? You are our only son. We are dependent upon you. Please don't forsake us like that. Don't go into the forest and leave us all alone."

But Kaushika was determined. He said, "Mother, this world is only a temporary bondage of the soul, and it is keeping me from my cherished aspiration of self-realization. My first duty is to attain wisdom. That is why God has put me on this earth, for wisdom — not to be a servant!"

Ignoring his Mother's appeal, Kaushika went into the forest to practice austerities. He performed his disciplines with great earnestness. As the years passed, he attained great *siddhis*, tremendous spiritual powers.

One day as Kaushika was meditating under a tree, a crane flew up into its limbs, and perched on the branch above him. Accidentally the bird knocked some dirt down onto the meditating yogi's head. Startled from his meditation, Kaushika cursed that bird with a look of fiery fury in his eyes, and immediately that crane fell lifeless to the ground.

"Oh my," he thought. "What have I done? I have attained

to such spiritual greatness that even the look from my eyes can cause injury to one who would show me disrespect."

That evening, Kaushika went to a village to beg for his food. He came to a house where a very gentle housewife greeted him, and bade him to wait one moment while she prepared some food for him.

Just at that time the lady's husband came home, and forgetting all else, she went to assist him. She offered her husband water for washing, and made him sit down to take food.

Kaushika became angry at the neglect shown to him. "Having invited me to wait a moment, this housewife is completely ignoring me," he thought.

Remembering the presence of the *brahmin* again, the housewife returned with apologetic tones. "Please take your food," she offered, "and forgive me for taking so long."

"Is this the way to treat a yogi?" he asked with voice trembling in anger. "After inviting me to wait, you ignored me completely. Have you no respect for my attainments?"

"Oh revered Brahmin. Please forgive me, but a woman's first duty is to her husband. When I saw him coming home tired and hungry, I forgot about everything and everyone else. I am so sorry to have offended you. Please take your food and forgive me."

"Don't you know the power of a *brahmin*? Have you no fear?" he chided her.

"Oh *Brahmin*, I have learned that a *brahmin* is one who controls his anger. So please do not threaten me, oh learned one. I am not like a crane that you can burn with a single glance."

"How does she know about the crane?" Kaushika thought.

But instantly the virtuous woman continued, "No doubt, oh Brahmin, you have attained great learning and tremendous powers in your years of discipline. But you have not yet understood the truth about virtue. Your spiritual attainment is little more than the ability to kill a bird with your anger. I have attained to real spiritual knowledge by serving my husband and family with pure love and devotion."

"Now you are to learn about true virtue. But I am not your teacher. If you want to know more about this subject, you should look for the man known as Dharmavidya, who resides in the City of Mithila. You go find him and he will be your Guru."

Kaushika was humbled. "I am very grateful to you, and I will do as you say." He bowed and departed in the direction of Mithila.

"This Dharmavidya must be a great ascetic," he thought as he approached the City of Mithila. "I will go find him first."

Entering into the city, he asked a man on the street. "I am looking for Dharmavidya," he said.

"You'll find him in that shop over there," came an incredulous reply. The man pointed to a butcher shop.

"What would an ascetic be doing in a shop, a butcher shop no less, where they cut up dead meat?" thought Kaushika.

He timidly walked up to the butcher shop, and, as he stood there gazing in perplexity, the proprietor stood up and came out to greet him. "Welcome, holy one. I am Dharmavidya, the man you seek. I know you have been sent to meet me by the virtuous woman who is a housewife in a far off village, and also I know for what purpose you have come."

Kaushika thought, "The woman knew about the crane that was slain by my glance, and this butcher knows about the woman who sent me. Certainly they must have some great knowledge, which I do not."

"Come sir," said Dharmavidya. "Let's go to my house. This is no place for a holy *brahmin* such as yourself."

"Such a sinful profession does not befit one such as you,

venerable sage. You must be ashamed of the work that you do," said Kaushika.

"No, I am not ashamed," replied the butcher. "I am engaged in my family trade, and I work hard and honestly at it. There is no reason why I should be ashamed for my work. There is no man alive who is completely free from causing injury to another life. As we walk, we cannot help but to trample forms of life on the ground. The air we breathe is full of living organisms which perish within us. And doesn't the farmer destroy numerous creatures when he plows his field?"

"But please, sir, come in, and accept the hospitality of my humble house. This is my wife and my children, and I look after them as best as I can. Come in and meet my aged parents. My parents are my deities, my wife and children and I attend upon them with devotion and love. I consider that caring for them is my greatest duty. And in doing one's duty cheerfully lies true virtue. That is what the blessed housewife sent you to learn."

"You, oh holy learned one, have run away from your responsibilities. You have deserted your aged father and mother. All one's learning and penances are useless if one has neglected one's duty."

Kaushika, the *brahmin*, bowed down to the butcher. "You have showed me the path of true virtue, oh pious man. I am indebted to you."

Returning immediately to his parents, he served them lovingly until the end of their days.

One Friend with a Prostitute
and the Other in the Temple

There were two friends who met while walking along a path. They came to a temple where spiritual dialogues were taking place. One friend said, "Come, my friend, let us hear the word of God."

His friend looked with surprise and declined, stating that he had a date with a prostitute instead. Thus the two friends parted, one to visit the temple to hear the word of God, and the other to enjoy himself with his lady friend.

But after a short time of sexual dalliance, the one man said to himself with great disgust, "Oh, may I be damned! My friend is sitting in the temple listening to the word of God. While I am sinning, he is certainly being saved. Certainly I am a fool!"

At the same time the friend, who was sitting in the temple listening to the spiritual talks, thought to himself, "Boy, am I a fool! My friend is enjoying the company of that prostitute, while I am listening to these dull speeches."

When these two men died, the servants of the God of Death came to the man who sat in the temple. But the man who was with the prostitute went directly to heaven.

God looks to the mind, not where you are, but with what quality of mind you are there. God receives the expressions of the heart.

The Greatest Sacrifice

After becoming victorious in the battle of Kurukshetra, King Yudhishthira decided to perform the Ashwamedha Sacrifice, which literally translates as the sacrifice of the horse. The rules of this sacrifice provide that a beautiful and strong horse is set free to roam at will, unimpaired, behind which, the King's army follows. Into any kingdom which that horse enters, that King has the choice to render tribute and acknowledge the sovereignty of the King of Hastinapura or to fight.

After many travels, Arjuna, who was leading the forces behind the horse, returned to Hastinapura and his family began the preparations for a great sacrifice. The sacrifice lasted weeks and months together, and in this sacrifice countless oblations were made to the fire, while singing the praises and chanting the mantras by which one can both please and unite with the Gods.

At the completion of the sacrifice, Yudhishthira and his brothers distributed thousands of gold coins among the participants, and all the *rishis* and the *munis*, the respected wise seers of divinity, were given rich presentations.

All the learned men assembled were given from the abundance of the Pandava Kingdom. The lame and the blind and the poor, everyone was given the fruits of the *yagya* according to the capacity of the five brothers.

"This is the greatest sacrifice any King has ever performed," declared one of the *brahmins*.

Another said, "He has given away three times the fees and charities ordained in the scriptures for such a sacrifice, and such an abundance of food! The heavens must be resounding with praise for the greatness of this sacrifice!"

As all the joyous people were proclaiming the greatness of Yudhishthira and the five Pandava brothers, and the magnificence of the sacrifice which they conducted, there entered just near to the sacrificial arena a very strange animal.

"Look, a mongoose! What kind of a mongoose is that? Half of his body is golden."

The mongoose walked directly up to the area where the sacrifice had been conducted and instantly began to roll on the ground.

Sadly and quite dejectedly, he rose up and said, "It hasn't happened here either. This sacrifice, oh learned ones, is not as great as that of the poor *brahmin*."

"What?" asked one of the learned pundits. "Could there be any sacrifice greater than this? The king has spared nothing to make it so. It was conducted with such great splendor, and according to the prescribed rituals in every detail."

"And yet," said the mongoose, "compared to the sacrifice of the *brahmin*..."

One pundit stood forth. "Please, we are learned men. Tell us of what *brahmin* you are speaking. What was his sacrifice and why was it greater than this?"

The mongoose began to relate his tale:

Once in a village near Kurukshetra there lived a *brahmin*. With him in his household were his wife, his son and his daughter-in-law. They lived a simple, austere life, contemplating the scriptures and attending the sacred fire of sacrifice, performing all the rites of worship and rules of meditation as the scriptures ordain.

That *brahmin* used to eat only one meal each day at noon and that too only a very frugal meal of a few grains of corn.

Then there came a time when a great famine descended on the land, and even those few grains of corn became difficult to obtain. For several days the household went hungry. Neither the father nor his son could find any food to bring home for their meals.

Then one morning, the *brahmin* came home after his daily search with a very small portion of barley. With great delight he gave it to his wife proclaiming, "Today, at last, we shall eat."

His wife and his daughter-in-law pounded the grain into flour, and they divided it into four equal portions, one for each member of the family. The father and son were busy reciting the morning scriptures, and when they had completed, the wife called them, "Come to eat."

But just as they were about to begin their meal, there was a knock at the door.

"Father, a guest!"

"Welcome sir, welcome to our home."

Even in his difficulties, the *brahmin* didn't forget his duties as a host.

"Here is some water to wash your feet."

And when the guest had washed, "Now please come and take your seat. I'll get some food for you to eat," said the old *brahmin*.

Immediately he went inside the kitchen, and returned with his portion of the barley. "Here, Sir, please forgive me, but this is all I can offer you," he offered.

Without any ceremony the guest gulped it down, and began to lick his fingers.

"He is still hungry," thought the *brahmin*. "What can I do now? He is my guest. How can I send him away hungry?"

His wife, seeing the perplexed attitude of her husband, came offering her share.

"I can't do that!" proclaimed the *brahmin*. "You, yourself, have not eaten for several days, and your body is worn out with work."

"No," said the wife. "If you, who have been suffering as long as I, can give away your share, why can't I give away mine? Please take this barley and give it to our guest."

The *brahmin* could not refuse. He took it and placed it before the guest. And in the same manner the guest gulped it down.

"He is still not satisfied." thought the *brahmin*. "And I can't blame him. Two hand fulls of barley can hardly appease a man's hunger."

Then the son came forward with his share. "Father, please take this share too. I know you will not be comfortable if you send that man away hungry. I am young and I can withstand the rigors of hunger."

"Oh my son, and you will always be my son, how can I

stand by and watch my own child go hungry?"

But the youth persisted and finally that *brahmin* took the other portion and gave it to the guest as well. And as before, the guest gulped it down.

"Oh my," thought the *brahmin*. "He is still looking for more."

And then his daughter-in-law persuaded him to give away her share too.

Said the *brahmin*, "Here Sir, won't you have some more?"

"No," replied the guest. "That is quite sufficient. You have passed the examination. I am pleased with all of you. You are prepared to sacrifice your lives for your *dharma*. Hunger even invades the thoughts of righteous men. Therefore, he who conquers his hunger, has won himself a place in heaven."

"Your sacrifice has impressed even the Gods. Moving beyond the necessities of this physical body, you have been true to your virtue, true to the righteousness of your *dharma*. Now come with me and live as one in *dharma* amongst the Gods."

"Ah," thought the *brahmin*, "He is a *deva*, a divine being from heaven."

Instantly a heavenly chariot descended, and the *deva* took the *brahmin* and his family up into the heavens.

I was a witness to all those wondrous happenings. As they left that place where the *brahmin* had lived with his family, I entered the room where he had served his guest. There, on the floor, I found a scattering of barley flour. Much to my astonishment, when I touched it with my body, one half of my body became golden.

Since that time every place where there has been a sacrifice conducted, I have taken it as my sacred duty to visit, and I have rolled over the grounds of several sacrificial areas in the hopes of turning the other half of my body into gold as well.

But as yet I have had no success.

To find men who can perform such a sacrifice is truly a difficult task. Great indeed was that *brahmin's* sacrifice.

Narad and Vishnu: The Farmer is My Devotee

Narad Muni was a great devotee. He used to sing God's name twenty-four hours a day. One time he fell into egotism, thinking: "I must certainly be God's greatest devotee. I am singing His name twenty-four hours a day."

Narad asked Vishnu, "Oh Lord, am I not your greatest devotee? Do you have any other devotee who sings your name as much as I do?"

Then Vishnu, the Lord of Universal Consciousness, replied, "No, you are not my greatest devotee. Come with me to the earth, and I will show you who my greatest devotee is."

When Vishnu and Narad went to the earth, they came to a farmer's house. The farmer got up in the morning and said, "Oh Vishnu," picked up his plow and went out to his field. He labored all the day long, and at evening went home, took his meal, said, "Oh Vishnu," and went to sleep.

Narad was astounded when he saw the behavior of the Lord's greatest devotee. "What kind of devotion is that?" thought Narad. "He said God's name once and then worked all day, and he said it again and slept all night."

Then Vishnu said, "Narad, walk around this field while carrying this glass full of milk. Make sure not to spill even one drop. If one drop spills, I won't drink it."

Then very carefully, very slowly, Narad began to walk around the field. Carefully watching his steps, he walked around the field. After some time he returned and said, "Here is your milk, Lord."

Vishnu asked, "Did you spill any?"

"No, Lord."

"How many times did you say my name?"

"Well, Lord, I was concentrating on the milk to be sure that I didn't spill any."

"How many times?"

"I didn't say your name at all."

"You mean that you were carrying one glass of milk around a field and you couldn't say my name once, while that farmer who is taking care of a wife and family and is performing my work in the world managed to say it twice! That is why he is my greatest devotee!"

The Sadhu Can Kill an Elephant

There was once a *sadhu* with great powers of attainment, because of which he was infatuated by egotism. The *sadhu* was a good man, and he performed his discipline with regularity, but still his ego persisted.

One day God decided to test him, and came to him in disguise. Approaching with great respect he said, "Oh Great Learned One, I have heard of your great attainments."

The *sadhu* welcomed him, and gave him a place to sit down.

At that time an elephant came walking down the path.

Then God said to the *sadhu*, "Do you think you have sufficient attainment to kill that elephant?"

The *sadhu* replied, "Certainly that can be performed," whereupon he took some dust, recited a mantra, and threw it at the elephant. Immediately the animal fell to the ground dead.

God began to laugh. "What incredible powers you have," he said. "You killed the elephant instantly!"

Then he thought a little while and asked, "Can you bring that elephant back to life?"

"Certainly I can," replied the *sadhu*. Then he took another hand full of dust, repeated a mantra and threw it at the ele-

phant. Immediately the elephant rose up as full of life as
before.

Then God said, "Oh what powers you have! Now you
please explain to me: you caused the elephant to die and you
caused the elephant to live. What effect has this had on your
life? Did you rise in spiritual knowledge as a consequence?
Did you realize the ultimate divinity?"

So saying, God became invisible. Surrender the ego so that
we can recognize God when He comes, rather than passing our
time trying to manipulate His creation.

Swami Purnananda Digambar's Renunciation

Swami Purnananda Digambar was such a great renunciate.
In all the world he had only two possessions: the simple cloth
which he wore about his loins, and a small *kamandelu* or begging bowl which traditionally every monk will carry.

Now, as he sat in the town square, discoursing with the citizens of Kanauja, everyone was amazed at the subtlety of his
wisdom, and the impeccable logic with which he presented his
ideals of truth and religious philosophy. He had such an aura
of light about him, and even the most earnest sceptic could not
help but to have tears in his eyes because of the stirring inspiration of this great Swami's words.

When Swamiji had finished his discourse, the good citizens stood in awe of his intellectual capabilities, and with one
accord they decided, "This is the man who should govern us.
There is no more fit candidate to be our king, than this man of
tremendous learning, whose wisdom, logic and wit combine to
inspire and instruct in every field of life. Moreover, he is a
renunciate of the highest standards, and our people will never
have to worry about trying to satiate the unfulfilled desires of
a tyrant king. This is our leader! This is the king for us!"

With one voice the people lifted the Swami upon their

shoulders, and placed him squarely on a throne in a palace. Then Swami Purnananda Digambar began to issue laws for the conduct of the population, and orders for their enforcement, and the entire kingdom began to live in harmony and joy. During the reign of that Swami everyone used to love to cooperate with his neighbor, and people rarely had occasion to speak a cross word. Farmers harvested abundance, merchants made a fair profit for their goods, and peace and prosperity was enjoyed by all.

The king maintained his ascetic ways, continued to wear his one loin cloth and to eat his frugal vegetarian meals from his begging bowl, even though he was lord of a most prosperous nation. This made him the object of even greater love and devotion by his people. The subjects looked up to him as to a father, and following his ways, no one in the kingdom spoke a lie or cheated, or intentionally caused harm to another. The Swami was the ideal king.

One day some of the people came to the king with the news that soldiers of another king's army were approaching the boundaries of Kanauja. "What shall we do?"

The king thought for a moment and replied, "Let us meditate."

Some time later the citizens returned and told, "That army has crossed over our territory and is approaching the city gates. What shall we do?"

The king thought for a moment and replied, "Meditate."

After a little more time the citizens came again and said, "Your Highness, that army is approaching the palace gates. What shall we do?"

The king thought for a moment and replied, "Meditate."

After a little more time the citizens came again and said, "Your Highness, that army has entered the palace. What shall we do?"

The king thought for a moment and replied, "Meditate."

After a little more time the citizens came again and said, "Your Highness, that army is about to enter your room. What shall we do?"

Then the king, that great renunciate Swami, said to his beloved subjects, "Now, my children, I shall demonstrate to you the powers of renunciation."

After saying that, he stood up, took up his begging bowl, and walked out of the palace, never to be seen again.

You Can't Take a Sewing Needle to Heaven

Since as long as she could remember, every day at Mina's house, ten monks were invited to partake at the noon meal. This was a tradition in her family for so many generations, which her father continued meticulously, and Mina could never recall a day when the guests were not received or when the blessings were not given.

On her wedding day it was no surprise to her, that along with all the other blessings which her family gave to her, came the admonishment of her father to continue this same tradition.

"My child," he said. "No matter what your status comes to be, with whatever capacity you have, please do not ignore to take the blessings of holy ones striving in the path of divinity. My child, practice generosity, be open-handed, and God will see that you dwell with increase.

"If ever, for any reason, you are not able to feed or share with others, come to me and I will provide, but do not neglect this tradition of our family."

Now in her new home, every day Mina invited ten spiritual aspirants to lunch. With what joy she prepared the dishes, and offered them at her altar of divinity, chanting the sacred texts which she had learned and practiced. And every day when her meditation was complete, she set the places and bid the monks come to take their seats for the noon-time meal. Every day they blessed her, and she dwelt with such contentment.

One day her husband came home at noon, and was so surprised to see the spectacle. "What is this!" he stammered. "All day long I work long hours under the stress of economic pressure, trying to manage my store efficiently so that we can enjoy a better standard of living. And without my knowledge, you are regularly feeding all of these no good monks who are making no contribution to society whatsoever! What is this? You have got to stop squandering my hard earned money! This nonsense has got to stop!"

Mina was so sorry to receive the rebuke from her husband. She went to her father's house, and explained to him the situation. "Oh Mina, don't be sad. I will give you food with which you can feed the poor. Then your husband will have nothing to get angry about. But do not neglect our tradition."

Now regularly her father sent over all the ingredients for Mina to prepare in her offerings, and every day Mina continued the practice of inviting the holy men of God. Again, on another day her husband came home to see the same practice continuing in his house, and this time his anger was without control.

"You disobeyed my order!" he scolded. "Still you are feeding these worthless beings! This practice has got to stop!"

"But," protested Mina, "this food was not purchased from your earnings. It is a gift from my father's house, to help me maintain my family tradition with my vow of generosity."

"I don't care where it came from!" shouted the husband. "I can't stand to see where it is going! These monks have retired from the world to contemplate God. Let God take care of them — not me! I don't want this practice to continue in my house! You can feed them today, as the food is already prepared, but from tomorrow the invitations will cease!"

Mina was so sad as she served the food to the monks that day, and all the monks asked her the cause of her sorrow. Mina explained that her husband had forbidden her to feed the holy men any longer, and that today would be their last meal.

One of the old monks looked at her with a gleam in his eye, and requested, "Are you sad because you can't give us food any longer?"

"Yes," replied Mina.

"Then we shall secure permission for your generosity to continue," said the old monk. "I will take care of everything."

That afternoon the old monk went and sat outside the husband's shop. He just sat there reciting his rosary.

"What is that old monk doing outside my store?" thought Mina's husband. "Certainly he is going to ask me for some alms, worthless creatures."

He tried not to pay any more attention, but every now and then he glanced out the window to see that the monk hadn't moved. Now it was time to close the store, and that same monk was still sitting there in the same place.

"Well," he thought. "If I am quick enough, maybe I can lock the door and move on, before he has a chance to talk to me."

He slipped through the door, quickly turned the key and started to move off at a fast pace.

"Young man," called the old monk.

Caught.

"How would you like to earn enough merit to go to heaven and to dwell there for a life time?" he enquired.

"Sure, I would," the husband responded.

"I was just sitting here in meditation, when I received a message from the Gods in heaven. They have one errand for you, which, if you complete it efficiently, they promise you a life time of heavenly happiness."

"What is it?"

"Do you know Rakesh the Tailor, who lives just up the street?"

"Yeah, sure I know Rakesh."

"Well, Rakesh is dying at this very moment. And the Gods in heaven have some work for him. If you will deliver the message, they will give to you the blessing of a life time full of happiness."

"That's crazy! I just saw Rakesh yesterday, and he was fine. You are surely telling me stories."

"Of course you will want to verify what I'm saying," replied the old monk. "Sure, go see for yourself the state of Rakesh's health. And when you see him, tell him that the tailor in heaven is sewing some clothes for the Gods, and he needs a number twelve sized needle. Just that. Tell him to take a number twelve sized needle with him to heaven, and you will receive a life time full of happiness."

"What nonsense," muttered Mina's husband as he walked off in a huff towards the end of the street. But as he reached the end of the block he paused for a moment in front of Rakesh's house. He heard the sound of wailing coming from within, and when he entered into the home he saw all of the family members gathered about in sorrow, while Rakesh lay on his death bed, getting ready to leave his body.

"Rakesh, Rakesh!" he called. "What happened to you?"

Very slowly Rakesh responded, "Now I see that each of us has a time and a purpose which only God can understand. Yesterday I was in the best of health, and now I am preparing to meet my Maker."

"It's true," thought Mina's husband. "Everything that the old monk said, it's all true..."

"Rakesh," he said. "You've got to do a favor for me. When

you die, would you please take a number twelve sized sewing needle to the tailor in heaven. He is preparing some clothes and this old monk got the message in his meditation that he needs the needle. Will you do that for me, please?"

"Are you crazy?" replied Rakesh. "When I go, all of this is going to stay here. I can't take anything with me. Only my *karma* is going with me, the actions I performed while I was on earth. Everything else is going to stay here. I can't even take a sewing needle to heaven!"

Mina was so happy that night when her husband came home and told her, "Mina, every day I want that you will not feed only ten monks, but you must feed fifteen! We must always remember it is by the grace of God that we are able to enjoy all of this, and to share with those noble souls who remind us who we really are and what we are doing here. From today we will always practice generosity in this family."

The Curse of Shiva

One day Shiva and Parvati went to visit some of their devotees. They went to the house of a very rich man, who was very much engaged in counting his money. When he looked up to see Shiva and Parvati, he said, "Oh, hello Shiva. Hello Parvati. I am so glad that you came to visit me. I was just counting the day's receipts. Please have a seat on the sofa and I will be with you just as soon as I am finished counting my money."

Shiva and Parvati sat down on the sofa and watched the man count his money. After some time had passed, Parvati said to Shiva, "I am very insulted. Doesn't this man know that everything he has comes from you? I am not going to stand for this kind of behavior from someone who professes to be a devotee. This conduct is offensive. Shiva, I request you to curse him."

Shiva said, "I curse you. Let your wealth increase."

Both Shiva and Parvati stood up and walked away. Parvati looked at Shiva incredulously and asked, "What kind of a curse is that?"

Shiva remained silent while they walked down the road a little bit to the home of a very poor man, who lived in one little hut. The only thing he owned was a cow, with whom he shared his humble accommodations.

When that devotee saw Shiva and Parvati walking up the road towards his house, he ran out of his hut to fall down bowing down at their feet. With such gratitude and appreciation he welcomed them. Then he ran back to his hut and got some milk. He poured the milk over Shiva's feet. He made cheese and sweets. He treated Shiva and Parvati with such love, humility, and pure devotion, and performed their *seva* with the greatest of love.

Parvati said to Shiva. "I am very pleased with the devotion of this devotee. Shiva, please give him a blessing."

Shiva said, "I bless you. Your cow will die."

Shiva and Parvati rose from their seats and left. They were on their way back to their home on Mount Kailasha, when Parvati asked of Shiva, "Shiva, I don't understand. I asked you to curse the rich devotee, and you said, 'Your wealth will increase.' I asked you to bless the poor devotee, and you said, 'Your cow will die.' What kind of justice is this?"

Shiva replied, "The rich devotee was busy with his wealth, so that he didn't have time to pay attention to others, not even to you and me. When you asked me to curse him, I gave him more wealth so he has even less time to think about God. You asked me to bless the poor devotee, and I took away his cow. He lost the last remaining attachment he had to this world. And see, he is coming along with us right now on the path to heaven."

The Sadhu and the Loin Cloth

There was once a *sadhu* who had only one loin cloth. His guru had told him, "Don't worry about your material possessions, just perform your spiritual discipline."

Everyday the *sadhu* would take a bath in the river and he would hang his loin cloth up in a tree to dry. Then he would sit down beneath the tree and practice his meditation.

One day when he finished his meditation, he got up to put on his loin cloth, but he found that some mice had chewed the cloth to shreds. He thought this was truly a difficult situation and he wondered what to do. So he went to the town and asked the people, "Could you please give me another piece of cloth to wear. The mice have chewed mine to shreds."

The village people said, "Look, we can't give you another piece of cloth every day. You must do something to protect your possessions from the forces of nature."

The *sadhu* said, "What should I do? I bathe in the river, and hang my cloth on the tree to dry. Then I sit for my worship. It was the mice that came and destroyed it."

The village people said, "Well then get a cat."

So the *sadhu* got a cat. He took the cat back with him to his tree, and the next morning he had his bath and put his cloth up in the tree to dry. Then he sat down at the foot of the tree to meditate. The cat came over to him, sat in his lap, and began to purr. "Meow. Meow. Please give me some milk. I am hungry."

The *sadhu* wondered where would he get some milk. So he went to the village and went from door to door and requested, "Would you please give me some milk for my cat?"

The village people said, "We can't give you milk everyday. Once in awhile is okay, but your cat will require milk every day. We can't accept the responsibility for your cat everyday."

The *sadhu* asked, "What should I do? I was meditating

peacefully on the bank of the river. But then I needed the cat to protect my one simple loin cloth from the mice. And now I need milk to feed the cat."

The village people said, "Get a cow."

So the *sadhu* got a cow, and brought the cow back to his tree.

The next morning the cow said, "I am hungry. Would you get me some grass?" The *sadhu* looked all around the river bank, but all he saw were a few trees and stones and sand.

He went back to the village and said, "People of the village, please give me some grass."

The village people said, "Look, we can't give you grass everyday. We go out and cut the grass for our cows. How can we give you grass everyday? You will sit on the bank of the river and meditate, while your cow will eat our grass? After all, the cow will give forth milk to feed your cat, to protect your loin cloth from the mice that are bothering you, isn't it?"

The *sadhu* said, "Well then, what should I do?"

The people said, "Get a boy to tend the cow."

The next day when the *sadhu* sat down to meditate, the boy he had hired came to him and said, "Isn't someone going to feed me? I am here to cut grass for your cow. Who is going to feed me?"

The *sadhu* asked, "Who will feed you?"

"Get a wife," the boy replied.

Some years later the man's guru came back in search of his disciple. Very near to the tree where the *sadhu* had meditated was a large mansion with servants caring for the crops in the fields and for all of the animals.

The guru asked one of the servants, "What happened to the *sadhu* who used to sit under this tree?"

The servant said, "Guruji, I don't know. I never saw a *sadhu*. I have been working here for several years now. I am an employee."

The guru said, "Where is the master of the house?"

The servant went and got the master of the house, whereupon the *sadhu* came running outside and bowing down said, "Guruji, it was all because of my loin cloth."

The Pundit and the Milkmaid

Krishna Priya was so happy when she heard that a new pundit had come to stay in the temple. She looked forward to the opportunity to learn about philosophy from such an educated man, someone who could expound on the scriptures from personal experience, who knew the spirit along with the letter of the law.

Soon after she got this news, a servant from the temple came to her house and asked her to provide milk to the temple daily for the pundit's worship. Krishna Priya was overjoyed at the potential to perform such an honored service and to have a steady customer for her earning some money.

The servant said, "This pundit is an extremely punctual individual. Please do not be late. Everyday he wants to take milk with his tea before he sits, and milk for the *puja*, and you, Krishna Priya, will be responsible."

Krishna Priya said, "I promise I will be there on time. He won't be delayed because of me."

The next morning Krishna Priya took the milk in a container very, very carefully, and walked down to the bank of the river. She went to the boatman and said, "Boatman, please ferry me across the river. I am bringing milk for the pundit's worship."

The boatman said, "Oh Krishna Priya, you will have to wait just a little bit. I am mending the sail on my boat and we won't be able to leave until my work is finished. You will just have to wait a little bit more."

Krishna Priya was very disturbed because the boatman was taking so much time and it was getting late. Finally the sail was mended and Krishna Priya got in the boat and the boatman took her across the river.

The pundit was pacing back and forth in front of the temple. "Krishna Priya," he said. "You were told that the milk was to be delivered to me in time for the worship. Now it is mid-morning, and the time for worship has passed. I am delayed because of you, and if you can't do a better job of being punctual, then I will have to find someone else to bring me my milk."

"Please give me another chance," Krishna Priya begged. "It was because of the boatman's sail. He was mending his sail and he told me that he couldn't take me across the river until he was done."

"All right young lady, you come again tomorrow. But be on time!"

The next morning Krishna Priya woke up long before the dawn. She milked her cow, and put the milk into her container and went down to the river. The boatman was not there. When the sun came up over the horizon, she saw the boatman on the other side of the river. She yelled, "Boatman, please come here. I need a ride across the river."

The boatman yelled back, "Krishna Priya, some passengers are just coming, and as soon as they get in the boat, I will come and get you. They are on their way right now. I can see them walking towards me a little distance away."

Krishna Priya was pacing up and down on her side of the river wondering what the pundit was going to say. She thought, "I am going to be late again, and I'm going to get in trouble."

Finally the boatman arrived, and Krishna Priya scurried onto the boat and cried, "Hurry Boatman! Take me across the river!"

When she reached the temple, the pundit was standing outside waiting and he was so angry. "I told you, young lady, don't be late. This is not a joke. This is the worship of God you are detaining! Can't you take any sense of responsibility? If you are late one more time, that is it!"

Krishna Priya was so sad. She needed the money, and she wanted so much to have the opportunity to serve God.

By the next morning she had hardly slept at all. She milked her cow long before the sun rose and put the milk in the container. She went down to the river and waited for the boatman. The sun rose and she was still waiting for the boatman. "Where did the boatman go? What happened to the boatman?" she thought.

Some other people came and they were also waiting for the boatman. In fact, they too were going to the temple, because the pundit was giving an important lecture this morning.

Finally the boatman arrived and said, "I got another fare to the next town and had to take the passengers to their destination. That is my job. Come. I will take you all across."

When Krishna Priya arrived at the temple, the pundit was already giving his discourse. In the discourse he said, "With the help of the name of God you can cross this ocean of world."

This discourse kindled the fire of devotion within Krishna Priya. When the pundit was finished with his discourse, Krishna Priya went up to him and said, "Punditji, here is your milk. I know I am late, but I have found the solution to this problem, and I won't be late again. Just give me one more chance."

The pundit said, "You have come late three times in a row. You told me you would be on time from the beginning, and three days in a row you have been late. What solution could you have possibly found?"

"Don't worry, Punditji, you will see tomorrow morning that I will be here right on time."

"Okay young lady, we will see tomorrow."

That night Krishna Priya slept so soundly. She woke up at a very leisurely time and she went with the grace of God to milk her cow. She put the milk in the container, walked down to the river and said the name of God, "Rama, Rama, Rama." And she walked right across the river.

At the appointed time she went to the pundit's door and knocked. She said, "Punditji, here is your milk. Right on time."

The pundit asked, "How did you get here so soon? The boat hasn't even come yet."

"Punditji, it was your grace that illuminated my ignorance. You, yourself, told me the solution to my problem, and I will be forever grateful to you for this wisdom. You told the entire congregation in the temple, 'With the help of the name of God you can cross this ocean of world.' I thought if the name of God can take you across the ocean of the whole wide world, then why can't I cross this little old river? So I sang the name of God, and I walked across the river."

The pundit said, "What do you mean that you walked across the river?"

She said, "Just what you told me to do, Punditji. I bow to you and I thank you so much for illuminating me in my time of doubt."

The pundit asked, "Did you actually walk across the river?"

Krishna Priya replied, "Yes, Sir."

The pundit said, "Let me see you do this."

Krishna Priya said, "Sure, Punditji. Come down to the river with me."

The two of them went down to the river and Krishna Priya said, "Rama, Rama, Rama." And she walked right out into the center of the river. Then she said, "Come on in, Punditji."

The pundit took one step and the water came up to his ankle.

"Take another step," Krishna Priya called.

He took another step and the water came up to his knees, and he pulled up his cloth.

Krishna Priya asked "Why aren't you singing the name of God instead of thinking about your cloth? How can you hope to cross the ocean of the world while thinking about your personal attachments?"

The Sadhu and the Ashura and the Fruits of their Karma

Swami Ramananda Giri was walking in the forest. He came to a clearing in the forest, whereupon he stepped on a thorn.

"Ouch!" he cried as the thorn entered into his flesh.

Swamiji went to sit underneath a tree and began to pull on the thorn to extract it from his foot. While he was sitting there doctoring his wound, an *ashura* came walking along the same path. He was a very devious man, constantly engaged in stealing and lying. When he reached exactly the same spot in the path, he looked down and found one coin. He picked it up, put it in his pocket, and very happily walked off.

Swamiji, befuddled by this turn of events, got up and walked to his Guru's ashram. "Guruji," he asked. "What is the cause of this circumstance? I have been performing severe *tapasya* for several years, purifying myself and making a contribution to society. I have been living my life as an example of *dharma* to all who would see. That *ashura* has been robbing, cheating, and squandering away the wealth of this nation with the utmost selfishness, trying to get whatever he could for himself. Why is it that I got a thorn and he got a coin?"

The guru prepared a horoscope. He said, "Swami, it says here in your horoscope that because of the astrological configuration of the stars, today you were supposed to be hanged. But because of your good *karma* and all of the good deeds you performed, you escaped with the prick of a thorn. It says according to the horoscope of that *ashura*, today he was supposed to have become a king. But because of his evil selfishness and his bad *karma*, he only got one coin. Therefore, be content with the knowledge that you will get the fruit of your *karma*."

The Meditating Swami and the Young Man in Love

Swami Alokanandaji was so enamored of his spiritual practices that he would sit down anywhere, wherever he was, whenever the time for worship arrived. One day he sat down along the path of the road and began to meditate.

Along the road came a young man deeply engrossed in day-dreaming about the girl with whom he was in love. He was totally oblivious to any other pedestrians, stragglers, or any other obstructions that may be in the way of his path. As the young man came dancing down the path, he inadvertently stepped upon the meditating Swami.

The young man was in such a degree of concentration on his beloved, that he was unaware that he had even stepped upon the meditating Swami, and merely continued on his way.

The Swami called to him from his meditation posture, "Hey, young man! I am a meditating Swami, and you have just stepped upon me! Is there any greater disrespect that you can show?"

The young man turned around quite startled, and said, "Swamiji, I am a young man intoxicated with the love of my beloved, while you are a meditating Swami. Why is it that I was not aware of you, so much as you are aware of me? If you had as much devotion to your meditation as I have towards mine, then you would have probably been enlightened already!"

But I Didn't Tell You Not to Hiss

There was once a very fearful snake who lived at the foot of a large banyan tree. The branches of this tree reached up toward the sun and created an umbrella that covered the entire forest floor. This cobra lived under the tree and he was extremely fierce. He was feared by all of the members of the nearby village. In fact, he had a reputation for being downright nasty and all of the village people warned everyone, "Don't go near that tree. If you are walking through the forest, take a long detour and go around the tree. Don't be attacked by that snake. Be weary of that snake!"

One day a *sadhu* came to the edge of the forest and all of the village people said, "*Sadhu Baba*, please don't go by this route. It will take you by the tree where you will meet that ferocious snake. That cobra has a habit of biting everyone that comes near and injecting anyone with poison without any mercy. He is extremely ferocious.

The *sadhu* said, "People be fearless. I know a mantra and when the snake hears my mantra, he will become very sweet and peaceful."

The *sadhu* walked into the forest and approached the tree where the snake was residing. The snake reared his head and opened his hood and began to hiss and spit. The *sadhu* began to recite the mantra. When the snake heard that mantra, he suddenly felt some intuitive power in his heart and sat down. The *sadhu* came up to him and said, "Oh King of Snakes, why is it that you are terrorizing these people? Can't you live in peace?

The various elements of this world all comprise a harmony. All of the elements of nature work together. They all live together, work together, and support each other. By antagonizing others you will never become part of this universal harmony of nature. Now I am going to teach you a mantra. I want you to learn this mantra and make its recitation until the mantra becomes the essence of your being."

The cobra learned the mantra and began to recite it. The *sadhu* went off and some months went by. The people of the nearby village said, "What happened? We have not heard anything from that king cobra snake in so long. He had been terrorizing the entire neighborhood and now he is silent. We wonder what happened to him. What did that *sadhu* do to him?"

Some of the adventurous young men of the village went off to explore the area near the tree where the snake used to reside. They saw the snake sitting on a rock reciting his mantra. The snake was reciting the mantra and he was so much absorbed into the mantra that he gave blessings of peace and love to everyone.

The young boys said, "Wow! What change has transpired in the life of that snake? He used to bite everyone and inject them with poison and his venom would be thrust into people, and they would become ill and die from his ferocious nature. Now he has become so passive. He just sits there doing *japa*, reciting his rosary."

Some boys saw the snake and remembering his old nature, they threw stones at him. Some boys grabbed sticks and beat the snake, so that the snake crawled back into his hole almost devoid of consciousness.

Many years passed when the *sadhu* came back to that forest. He asked the people of the village, "Do you remember that snake who lived by the big banyan tree? Whatever happened to him?"

The people replied, "Oh, he died a long time ago. He was so ferocious that some of the boys hit him with sticks and threw stones at him. They beat him until he died."

The *sadhu* said, "I don't believe that he would have died without realizing the fullest experience of the mantra I taught him."

The *sadhu* went into the forest and found the tree. At the base of the tree there was a little hole. Inside the hole was the king cobra snake. He had withered away, dried up, and shriveled up so that he was very thin and weak. When the snake heard his guru's voice outside, he came crawling out from his hole.

The teacher said, "Hey, Mr. Snake, what happened to you? You were so fit and now you are so weak."

The snake said, "Oh, Guruji, I practiced the mantra that you taught to me, and I recollected all of the great teachings of wisdom that you shared with me. I really took it to heart and realized that I had to change my nature. I resolved not to bite, cause injury, or kill anyone anymore. Those boys did not know how I had changed my behavior. They were not at fault because they remembered me as the ferocious snake. They came and attacked me with stones and beat me with sticks. I didn't do anything to retaliate because I was practicing nonviolence. I just went back into my little hole. I even became a vegetarian, and came out once in a while to eat dry leaves or whatever else I could find. I stopped all of my violent actions. You see this is the result. I have no anger toward those children. They didn't know what they were doing."

The *sadhu* looked at his disciple and said, "Snake, certainly I told you to abjure and abstain from violence, and change your nature so you don't kill innocent beings, harm others, or create division in this world. But I never told you not to hiss! If you would hiss, you would frighten people away and you would be safe to live your life in peace."

He Knew He Was the Brother of God

Kalyani had only one young son whose name was Rohit, named after the Sun. Just the two of them lived together in a little thatched hut at the edge of the forest. After some years, Rohit grew up into a fine young boy and Kalyani said, "Rohit, it is time for you to go to school. The school lies at the end of the path just on the other side of the forest."

Rohit said, "Mother, I have never been on the path through the forest by myself. The forest looks so dark. There is not much sunlight that shines there and it is cold and scary. I don't want to go to school through the forest on the path by myself."

Kalyani said, "Well, your brother lives in the forest. His name is Madhusudana. If you call his name, "Madhusudana," he will walk with you through the forest to school."

Rohit said, "I didn't know that I had a brother named Madhusudana."

His mother said, "Yes, you do. Now here is your lunch and your books. Have a good day at school."

Rohit walked into the forest, and after a little time, the forest became dark and he got scared. He said, "It is so dark and cold in here. I don't know if I am going to get to the end of this path. What will happen if I get lost? My mom told me that if I got scared to call my older brother, "Madhusudana."

"Hey Madhusudana! Madhusudana!" Rohit began to call. Suddenly Madhusudana appeared. He was a beautiful young boy playing his flute. He was blue all over, with peacock feathers in his hair.

"Hello, Rohit," he said. "Come with me. I will walk with you through the forest up to the school." And he did. He took his little brother right through the forest to the school.

After school, when Rohit was walking home through the

forest, he got scared again.

He called, "Madhusudana! Madhusudana!"

His brother Madhusudana appeared from behind a tree and walked with him all of the way home. In this way everyday Rohit used to walk to school with his older brother Madhusudana.

One day the teacher at the school said, "Class, we are going to have a feast tomorrow and I would like everyone to bring some food for the feast." He went around the classroom and assigned one dish to each of the children. He came to Rohit and said, "Rohit, I would like for you to provide the yogurt."

That night Rohit went home to his mother and said, "Mother, there is going to be a festival in the school tomorrow, and we are going to have a feast. The teacher wants me to bring the yogurt."

His mother said, "Oh, my son, where will I get so much yogurt to feed the whole school? You see that I am alone. I have to work all day long. We don't have the money to purchase it. Where can I get that much yogurt? Why don't you ask your older brother Madhusudana when you go to school tomorrow. Ask him to help you provide the yogurt."

Rohit was on his way to school when he called, "Madhusudana! Madhusudana!" And Madhusudana appeared to him and walked with him to school. As they were walking through the forest, Rohit said, "Madhusudana, the teacher asked me to bring yogurt for the feast at the school today. Mom told me to ask you how to provide it."

"Okay," replied Madhusudana. "Here is a cup of yogurt for you." He gave Rohit a cup full of yogurt, and again Madhusudana said, "Take this yogurt and offer it at your school."

Rohit was very happy. He brought his cup of yogurt to the

teacher and the teacher said, "You foolish child, we have so many students in this school. You only brought one cup of yogurt. What kind of a feast is this? This is not enough for even one or two students. You have ruined the whole feast!" He put the yogurt aside and apportioned all of the other things to the students.

At the end of the feast, Rohit was feeling very badly because he was responsible for ruining the whole feast by not bringing enough yogurt. The teacher saw the boy sulking in a corner and said, "Oh well, let's give everyone a little spoonful of your yogurt, and see how far it goes. We will give everybody a little taste of your yogurt."

The teacher took the little cup of yogurt and started to portion it out. But no matter how much he took out from the pot, the pot was always full. He went around the classroom giving everyone a full portion of yogurt, and yet there was still more in the pot.

"Where did you get this yogurt?" the teacher asked.

"I asked my mother for the yogurt, but she said that we do not have enough yogurt to feed the whole class. She told me to ask my older brother, Madhusudana," came Rohit's reply.

The teacher said, "Wait a minute, Rohit! You don't have an older brother. I have been teaching at this school for over 20 years, and I have never seen your older brother."

Rohit replied, "I do too have a brother! His name is Madhusudana. He lives in the forest. He walks with me to school everyday and he walks me home. He gave me this yogurt."

"What stories are you telling me? This isn't a true story. You show your older brother to me and then I will believe you."

Rohit said, "I am not making this story up. You come with me into the forest and you will meet my older brother,

Madhusudana."

The teacher followed Rohit into the forest. After some time of walking in the forest, Rohit called, "Madhusudana! Madhusudana! Please come to me. My teacher doesn't believe that I have an older brother!"

Then from behind the tree there were a few notes of the flute heard. And then a few more notes were heard. Then came a voice from behind the tree, "Your teacher is not fit to see me. He doesn't have the eyes of faith by which I am seen. But just so that he believes you, I will let him hear the sound of my flute."

The Sadhu Who Would Ask the King for Wealth

Purnananda Giri was a great renunciate. He sat at the foot of a tree performing his *sadhana* and *tapas* with regularity, sincerity, and pure devotion. Over the years countless people came to take darshana of this great saint. Purnananda Giri thought, "I am a poor man and I have nothing to give these people. I shall go to the king and ask him for assistance."

The next morning he went to the king's palace and said to the guard, "Captain of the Guard, I would like to see the king."

The Captain of the Guard said, "The king is in his temple praying right now. But seeing that you are such a great saint and highly respected person, go right in. Sit down and wait until the king is done with his prayer. Certainly the king will grant the wish of any devotee he meets when he rises from his worship."

Purnananda Giri went into the temple and he saw the king sitting before the altar with outstretched arms saying, "Lord, please give me wealth so that I can take care of all of the people of my kingdom."

When Purnananda Giri heard this prayer, he looked deeply within his own self and stood up. He began to walk out. The king turned around from his worship and motioned to the *sadhu* to sit down. Purnananda again resumed his seat.

The king again with outstretched arms said, "Lord, please give me wealth with which I can entertain all of the people of my kingdom."

Hearing this prayer, the *sadhu* again rose and began to walk out. Once again the king turned around and looked at him with curiosity, then motioned for him to sit down. Once again the *sadhu* sat down.

For the third time the king with outstretched hands said, "Lord, give me wealth."

Then the king bowed down at the altar. When he rose he saw the *sadhu* by the door ready to walk out. He called, "*Sadhu Baba*, you must have come here with some special desire in your mind. What is it that you want? Why do you keep walking out?"

Swami Purnananda Giri turned to the king and said, "Your Highness, I am a poor *sadhu* and I do my meditation at the foot of a tree. Everyday numbers of people come to visit me, and I have no wealth with which to take care of them. Therefore, I thought I would come to the king and ask Your Highness if you would be so kind as to give me some wealth with which to serve the people that come to visit me."

The king said, "Well, why were you walking out before you made the request?"

The Swami replied, "Your Highness, I saw that you, yourself, were in want. You, too, were beseeching a higher power to give you wealth with which to serve. Therefore, I thought it would be more appropriate for me to take my prayer directly to God instead of disturbing the king."

The King's Barber and the Seven Jars of Gold

The King's barber was the happiest of men. He was always singing and full of delight. He was always full of joy and inspiration. Everyday he came to shave the King.

One day when he was walking in route to the King's palace, he heard a voice call out from behind a tree. "Barber, would you like to have seven jars full of gold?"

The barber said, "Of course, I would like to have seven jars full of gold."

The voice said, "Go home and they will be there waiting for you."

The barber ran towards his village, and when he got near to his home his wife came running outside, "Husband, husband, you will never believe what happened," she called.

"What happened?" asked the husband.

"I was digging in the garden and my spade hit something solid and I found ..."

The barber interrupted her, "You found seven jars full of gold."

"How did you know?"

"The voice said that it would be so. Quickly let me see the seven jars of gold!"

The husband and wife together brought the seven jars into their humble cottage. One by one they opened the lids and peered inside. They opened up the lid of the first jar and they saw that it was full of gold. They opened up the lid of the second jar and it was full of gold. It was the same with the third, forth, fifth, and sixth jars. Much to the couple's delight, the jars were all filled with gold!

The barber opened up the lid of the seventh jar, but it was only half full. The barber turned to his wife and said, "This can't be."

The voice said, "Seven jars filled with gold. There are only six and a half."

The barber said, "Wife, do you have any gold?"

She said, "Yes, dear, I have the golden ornaments that were presented to me on my wedding day."

The barber said, "Bring them here, and we will put them in the jar to see if we can fill it up. The wife brought all of her golden ornaments and watched with dismay as her husband put all of the jewelry into the jar. But the jar still wasn't full.

The husband said, "Wife, do we have any other gold, money, or coins?"

The wife said, "Yes, husband, we have our life savings in the bank."

The husband said, "Go bring all of the gold from the bank. I won't be content until the seventh jar is full."

So the wife went off to the bank and returned shortly with a bag of gold containing all of their life savings. The husband put all of that gold into the jar. And yet the jar was not full.

The next day the husband was very pensively beset with thought as he walked into the palace to shave the King. The King said, "Oh, my barber has come! He is the happiest man in the world. Barber, why aren't you smiling today?"

The barber said, "Oh, King, I have been working for you for many years. You have always been generous and kind. But today I am beset with some financial problems. Therefore, I am not so happy today as usual."

The king said, "Prime Minister, double the salary of the barber. Give him double the wages. Will that make you happy?"

"Oh yes, King. I am sure that will relieve my problems."

This day the barber took home double the wages. He put them all into the pot. And yet the pot was not full.

Now he became totally beset with care. He began to fast. He even began to cut down the rations of his family, and he put all that he could save into the jar. And yet the jar was not full.

Some weeks went by in this way, and the barber became very thin. The king was really concerned, "Barber, why do you appear so thin and worried. I doubled your salary as soon as you asked, and we thought that would relieve your problem."

The barber said, "Your Highness, I am still facing those financial difficulties."

"What?" said the king. "When you had half the salary, you did not have any financial difficulties. Now with double the salary, you are experiencing financial difficulties? Did you accept the seven jars of gold from that *yaksha*?"

"How did you know, Your Highness?"

"That *yaksha*, one who inspires greed, offered me those same seven jars of gold, but I knew that the seventh jar was the jar of uncontrolled desire. It can never be filled! You can never fill that jar of desire! Therefore, I did not accept those seven jars of gold. You can see how content I am today. Those jars of gold are the cause of all your problems. Give them back immediately or you will never have any peace!"

The barber was so happy to find the solution to his problem. He ran out from the King's palace and shouted to the *yaksha*, "Take back your seven jars of gold! I do not need your gold! It will never make me happy! "

When he went home, his wife came running out from the house to meet him. "My husband!"

"Don't tell me," interrupted the husband. "The jars of gold have all vanished."

"Yes, my husband, along with all of my golden ornaments, all of our life savings, and all that we had saved and put into the jars these many months. Everything has been given back!"

The Married Monks of Jaipur

Bindugupta was the King of Jaipur. One day he summoned the abbot of the Govinda Temple, which was nearby to his palace estate. "Abbot," he said. "I would like for all of the monks that reside in your ashram to come to my palace to perform worship for me and my family."

The abbot said to the king, "Your Highness, my monks are all renunciates. They don't pray for kings. They pray for God and self realization. They pray for the purity of enlightenment. If you want prayers for the king and the king's family, then go to the temple. Don't give orders for the monks to come to your palace."

The king summoned his prime minister and said, "See the fun. I am the king of this nation, and those *sadhus* are giving me disrespect. How can I have *sadhus* that are so egotistical, they won't even come to the palace when the king summons them? How can I support temples, where the abbot tells me that I have to go to them? What shall we do about this?"

The prime minister asked, "How many monks reside in that ashram?"

"Five thousand monks."

"Well, Your Highness, I propose that we offer the abbot a presentation of five thousand beautiful young ladies, who will serve those wonderful ascetics and make sure that they have no obstructions in their spiritual discipline."

Thinking this to be an excellent idea, the king made presentation of five thousand beautiful young ladies to the monastery, and within a short time that certainly took care of the problem. The monks began to come to the palace regularly, requesting, "Oh King, may I have some alms to celebrate the birth of my son? Oh King, may I have some alms to give my child an education. Oh King, my wife and my family require so many things. Would you please help us out?"

The Businessman and the King

Kalidas Sreshti was one of the greatest business men in Takshashila. He was a very wealthy man and highly respected by the community. Regularly he was seen at the homes of ministers and officials of the King's government.

One day this businessman went into his shop filled with quality merchandise, and he took every item of merchandise from off of the shelf. He went outside and proceeded to distribute all of the articles in his possession to the poor and needy. Next he went to the bank and withdrew all of the sums of money that he had on deposit. And he gave everything away.

Then he went to the office of the Official Keeper of Records and prepared the Deeds of Title to his lands and property. He signed away all of his possessions into the names of the poor.

The whole bazaar was amazed with this information. Every person on every corner was talking about the fact that this very wealthy merchant gave all of his possessions away. Not only did the traders and shopkeepers talk about this, but so also did the King's officials. Even the police and the King's guards and the ministers got hold of this news. Everyone in Takshashila was talking about Kalidas Sreshti and how he gave away everything he possessed.

And there he was sitting on the bank of the river on a large stone reciting the name of God: "Rama, Rama, Rama."

The whole community was amazed by this news. Why would the wealthiest man of the community give up all of his inventory of goods, all of his money and hard earned wealth, property, and everything he possessed, how could he give it away and sit on a large stone at the bank of the river saying, "Rama, Rama, Rama?"

Even the king was curious as to what possessed this man

to make such a tremendous sacrifice. One afternoon the king along with his retinue went to see the *sadhu*, who was sitting on a rock saying the name of God. With folded palms the King said, "Sreshtiji, you were the wealthiest, most dynamic, and successful businessman in our entire community. Why did you give everything away? What did you get for it?"

The businessman turned to the king and said, "Your Highness, I used to be a businessman, practicing fair and honest business in this community. From time to time my work took me to the Tax Collector, the Registrar, and other officials of the kingdom, and with folded palms I requested them to assist me in my work. I went to the ministers and other members of the royal cabinet and even before Your Highness, Yourself. I came to you all on numerous occasions with folded palms requesting your assistance in the various functions I performed.

"Your Highness, I have given up all of my possessions to the poor, and I am sitting here by the bank of the river on this large rock. Now even Your Highness, Himself, along with all of the retinue of ministers and officials, comes with folded palms to pay a visitation to me. What else shall I seek to gain? When the King, Himself, can come to visit me, certainly I have gained all."

The Fisherman's Wife Sleeps at the Florist's Home

Dipta wasn't just an ordinary fisherman's wife. She was a loving, joyous, and efficient helper. Everyday she would take her husband's basket full of fish to the marketplace. She would sit there the whole day until she sold all of the fish to her customers. When she was done, she would clean up her space, and then do the necessary shopping. Finally, she would take the balance of her hard earned money home.

One evening it was rather late when Dipta closed her market stall for the day and finished all of her chores. As she was walking home with her friend, the florist's wife, it started to rain. The friend said, "Dipta, you come to my house. There is no sense in your trying to go home in this stormy, dark and cold rainy night. You will have nothing but difficulties. Spend the night at my house and you can go home in the morning when the storm passes.

That is just what Dipta decided to do. She went to her helpful friend's house. She had such a loving friend, whose husband was a florist, and they had a lovely house which was always full of flowers. In fact, there were flowers everywhere.

Her friend made Dipta a fine meal and then they lay down to sleep.

Dipta tossed and turned from one side to the other. "I wonder why I can't sleep? This is a terrible thing."

She got up and walked around her bed. She looked high and low, but could find no reason why she couldn't sleep. She lay down again and began to toss and turn from one side to the other.

Finally her friend noticed the difficulty that Dipta was having in going to sleep. So she brought her fish basket and put it by her pillow. When Dipta took one scent of that familiar aroma, she was so comfortable that she went right to sleep.

The Salt Water of the Desert

In the distant land of Rajasthan there was a very poor herder who roamed in the barren reaches of the western desert with a few goats. The area was extremely dry, and water was very rare. Every morning he used to collect the dew from off the leaves, let the water condense to form into a small cupful, and that would be his daily ration of water.

One day this poor herder found a well of some salty, brackish water in the middle of the desert. There was no one around for miles. The man was amazed. He had never seen so much water collected in one place. He tasted the water and it was a bit foul, but it was wet and refreshing.

He bathed himself and still there was water. He was so amazed. He said, "This water supply is so wonderful. All of the wonderful things of our existence belong to the king. I better bring a cup of this water to the king, and let him know how wealthy he is. Imagine, in his kingdom there is an abundant well of water like this. As much water as you desire is available.

With that, the poor herder took one cup of water and went off to find the king. It was well into the night when the herder found the king's palace. The Captain of the Guard told the herder to go away and come back in the morning.

When the herder returned first thing in the morning, he said to the Captain of the Guard, "I have brought a cup of water for the king."

The Captain said, "You are crazy. Go away from this door. What does the king need with a cup of water?"

"Really," said the herder. "It came from a well in the desert. There is such an abundance of water, I thought the king should be informed about this wealth."

The Captain of the Guard said, "Wait here. I will show this to the minister." And he carried the cup of water to the minister.

The minister smelled it and said, "Take the man to a waiting room, and we will inform him of the king's decision."

The minister took the cup of water to the king and told him the story. A herder from the desert has brought this cup of water, because he had never seen so much water as is in a well before, and this all belongs to the king.

The king said, "Call the herder."

The minister called the herder.

The king said, "Herder, you are a faithful servant of this nation. You have discovered this abundant source of water and came to offer it to our people. I make you the Official Custodian of the Waters of the Desert, and give you the official responsibility for this well. You guard and nurture that well, and make sure it's waters are not abused, but are shared with equality for all."

Then the king called the Captain of the Guard and secretly ordered, "Escort this man back to his well. But make sure he doesn't see the rivers like the Ganges or Jamuna along the way."

The Wish Yielding Tree and the Lion

There was a tree called the *Kalpavriksha*, the tree which yields the fruit of any wish one may so desire.

One day a young man was wandering through a very hot, desolate plain, when he began to thirst. Over there in the distance he spied a single tree, just one tree in the hot dusty plain. It was so hot and he was so happy to make his way to the foot of that tree. He just wanted to rest a moment in the shade. He had no idea that this was the Kalpavriksha, the tree which yields the fruit of anything one might desire.

He said to himself, "What a pleasure to feel the shade and get the sun off from shining directly on my head. If only I had something to drink, something nice, cool, clear and refreshing."

Suddenly there was a goblet of cool, clear water. So joyously he quenched his thirst.

"This ground is so hard," he thought. "If only there was some cushion for me to sit upon or maybe a bed or couch to stretch out on."

Immediately there was a luscious bed with cushions and pillows. The young man sat down on the bed and reclined against the pillows. He heaved a sigh of relaxation.

Then the young man thought, "I am hungry. I wish I could find a tasty meal."

Instantly he was surrounded by delectable dishes. He ate with such contentment. When he finished his meal, he laid down and thought, "It would be wonderful if a young lady would come and rub my legs. Wouldn't that be comfortable?"

Instantly a young lady appeared and began to press the soles of his feet. He was the happiest of men.

As he lay there in perfect contentment, his mind began to recount the activities of the last few moments of this experience. He thought, "Gee, I wanted some shade and a tree appeared. I wanted a cushion and the couch appeared. I got hungry and the food appeared. I got cramps in my legs and the young lady appeared to rub my feet. What would happen if a lion came?"

Suddenly a lion pounced upon the young man and ate him up.

A Thief Becomes a Sadhu

One night, late in the evening, a thief broke into the palace and went to the king's private chambers. He had the intention of stealing as many of the jewels as he could carry. He tiptoed into the king's boudoir, where all the royal ornaments were on display, and as the thief was about to take the jewels, he heard the king in the next room talking to the queen.

The king said, "I am so tired of searching for a suitable groom for our daughter. I have searched among all of the princes from the neighboring kingdoms, and there is not one suitable among them. Tomorrow I am going to go to the bank of the river, and I am going to find the first *sadhu* that says, "Yes," and have him marry our daughter."

The thief heard this news. He thought, "If I steal all of the king's jewels, it will only last me for a short while, but if I marry the royal princes, I will be fixed for life."

The thief renounced his intention to steal the jewels, and he tiptoed out from the king's apartment empty-handed.

First thing in the morning that thief went down to the bank of the river and took a seat near the other *sadhus*, and began to say the name of God. "Rama, Rama, Rama."

It was mid-morning when the king appeared on the bank of the river along with his ministers. He went to the first *sadhu* and said, "*Sadhu Baba*, will you marry my daughter?"

The *sadhu* said, "No, Your Highness, I am a *sadhu*. Why will I marry your daughter?"

The king went to the second *sadhu* and said, "*Sadhu Baba*, will you marry my daughter?"

The *sadhu* said, "No, Your Highness, I am past the age of marriage and I have no such inclination. I am a *sadhu*."

There on the next rock was the thief in the disguise of a *sadhu*. The king came to the thief and said, "*Sadhu Baba*, will you marry my daughter?"

The *sadhu* thought within himself, "Just by pretending to be a *sadhu*, I have become worthy of such respect, and I am receiving such generosity. What if I really became a *sadhu*?"

Suddenly he heard the words come out of his mouth, "No, Your Highness, I am a *sadhu*, and I have no need of a wife." He rose up from his seat and walked off into the forest. Later he became a great saint.

The Merchant's Devoted Servant

There was a very wealthy merchant who had a very devoted servant. This servant was very much trusted by his master and had great respect for his employer. This servant had full faith that all that the master had attained in life was from the blessings from his guru.

Whenever the master's guru would come as a guest to the employer's home, this servant would volunteer to perform all of the guru's personal services. He would wash his clothes, rub his feet, see about his food, perform the guru's errands.

He said to himself, "I must try my best to get as close to this guru as possible. Maybe he will bless me, too."

One day he asked the guru, "Guruji, would you please give me the mantra that you gave my master, by which he became so successful. May I have initiation from you?"

The guru replied, "Next time."

The simple servant was so joyously grateful, and he went into his room, closed the door, and didn't come out.

Some months later the guru returned to the master's house. The master came running out to meet the guru and said, "Guruji, what did you do to my servant?"

Guruji said, "I didn't do anything to your servant. What is the problem?"

"Guruji, ever since you were here last time, you must have said something to that servant. He went into his room that day and closed the door, and I haven't seen him since."

"That can't be," replied the guru. "He asked me for initiation and I said, 'Next time.'"

"Well, Guruji, I haven't seen him since you left. He has been inside of his room, and he won't come out."

The guru said, "I shall see into this matter." He went to the servant's room and opened up the door. There he saw the faithful servant sitting in his *asana*, lost in deep meditation, repeating the mantra, "Next time, next time."

Narad Muni and the Meditating Sadhus

Three *sadhu*s were meditating under a tree. One day Narad Muni came walking down that path.

The first *sadhu* asked, "Narad, how long will it take me to get enlightenment?"

Narad looked deeply into his own self and said, "It will take you 10,000 years."

The *sadhu* said, "10,000 years? Oh, no!"

The second *sadhu* asked, "How long will it take me to get enlightenment?"

Narad looked deeply within his own self and said, "It is going to take you 20,000 years."

The *sadhu* said, "20,000 years? Oh, no! Such a long time!"

The third *sadhu* said, "Narad, how long is it going to take me to get enlightenment?"

Narad said, "It is going to take you 50,000 years."

The *sadhu* jumped up and began to dance and said, "You mean I am really going to make it? Thank you!"

Glossary

achara	behavior
agnya chakra	the energy center located in the third eye which orders and discriminates experience
arati	the dance of praise of the deity which is the culmination of every worship
arpana	offering
asana	sacred seat for worship and meditation
bedi	a raised platform for sitting
bel	a certain fruit that grows in tropical climates
belgach	the tree which bears the bel fruit
bhaktas	devotees
bhakti	devotion
bhava	an intense attitude
bhikshapatra	a begging bowl
bhumi shuddhi	the ceremony of purification
brahmin	a learned person
chai	an Indian preparation of tea with milk and spices
Chandi homa, *Chandi yagya*	an offering of the mantras of the *Chandi Path* to a consecrated fire
Chandi, *Chandi Path*	seven hundred verses of praise to the Divine Mother
dakshina	an offering of money to a deity or priest
Dakshina Achara	preferred behavior, the behavior which reduces the necessity to act in the world
darshan	intuitive vision of God
deva	shining one, a god
dhaki	a special kind of Indian drum
dharma	the ideal of perfection
Ekadashi	the eleventh day of the lunar fortnight
gamcha	a towel made of thin Indian cloth
ganja	intoxicating marijuana leaves

ghat	the stairs to a body of water where religious ceremonies are performed
gundas	thugs or thieves
gyanis	wise people
hawan	ceremony of the sacred fire
hawan kunda	a pit for the sacrificial fire ceremony
homa	a consecrated fire
jal	water
japa	recitation of mantras with a rosary
Jaya Maa!	victory to the Divine Mother!
kamandelu	a *sadhu's* water pot or begging bowl
karma yoga	actions which bring us into union
kirtan	singing about God
kripa	grace, defined as what you do is what you get
Kula Achara	the behavior of excellence
kurtas	shirts
lingam	a symbol of Lord Shiva
mahayagya	great fire sacrifice
mahut	caretaker of an elephant
mala	rosary
mangal arati	the opening ceremony of morning worship
masala	the mix of rice, barley, sesame, ghee, milk and sugar offered to the sacred fire
mast	totally absorbed, full of joy, intoxicated with God
maya	the illusion of the world
mudras	hand gestures of philosophical meaning
murtis	symbolic figures of the Gods and Goddesses
Namaskar	Sanskrit greeting meaning "I bow to the divinity within you."
Namaste	Sanskrit greeting meaning "I bow to the divinity within you."
navaratri	a festival of nine nights of worship

pithas   places of pilgrimage
prakriti   nature
prana pratishta   establishment of life within a deity
pranayam   control of the rhythm of breathing
prasada   consecrated food offering
pravachan   discourse to explain the meaning of scripture
puja   formal worship
pujari   a priest who offers worship
purusha   divine consciousness
rickshawala   the driver of a hand-pulled conveyance
rishis   seers of divine wisdom
rudraksha   a sacred bead worn by *sadhus*
sadhana   spiritual discipline or practices
sadhika   a female practitioner of spiritual discipline
sadhu   a male practitioner of spiritual discipline
samadhi   pure intuitive absorption in meditation
sangeeta   singing songs for God
sankalpa   a spiritual promise or vow of worship
sannyasi   a renunciate of worldly life
satsangha   communion with truth, spiritual fellowship
seva   action which demonstrates an offering of love
                        and respect, selfless service
*Shaiva Achara*the behavior of practice
shaivites   followers of Lord Shiva
shakha   branches of philosophy
shakti   energy
shanti   peace
Shata Chandi Vrat   the vow of singing the
                   Chandi Path 100 times
Siddhanta Achara behavior according to the scriptures
siddhi   the attainment of perfection

swaha	the word by which offering to the consecrated fire is made
tapasya	purifying austerities
tata-stu	I grant you that! Let it be so!
tilak	a mark of blessing placed upon the forehead
tirthastans	the places of special religious pilgrimage
tulasi	the holy basil plant
Vaishnava Achara	the behavior of devotion
vaishnavas	followers of Lord Vishnu
Vama Achara	the behavior which seeks perfection of every action one performs in the world
Vedic Achara	the behavior of knowledge
yagya	ceremony of fire sacrifice
yaksha	one who inspires greed
yantra	a mystical diagram which shows a road map to Godliness
yatra	spiritual pilgrimage
Yoga Achara	the behavior of union

Yes, the *sadhu* is going to make it! And we're all going to make it too! That is Shree Maa's blessing. She blesses all devotees that we also will make it to our goal. She shows us the way to reach perfection, and she will be there to greet us with her pure love when we arrive. Her life is a living teaching that inspires all to greater clarity. Watch her example and learn how to reach God through effervescent joy! Follow your disciplines of meditation and spiritual practices, and find a way to manifest Shree Maa's teachings in making each act in our lives a manifestation of unselfish love and divine awareness. Let us celebrate in our capacity to serve and surrender to the Divine Mother. Shree Maa shows us that the truth of our surrender is infinite love. May we always dwell in her blessings! Namaste.

Books by Shree Maa and Swami Satyananda Saraswati

Annapūrṇa Thousand Names
Before Becoming This
Bhagavad Gītā
Chaṇḍi Pāṭh
Cosmic Pūjā
Cosmic Pūjā Bengali
Devī Gītā
Devī Mandir Songbook
Durgā Pūjā Beginner
Ganeśa Pūjā
Gems From the Chaṇḍi
Guru Gītā
Hanumān Pūjā
Kālī Dhyānam
Kālī Pūjā
Lakṣmī Sahasra Nāma
Lalitā Triśati
Sahib Sadhu
Shree Maa - The Guru & the Goddess
Shree Maa, The Life of a Saint
Śiva Pūjā Beginner
Śiva Pūjā and Advanced Fire Ceremony
Sundara Kāṇḍa
Swāmī Purāṇa
Thousand Names of Ganeśa
Thousand Names of Gayatri
Thousand Names of Viṣṇu

Cassette Tapes and CDs by Shree Maa and Swamiji
Chaṇḍi Pāṭh
Durgā Pūjā Beginner
Lalitā Triśati
Mantras of the Nine Planets
Navarṇa Mantra
Oh Dark Night Mother
Sādhu Stories from the Himalayas
Shree Maa at the Devi Mandir
Shree Maa in Mendocino
Shree Maa in the Temple of the Heart
Shiva is in My Heart
Śiva Pūjā Beginner
Śiva Pūjā and Advanced Fire Ceremony
The Goddess is Everywhere
The Songs of Ramprasad
The Thousand Names of Kālī

Devi Mandir Publications
5950 Highway 128
Napa, CA 94558 USA
Phone and Fax: 01-707-966-2802
http://www.shreemaa.org
info@shreemaa.org

Namaste